# MAKE A STARTUP

AF592169

ARVIND UPADHYAY

Copyright © Arvind Upadhyay
All Rights Reserved.

This book has been published with all efforts taken to make the material error-free after the consent of the author. However, the author and the publisher do not assume and hereby disclaim any liability to any party for any loss, damage, or disruption caused by errors or omissions, whether such errors or omissions result from negligence, accident, or any other cause.

While every effort has been made to avoid any mistake or omission, this publication is being sold on the condition and understanding that neither the author nor the publishers or printers would be liable in any manner to any person by reason of any mistake or omission in this publication or for any action taken or omitted to be taken or advice rendered or accepted on the basis of this work. For any defect in printing or binding the publishers will be liable only to replace the defective copy by another copy of this work then available.

As a successful scaled company, you cannot run the ship the way you used to. You'll get run over by a swarm of start-ups.

No problem, no opportunity. No one will pay you to solve a nonproblem. —Vinod Khosla, Founder, Sun Microsystems and Khosla Ventures

HAVE YOU EVER come up with an idea for a new product or service that you thought would be very cool, but didn't take any action because you thought it would be too risky? Or maybe you just didn't know how to take the next step? Or at work, have you had what you thought could be a big idea for your company—perhaps changing the way you develop or distribute a product, provide customer service, or hire or train your employees? The fact is, most of us have these kinds of ideas at one time or another. But neither we, nor our companies, are very good at taking advantage of them. Why? Because typically there is significant uncertainty around whether these ideas will work. They are risky. And most individuals—and especially companies—are programmed to avoid risk. But what if you could take much of the risk out of it? What if you knew a process to quickly test and validate whether the idea had merit? The key message in this book is that new tools and perspectives for validating big ideas characterized by high uncertainty are emerging in many disparate fields. Whether you call it lean start-up, design thinking, or agile software development, these new methods are revolutionizing the way managers successfully create, refine, and bring new ideas to market. These and other tools help entrepreneurs, designers, and software developers lower uncertainty and risk through cheap and rapid experimentation. To help managers apply these new practices inside established companies, we offer a new method for managing innovation that we call the innovator's method: an end-to-end process for creating, refining, and bringing ideas to market. Drawing on our research of hundreds of established companies and startups, we show you when and how to apply the innovator's method, taking you step-by-step through these new practices. We answer such questions as: How do we know whether this idea is worth pursuing? Have we found the right solution? What is the best business model for this new offering? We focus on the "how"— how to test, validate, and commercialize ideas using the best tools from lean start-up, design thinking, and similar techniques used by a few corporations and most successful start-ups. We acknowledge that the innovation process is messy and unpredictable—and no process can fully remove the uncertainty. But these tools can be applied to create new innovations for customers or solve internal problems that have an element of uncertainty, whether in HR, finance, or another area. Let's start with a story. Rent the Runway In 2008, Jenn Hyman, a second-year MBA student at Harvard Business School, spent Thanksgiving at her home in New York. During her visit, Hyman noticed her sister, Becky—an accessories buyer at Bloomingdale's—struggling to decide what to wear to an upcoming wedding. "Becky desperately wanted to buy a $1,500 Marchesa dress," said Hyman. "She felt compelled to buy a new dress— because she knew photos would soon appear on Facebook and she didn't want to be seen twice in the same outfit." 1 As she watched her sister wrestle with the cost of the dress, her sister's emotion was a clue to an important job-to-be-done for young women: helping them feel special and confident. Hyman realized that other fashion-oriented young women might have a similar challenge, an observation backed up by her years spent building a wedding event business at Starwood hotels and working in marketing and sales at Wedding.com. Hyman's insight led her to hypothesize a potential solution: instead of purchasing designer dresses, women might prefer the option of renting designer dresses online for special occasions. Like many gifted young individuals—budding entrepreneurs and talented young managers—Hyman had used her powers of observation to generate a potentially valuable business idea. But what should she do next? Pop quiz: imagine she came to you. What would you advise? For most business professors and executives, the answer would be, "Write a business plan." The plan would identify the customer need, describe the product or service, estimate the size of the market, and estimate the revenues and profits based on projections of pricing, costs, and unit volume growth. After all, without this type of analysis, how can we know whether an idea is worthy of investment? Indeed, Hyman received just this type of advice. She didn't do it. Instead, Hyman recruited classmate Jenny Fleiss to help her test their proposed solution. Hyman and Fleiss set up an experiment to answer two key questions: 1. Will middle-to upper-class young women rent a designer dress if it is available at one-tenth the retail price? 2. Will women who rent dresses return them in good condition? Then Hyman and Fleiss borrowed or bought 130 dresses from designers like Diane von Furstenberg, Calvin Klein, and Halston and set up an experiment to rent dresses to Harvard undergrads. They advertised around campus, rented a rent dresses to Harvard undergrads. They advertised around campus, rented a location, and invited young women. The experiment answered both questions. Of the 140 women who came in to view the dresses, 35 percent ended up renting one, and 51 of 53 mailed them back in good condition (the other two had stains that were easily removed). This experiment resolved some of the uncertainty reflected in the two questions it was designed to answer. But would women rent dresses they couldn't try on? To answer that question, Hyman and Fleiss set up another experiment, this time on the Yale campus, allowing women to see the dresses before renting but not allowing them to try them on. In the second trial they had more dress options, because the first pilot revealed that many women didn't rent because they couldn't find an option they liked. The Yale pilot showed two things: women would rent dresses when they couldn't try them on, and the percentage of women who rented increased to more than 55 percent because they had more options. Now Hyman and Fleiss were ready to test the big idea: Would women rent dresses they could not physically see? The entrepreneurs took photos of each dress and ran a test in New York, where one thousand women in the target audience were given the option to rent a dress from PDF photos. The final experiment showed that roughly 5 percent of women looking for special occasion dresses were willing to try the service—enough to demonstrate the viability of renting high fashion over the web. So Hyman and Fleiss gathered data on whether designers would go for their idea and whether they could use designers' websites as their rental channel. Less than two weeks after conceiving the idea, the two women cold-called Diane von Furstenberg, an influential fashion designer and president of the Council of Fashion Designers of America. The initial idea Hyman proposed to von Furstenberg was to set up a rental option on the websites of existing designers. Hyman's start-up would take care of fulfillment—taking the order, shipping the dress, and dry-cleaning the returns. Von Furstenberg was intrigued by the idea and helped Hyman and Fleiss set up meetings with more than twenty designers. The initial response from most designers was extremely negative. "We were going to designers asking to buy their inventory so we could rent it at the same time it's available at Saks Fifth Avenue and Niemen Marcus for 10 percent of the retail price," said Hyman. "In the first meetings their response was basically, 'over my dead body.'" 2 Designers were worried about cannibalization. Renting dresses instead of selling them seemed like a bad idea. Hyman and Fleiss realized that to make their idea work, they would need to Hyman and Fleiss realized that to make their idea work, they would need to have their own website and inventory. So the idea of Rent the Runway—using the Netflix model to rent a wide variety of high-fashion dresses from multiple designers—was born. Now that Hyman and Fleiss had resolved concerns about whether there would be demand for their product—and what their initial solution might look like—they were ready to launch. But the change in business model meant they needed capital to purchase inventory. The typical advice when you're going for capital is to make sure you have a top-notch business plan and get capital as cheaply as possible. They didn't do it. Instead, as they took the idea to potential investors (including Bain Capital, which ended up financing their first round), they still had no formal written business plan. When asked why, Hyman replied, "We're anti-business plan people. We think that so many people just sit around all day and strategize but they don't act." Fleiss concurred, saying,

"We had a bias for action, not business planning." In fact, one reason Hyman and Fleiss chose Bain Capital, even though it wasn't necessarily the cheapest capital, was the attitude of partner Scott Friend. "He shared our commitment to learning by doing," said Fleiss. 3 With capital in hand, the two women were ready to build the team. The typical advice is to hire experts to head each functional area, perhaps someone who can leverage significant corporate experience to take the team to the next level. They didn't do it. Instead, Hyman took on marketing, and Fleiss took on finance. They then looked for individuals having broad skills who could wear different hats. "Having Jenn serve as CMO and me as CFO is typical of our fluid approach to allocating responsibilities," said Fleiss. "We need managers who can wear different hats. We learned about the value of all-around athletes when Lara joined on an unpaid trial basis to help with our college market tests. Although she had years of experience at Coach, she wasn't afraid to move dress racks. Brooke, our director of customer insight, has had several different roles but she's never worried about the title . . . We make heavy use of unpaid internships to test whether employees have the same hungry jack-of-all-trades attitude." 4 With a small team in place, the typical advice would be to carefully develop a flawless website and service with broad appeal, adding features that might attract a wider set of customers. They didn't do it. Instead, Rent the Runway quickly launched a beta version of its service for five thousand invited members on November 2, 2009. RTR started with eight hundred dresses from thirty designers—a relatively small inventory. "We followed the minimum viable product approach," said Fleiss. "At the outset we just wanted to provide the capability to rent dresses. Nothing fancy." But with the help of a New York Times article titled "A Netflix Model for Haute Couture," initial demand for the small inventory proved almost overwhelming. 5 Now with proven demand and increasing customer feedback on how to improve the service, RTR was prepared to invest in a complete solution. Over the ensuing months, as demand continued to increase, it expanded its inventory to more than thirty thousand dresses with help from a $30 million round of financing. "Our revenue growth is amazing," Hyman told us at the end of RTR's first year. "This is a dream come true." But a more visible sign of success, perhaps, is that "its inventory dressed 85 percent of the ladies who attended President Obama's second inauguration.

# Contents

# Foreword

At some point soon, please take a trip physically or virtually to New York City, Hong Kong, Singapore, and Dubai. In New York, go to the intersection of $6^{th}$ Avenue and $57^{th}$ Street and start walking south, away from Central Park. On the left side you will see Rockefeller Center—a set of skyscrapers that were built in the 1930s. Then look to your right, where you will see a set of even bigger skyscrapers designed and built in the 1960s. These are masses of rectangles and right angles reaching into the sky, differentiated only by the type of siding that was used and whether they had sixty or seventy stories. Then go to Hong Kong, Singapore, and Dubai and contrast their skylines with those on the Avenue of the Americas in New York. Most skyscrapers in these cities that have been built in the last fifteen years are unique to the world. Most are very attractive—and some are truly stunning. The curves, angles, accents, and statements are unique to each building. What has changed? Have the architects simply become more daring and creative? Are the architects in those cities simply better at design than American architects? The answer: No. Rather, the software that architects have been using in Hong Kong, Singapore, and Dubai—and around the world—has become so sophisticated that if an architect changes an angle, adjusts the weight-bearing or a new curve in an H-beam, or adds a new type of weld to be used in an ornament jutting out on the $23^{rd}$ floor, the software automatically recalculates the design of every other piece, showing what each one needs to do and where it must be placed to account for interdependencies mandated by the unusual element of each piece. The software's power to calculate all the interdependencies among the elements of these massive skyscrapers has yielded a set of rules that say "If this, then that." These rules are not of the sort that say "Don't do this, because we have no idea what will happen." The rules of causality actually emancipate artistry in design. The reason why skyscrapers designed in 1960s had so little differentiation is that there was little latitude for creativity: anything that was not a standard straight beam or a 90-degree angle was risky and very, very costly. Even the best architects struggled to come up with all the adjustments they needed to implement elsewhere in the structure to account for anything that was unusual. So how does this relate to management? Historically, management is about "straight lines" and "right angles." The tools of traditional business planning— the "software"—that managers use today have helped them perfect the art of analyzing, planning, and executing when the problem is standard and the interdependencies are known. But innovation is about uncertainty and nonstandard processes—"curves" and "weird angles"—and the management literature and the tools we use have not yet caught up with the new kinds of problems that managers and innovators face. New "software" is needed—a new set of guidelines and rules—that managers can use for facing high uncertainty problems. Furthermore, although most companies are laced throughout with interdependencies, most executives actually know little of what they are or how they interact. Some interactions in a company are static, occurring at a given point in time. Others are dynamic, doing their work over time. The reason why many executives and employees adhere to standard processes is that changes in interdependent processes are time-consuming, risky, and costly. Standard processes mitigate innovation, but many managers instinctively opt for less innovation nonetheless in their quest for order. Executives face these paradoxes in part because so few researchers of business have achieved the comparable exquisite understanding of business interdependencies that software has brought to architecture. Many more of us must follow the lead of these few, because the impact these researchers have had on understanding systemic interdependencies of processes and organizational structure has been profound. For example, Steven Spear and Kent Bowen conducted a remarkable study of the Toyota Production System, examining the complete process of production in industries from health care to aluminum. From this deep understanding they were able to distill four rules for managing (summarized in the HBR article "Decoding the DNA of the Toyota Production System") that went beyond what prior researchers had tried to describe in simplistic terms. Similarly, in The Anatomy of Peace, Terry Warner and his colleagues at the Arbinger Institute chronicled the interdependent process by which conflict is created and resolved. Edgar Schein studied from beginning to end the process through which culture is created and resists change, summarized in his book Organizational Culture and Leadership. And finally, Chet Huber wrote Detour: My Unexpected, Amazing, Life Changing Journey with OnStar.

# Preface

"With traditional career doors slamming shut, it's easy to panic, but Chris Guillebeau sees opportunities everywhere. Making a career out of your passion sounds like a dream, but in this straightforward, engaging book he shows you how to get it done, one simple step at a time." —Alan Paul, author of Big in China "Business, like traveling, is often improved by starting poor. You are forced to improvise, innovate, and stay close to reality. You can't buy solutions, so you have to create your own. Suddenly you have the first part of success—something of value. I got all this from The $100 Startup, which is full of practical advice about inventing your own livelihood. I've done a handful of $100 startups myself, several of which I later sold. Chris Guillebeau knows what he is talking about. Listen to this book! —Kevin Kelly, author of What Technology Wants "This book is more than a 'how to' guide, it's a 'how they did it' guide that should persuade anyone thinking about starting a business that they don't need a fortune to make one." —John Jantsch, author of Duct Tape Marketing and The Referral Engine "Is that giant knot in your stomach keeping you from starting your own business or pursuing the career of your dreams? Chris Guillebeau's seasoned, practical advice and his efficient blueprint for entrepreneurial success will alleviate your anxieties and get you on the path to being responsible for—and in control of—your future." —Erin Doland, editor-in-chief of Unclutterer.com and author of Unclutter Your Life in One Week "You can't grow a thriving business on wishes and dreams. You need the kind of nuts-and-bolts wisdom that only comes from hard-earned experience. Chris Guillebeau has been in the trenches for years, and in The $100 Startup he guides you step-by-step through how he and dozens of others have turned their passions into profits. It's essential reading for the solopreneur!" —Todd Henry, author of The Accidental Creative "Starting your own business doesn't have to be expensive or difficult. Follow Chris's advice, and you'll help people, have fun, and never work for 'the man' again." —Josh Kaufman, author of The Personal MBA: Master the Art of Business

# Prologue

Imagine a life where all your time is spent on the things you want to do. Imagine giving your greatest attention to a project you create yourself, instead of working as a cog in a machine that exists to make other people rich. Imagine handing a letter to your boss that reads, "Dear Boss, I'm writing to let you know that your services are no longer required. Thanks for everything, but I'll be doing things my own way now." Imagine that today is your final day of working for anyone other than yourself. What if—very soon, not in some distant, undefined future—you prepare for work by firing up a laptop in your home office, walking into a storefront you've opened, phoning a client who trusts you for helpful advice, or otherwise doing what you want instead of what someone tells you to do? All over the world, and in many different ways, thousands of people are doing exactly that. They are rewriting the rules of work, becoming their own bosses, and creating a new future. This new model of doing business is well under way for these unexpected entrepreneurs, most of whom have never thought of themselves as businessmen and businesswomen. It's a microbusiness revolution—a way of earning a good living while crafting a life of independence and purpose. Other books chronicle the rise of Internet startups, complete with rants about venture capital and tales of in-house organic restaurants. Other guides tell you how to write eighty-page business plans that no one will ever read and that don't resemble how an actual business operates anyway. This book is different, and it has two key themes: freedom and value. Freedom is what we're all looking for, and value is the way to achieve it.

CHAPTER ONE

# Good is the enemy of great.

one of the key reasons why we have so little that becomes great. We don't have greatschools, principally because wehavegoodschools. We don't have great government, principally because we have good gov ernment. Few people attain great lives, in large part because it is just so easy to settlefora goodlife.The vast majority ofcompanies never become great, precisely becausethe vast majority become quite good—and that is their main problem. This point became piercingly clear to me in 1996, was having dinner with a group of thought leaders gathered for a discussion about organizational performance. Bill Meehan, the managing director of the San Francisco office of McKinsey& Company, leaned over and casually confided, "You know, Jim, we love Built to Last around here. You and your coauthor did a very fine job on the research and writing. Unfortu nately, it's useless." Curious, I askedhim to explain. "The companies you wrote about were,forthe most part, always great," he said. "They never had to turn themselves from good companies into great companies. They had parents like David Packard and George Merck, who shaped the character of greatness from early on. But what about the vast majority of companies that wake up partway through life and realizethat they're good, but not great?" I now realize that Meehan was exaggerating for effectwith his "useless" comment, but his essential observation was correct—that trulygreatcom-

How on earth did a companywith such a long historyof being nothing special transform itselfinto an enterprise that outperformed some of the best-led organizations in the world? Andwhywas Walgreens able to make the leap when other companies in the same industrywith the same oppor tunities and similar resources, such as Eckerd, did not make the leap? This singlecase capturesthe essence of our quest. This book is not about Walgreens per se, or any of the specific compa- nieswe studied. It isaboutthe question—Can a good company becomea great company and, if so, how?—and our search for timeless, universal answers that can be applied byanyorganization.

UNDAUNTED CURIOSITY

People often ask, "What motivates you to undertake these huge research projects?" It's a good question. The answer is, "Curiosity." There is noth ing I find more exciting than picking a question that I don't know the answer to and embarking on a quest for answers. It's deeply satisfying to climb into the boat, like Lewis and Clark, and head west, saying, "We don't know what wellfind when we get there, butwe'll besure toletyou know when weget back." Here is the abbreviated story ofthis particular odyssey ofcuriosity. Phase 1: The Search With the question in hand, I began to assemble a team of researchers. (When I use "we" throughout this book, I am referring to the research team. In all, twenty-one people worked on the project at key points, usu allyin teams of four to six at a time.) Ourfirst task was to find companies thatshowed the good-to-great pat tern exemplified in the charton page 2.Welaunched a six-month "death march offinancial analysis," looking for companies that showed the fol-lowingbasicpattern:fifteen-year cumulativestockreturns at or belowthe generalstock market, punctuated by a transition point, then cumulative returns at least three times the market over the next fifteen years. We picked fifteen years because it would transcend one-hit wonders and lucky breaks (you can't justbe lucky forfifteen years) and would exceed the average tenure ofmostchiefexecutive officers (helpingus to separate great companies from companies that just happened to have a single great leader). We picked three times the market because it exceeds the performance of most widely acknowledged great companies. For per spective, a mutual fund ofthe following "marquis set"of companiesbeat the market by only 2.5 times over the years 1985 to 2000: 3M, Boeing, Coca-Cola, GE, Hewlett-Packard, Intel, Johnson & Johnson, Merck, Motorola, Pepsi, Procter & Gamble,Wal-Mart, and Walt Disney. Not a bad set to beat. From an initialuniverse ofcompanies that appearedon the Fortune 500 in the years 1965 to 1995, we systematically searched and sifted, eventually finding eleven good-to-great examples. However, a couple of points deserve brief mention here. First, a company had to demonstrate the good-to-great pat tern independent ofits industry; ifthe whole industry showed the samepat tern, we dropped the company. Second, we debated whether we should use additional selection criteria beyond cumulative stock returns, such as impacton society and employee welfare. We eventually decided to limit ourselection to the good-to-great results pattern, aswe could not conceive of any legitimate and consistent method forselecting on these other vari ables without introducing our own biases. In the last chapter, however, I address the relationship between corporate values and enduring greatcom panies, but the focus ofthisparticular research effort ison the very specific question of how to turn a good organization into one that produces sus tained greatresults. Atfirst glance, wewere surprised bythe list. Who would have thought that Fannie Mae would beat companies likeGE and Coca-Cola? Or that Walgreens could beatIntel? The surprising list—a dowdier group would be hardto find—taught usa key lesson right up front. It ispossible to turn good intogreat in the most unlikely ofsituations. Thisbecame the first of many surprises that led us to reevaluate our thinking about corporate greatness.

Phase 2: Compared to What? Next, we took perhaps the most important step in the entire research effort: contrasting the good-to-great companies to a carefully selected set of "comparison companies." The crucial question in our study is not, What did the good-to-great companies sharein common?Rather, the cru cial question is, What did the good-to-great companies share in common that distinguished them from the comparison companies? Think of it this way: Suppose youwanted to study whatmakes gold medal winners in the Olympic Games. If you only studied the gold medal winners by them- selves, you'd find that they all had coaches. But if you looked at the ath letesthat made the Olympic team, but neverwona medal,you'd find that they also had coaches! The key question is, What systematically distin guishes gold medal winners from those who never won a medal? We selected two sets of comparison companies. The first set consisted of "direct comparisons"—companies that were in the same industry as the good-to-great companies with the same opportunities and similar resources at the time of transition, but that showed no leap from good to great. (See Appendix LB for details ofourselection process.) The second consisted of "unsustained comparisons"—companies that made a shortterm shift from good to great but failed to maintain the trajectory—to address the question ofsustainability. In all,thisgave us a total studyset of twenty-eight companies: eleven good-to-great com panies, eleven directcomparisons, and six unsustained comparisons.

Phase 3:

Inside the Black Box We then turned our attention to a deep analysis of each case. We col lected all articles published on the twenty-eight companies, dating back fifty years or more. We systematically coded all the material into cate gories, such as strategy, technology, leadership, and so forth. Then we interviewed most of the good-to-great executives who held keypositions of responsibility during the transition era. We also initiated a wide range of qualitative and quantitative analyses, looking at everything from acquisi tions to executive compensation, from business strategy to corporate cul ture,from layoffs to leadership style, from financial ratios to management turnover. When all was said and done, the total project consumed 10.5 peopleyears of effort. We readand systematically coded nearly 6,000 arti cles, generated more than 2,000 pages of interview transcripts, and cre ated 384million bytes ofcomputerdata. (SeeAppendix l.D fora detailed list of all our analyses and activities.) Wecame to think ofourresearch effort asakinto looking insidea black box. Each step along the way was like installing anotherlightbulb to shed lighton the inner workings ofthe good-to-great process.

With data in hand, we began a series of weekly research-team debates. For each of the twenty-eight companies, members of the research team and I would systematically read all the articles, analyses, interviews, and the research coding. I would make a presentation to the team on that spe cificcompany, drawing potential conclusions and asking questions. Then we would debate, disagree, pound on tables, raise our voices, pause and reflect, debatesomemore,pauseand think,discuss, resolve, question,and debate yet again about "whatit all means."

The core of our method was a systematic process of contrasting the good-to-great examples to the comparisons, always asking, "What's differ ent?" We also made particular note of "dogs that did not bark." In the Sher lock Holmes classic "The Adventure of Silver Blaze" Holmes identified "the curiousincident ofthe dogin the night-time" asthe keyclue. It turns out that the dog did nothing in the nighttime and that, according to Holmes, was the curious incident, which led him to the conclusion that the prime suspect must have been someone whoknewthe dogwell. In ourstudy, whatwedidn't find—dogs that wemighthave expected to bark but didn't—turned out to be some ofthe best clues to the inner work ings of good to great. When we stepped inside the black box and turned on the lightbulbs, we werefrequently justas astonished at whatwe did not see as what we did. For example: • Larger-than-life, celebrity leaders who ride in from the outside are negatively correlated with taking a company from good to great. Ten of eleven good-to-great CEOs came from inside the company, whereas the comparison companies tried outside CEOs six times more often. • We found no systematic pattern linking specific forms of executive compensation to the process of going from good to great. The idea that the structure of executive compensation is a keydriver in corpo rate performance is simplynot supportedby the data. • Strategy per se did notseparate the good-to-great companiesfrom the comparison companies. Both sets of companies had well-defined strategies, and there is no evidence that the good-to-great companies spent more time on long-range strategic planning than the compari son companies.

• The good-to-great companies did not focus principally on what to do to become great;they focused equallyon what notto do and what to stop doing.

• Technology and technology-driven change has virtually nothing to do with igniting a transformation from good to great. Technology can accelerate a transformation, but technology cannot cause a transfor mation.

• Mergers and acquisitions play virtually no role in igniting a transfor mation from good togreat; two bigmediocrities joined together never makeone great company.

• The good-to-great companies paid scant attention to managing change, motivating people, or creating alignment. Under the right conditions, the problems ofcommitment, alignment, motivation, and change largely melt away.

• The good-to-great companies had no name, tagline,launch event, or program to signify theirtransformations. Indeed, some reported being unaware of the magnitude of the transformation at the time; only later, in retrospect, didit become clear. Yes, they produced a truly rev olutionary leap in results, but not bya revolutionary process.

• The good-to-great companies were not, by and large, in great indus tries, and some were in terrible industries. In no case do we have a company that justhappened to be sitting on the nose cone ofa rocket when it took off. Greatness is not a function of circumstance. Great ness, it turns out, islargely a matterof conscious choice.

Phase 4: Chaos to Concept I've tried to come up with a simple way toconvey what was required togo from all the data, analyses, debates, and "dogs that did not bark" to the final findings in this book. The best answer I cangive is thatitwas an iter ative process oflooping back andforth, developing ideas and testing them against the data, revising the ideas, building a framework, seeing it break under the weight of evidence, and rebuilding it yet again. That process was repeated over and over, until everything hung together in a coherent framework ofconcepts. We allhave a strength ortwo in life, andIsuppose mine is the ability to take a lump of unorganized information, see pat terns, and extract order from the mess—to go from chaos to concept. Thatsaid, however, I wish to underscore again thatthe concepts in the final framework are not my "opinions." While I cannot extract my own psychology and biases entirely from the research, each findingin the final framework met a rigorous standard before the researchteam would deem itsignificant. Every primary concept in the finalframework showedup as a change variable in 100 percent of the good-to-great companies and in less than 30 percent of the comparison companies during the pivotal years. Any insight that failed this test did not make it into the book as a chapter-levelconcept. Here, then, is an overview of the framework of concepts and a preview ofwhat's to come in the restofthe book. (See the diagram below.) Think of the transformation as a process of buildup followed by breakthrough, broken into three broad stages: disciplined people, disciplined thought, and disciplined action. Within each of these three stages, there are two key concepts, shown in the framework and described below. Wrapping around this entire framework is a concept we came to call the flywheel, which captures the gestalt of the entire process of going from good to great.

Level 5 Leadership. We were surprised, shocked really, to discover the type of leadership required for turning a good company into a great one. Compared to high-profile leaders with big personalities who make head linesand become celebrities, the good-to-great leadersseem to have come from Mars. Self-effacing, quiet, reserved, even shy—these leaders are a paradoxical blend of personal humility and professional will. They are more like Lincoln and Socrates than Patton or Caesar. First Who ... Then What We expected thatgood-to-great leaders would begin by setting a new vision and strategy. We found instead thatthey first got the right people onthe bus, the wrong people offthe bus, and the right people in the right seats—and then they figured outwhere to drive it.The old adage "People are your most important asset" turns outto be wrong. People arenot your most important asset. The right people are. Confront theBrutal Facts (YetNever Lose Faith). We learned that a for mer prisoner ofwar had more toteach us about what ittakes tofind a path to greatness than most books on corporate strategy. Every good-to-great company embraced what we came to call the StockdaleParadox: You must maintain unwavering faith that you can and will prevail intheend, regard less ofthe difficulties, AND atthe same time have the discipline to con front the most brutal facts ofyour current reality, whatever they might be. The Hedgehog Concept (Simplicity within the Three Circles). To go from good to great requires transcending the curse of competence. Just because something is your core business—just because you've been doing itfor years or perhaps even decades—does notnecessarily mean you can be the bestin the world at it.And ifyou cannotbe the bestin the world at your core business, then your core business absolutely cannot form the basis ofa great company. Itmust be replaced with a simple concept that reflects deep understanding ofthree intersecting circles. A Culture ofDiscipline. All companies have a culture, some companies have discipline, but few companies have aculture ofdiscipline. When you have disciplined people, you don't need hierarchy. When you have disci plined thought, you don't need bureaucracy. When you have disciplined action, you don'tneedexcessive controls. Whenyou combine a culture of discipline with anethic ofentrepreneurship, you get the magical alchemy ofgreatperformance. Technology Accelerators. Good-to-great companies think differently about the role oftechnology. They never use technology as the primary means ofigniting a transformation. Yet, paradoxically, they arepioneers in the application of carefully selected technologies. We learned that technology by itselfis never a primary, root cause of either greatness or decline. TheFlywheel and the DoomLoop. Those who launch revolutions, dra matic change programs, and wrenching restructurings will almost cer tainly fail to makethe leap from good to great. No matter how dramatic the end result, the good-to-great transformations never happened in one fell swoop. There was no single defining action, no grand program, no one killer innovation, no solitary lucky break, no miracle moment. Rather, the process resembled relentlessly pushing a giantheavy flywheel in one direction, turn upon turn, building momentum until a point of breakthrough, and beyond. From Good to Great to Built to Last In an ironic twist, I now see Good to Great not as a sequel toBuilt to Last, but as more ofa prequel. Thisbook is abouthow toturna good organization intoonethatproduces sustained great results. Built to Last isabouthow you take a company with great results and turn it into an enduring great company oficonic stature. Tomake thatfinal shift requires core values and a purpose beyond just making money com binedwith the key dynamic ofpreserve the core/stimulate progress.

Good to Sustained Built to Enduring Great -> Great f Last -> Great Concepts Results Concepts Company

Ifyou are already a studentofBuilt to Last, please set aside yourques tions aboutthe precise links between the two studies asyou embark upon the findings in Good to Great. In the last chapter, I return to this question and link the twostudiestogether. THE TIMELESS "PHYSICS" OF GOOD TO GREAT I had justfinished presenting my research to a set of Internet executives gathered at a conference, when a hand shot up. "Will your findings con tinue to apply in the new economy? Don't we need to throw out all the oldideas andstart from scratch?" It'sa legitimate question, aswedolive in a time of dramatic change, and it comes up so often that I'd like to dis pense with it right up front, before heading intothe meatofthe book.

Yes, the world ischanging, andwill continue to do so. Butthat does not mean we should stop the search for timeless principles. Think of it this way: While the practices ofengineering continually evolve and change, the laws of physics remain relatively fixed. I like to think of our work as a search for timeless principles—the enduring physics of great organiza tions—that will remain true and relevant no matter how the world changes around us. Yes, the specific application will change (the engi neering), but certain immutable laws oforganized human performance (the physics) will endure. Thetruth is, there's nothing new about being ina new economy. Those who faced the invention ofelectricity, the telephone, the automobile, the radio, orthe transistor—did they feel it was any less ofa new economy than we feel today? And in each rendition ofthe new economy, the best leaders have adhered to certain basic principles, with rigor and discipline. Some people will point outthat the scale and pace ofchange is greater today than anytime in the past. Perhaps. Even so, some ofthe companies in ourgood-to-great study faced rates ofchange that rival anything in the new economy. For example, during the early 1980s, the banking industry was completely transformed in about three years, as the full weight of deregulation came crashing down. Itwas certainly a new economy for the banking industry! Yet Wells Fargo applied every single finding inthis book to produce great results, right smack in the middle of the fast-paced change triggered byderegulation.

This might come as a surprise, butIdon't primarily think ofmy work as about the study ofbusiness, nor do Isee this as fundamentally a business book. Rather, I see my work as being about discovering what creates enduring great organizations of any type. I'm curious to understand the fundamental differences between great and good, between excellent and mediocre. I justhappen to use corporations as a means of getting inside the blackbox. I do thisbecause publicly traded corporations, unlike other types of organizations, have two huge advantages for research: a widely agreed upon definition ofresults (so we can rigorously select a study set) and a plethora ofeasily accessible data. That good is the enemy ofgreat is not just a business problem. It is a human problem. Ifwe have cracked the code on the question ofgood to great, we should have something of value to any type of organization. Good schools might become great schools. Good newspapers might become great newspapers. Good churches might become great churches. Good government agencies might become great agencies. And good com paniesmight become greatcompanies. So, I invite you to join meonan intellectual adventure todiscover what ittakes toturngood into great. I also encourage you toquestion andchal lenge what you learn. As one ofmy favorite professors once said, "Thebest students arethose who never quite believe theirprofessors." True enough. But he also said, "One ought not to reject the data merely because one does not like what the data implies." I offer everything herein for your thoughtful consideration, not blind acceptance. You're the judge and jury. Let the evidence speak.

CHAPTER TWO

# Leadership Level 5

In 1971, a seemingly ordinary man named Darwin E. Smith became chief executive of Kimberly-Clark, a stodgy old paper company whose stock had fallen 36 percent behind the general market over the previous twenty years. Smith, the company's mild-mannered in-house lawyer, wasn't so sure the board had madethe right choice—a feeling further reinforced whena director pulled Smith asideand reminded him that he lacked some of the qualifications for the position.2 But CEO he was, and CEO he remained for twentyyears. What a twenty years it was. In that period, Smith created a stunning transformation, turning Kimberly-Clark into the leading paper-based consumer products company in the world. Under hisstewardship, Kim berly-Clark generated cumulative stock returns 4.1 times the general mar ket, handily beating its direct rivals Scott Paper and Procter & Gamble and outperforming such venerable companies as Coca-Cola, HewlettPackard, 3M, and General Electric. It was an impressive performance, one ofthe bestexamples in the twen tieth century oftaking a good company and making it great. Yet few peo ple—even ardentstudents of management and corporate history—know anything about Darwin Smith. He probably would have liked it that way. A man who carried no airs of self-importance, Smith found his favorite companionship amongplumbers and electricians and spenthis vacations rumbling around his Wisconsin farm in the cab of a backhoe, digging holes and moving rocks.3 He never cultivated hero status or executive celebrity status.4 When a journalist asked him to describe his manage ment style, Smith, dressed unfashionably like a farm boywearing hisfirst suit bought at J. C. Penney, just stared back from the other side of his nerdy-looking black-rimmed glasses. After a long, uncomfortable silence, he said simply: "Eccentric."5 The Wall Street Journal did not write a splashy feature on Darwin Smith. But ifyouwere to think ofDarwin Smithassomehow meekorsoft, you would be terriblymistaken. His awkward shyness and lack of pretense was coupled with a fierce, even stoic, resolve toward life. Smith grew up as a poor Indiana farm-town boy, puttinghimselfthrough college byworking the day shiftat International Harvester and attending Indiana University at night. One day, he lostpartofa finger on the job. The story goes that he went to class that evening and returned to work the next day. While that might be a bit of an exaggeration, he clearly did not let a lostfinger slow down his progress toward graduation. He keptworking full-time, he kept going toclass at night, and he earned admission toHarvard Law School.6 Later in life,two months after becoming CEO, doctors diagnosed Smith with noseand throat cancer, predicting he had less than a yearto live. He informedthe board but made it clear that he was not dead yet and had no plans to die anytime soon. Smithheld fully to hisdemandingwork sched ule while commuting weekly from Wisconsin to Houston for radiation therapy andlived twenty-five more years, most ofthemas CEO.7 Smith brought that same ferocious resolve to rebuilding KimberlyClark, especially when he made the most dramatic decision in the com pany's history: Sell the mills.8 Shortly after he became CEO, Smith and his team had concluded that the traditional core business—coated paper—was doomed to mediocrity. Its economics were bad and the com petition weak.9 But, theyreasoned, ifKimberly-Clark thrustitselfinto the fire ofthe consumer paper-products industry, world-class competition like Procter& Gamble would force it to achieve greatness or perish. So, like the general who burned the boats upon landing, leaving only one option (succeed or die), Smith announced the decision to sell the mills, in whatone board member called the gutsiest move he'd ever seen a CEO make. Sell even the mill in Kimberly, Wisconsin, and throw all the proceeds into the consumerbusiness, investing in brandslikeHuggies and Kleenex.10 The business media called the move stupid and Wall Street analysts downgraded the stock.11 Smith never wavered. Twenty-five years later, Kimberly-Clark owned ScottPaper outright and beat Procter & Gamble in six of eightproductcategories.12 In retirement, Smith reflected on his exceptional performance, saying simply, "I never stopped trying to become qualifiedforthe job Darwin Smith standsas a classic exampleof what we came to call a Level 5 leader—an individual who blends extreme personal humility with intense professional will. We found leaders of this type at the helm of every good-to-great company during the transition era. Like Smith, they were self-effacing individuals who displayed the fierce resolve to do what ever needed to be done to make the companygreat .

The term Level 5 refers to the highestlevel in a hierarchyof executive capabilities that we identified in our research. (See the diagram on page 20.) While you don't need to move in sequence from Level 1 to Level 5—it might be possible to fill in some of the lower levels later—fully developed Level 5 leaders embody all five layers of the pyramid. I am not goingto belabor all five levels here, as Levels 1 through 4 are somewhat self-explanatory and are discussed extensively by other authors. This chapter willfocus instead on the distinguishing traits of the good-to-great leaders—namely level 5 traits—in contrast to the comparison leaders in our study. But first, please permit a brief digression to set an important context. We were not looking for Level 5 leadership or anything like it. In fact, I gave the research team explicit instructions to downplay the role of top executives so that we could avoid the simplistic "credit the leader" or "blame the leader" thinking common today. To usean analogy, the "Leadership isthe answer to everything" perspec tive isthe modern equivalent ofthe "God isthe answer to everything" per spective that held back our scientific understanding of the physical world in the Dark Ages. In the 1500s, people ascribed all events they didn't understand to God. Why did the crops fail? God did it. Why did we have an earthquake? God did it. What holdsthe planets in place? God. But with the Enlightenment, we began the search for a more scientific understand ing—physics, chemistry, biology, and so forth. Not that we became athe ists, but wegained deeperunderstanding abouthowthe universe ticks. Similarly, every time we attribute everything to "Leadership," we'reno different from people in the 1500s. We're simply admitting ourignorance. Not that we should become leadership atheists (leadership does matter), but every time we throw our hands up in frustration—reverting back to "Well, the answer must beLeadership!"—we prevent ourselves from gain ing deeper, more scientific understanding aboutwhat makes great com panies tick. So,early in the project, I keptinsisting, "Ignore the executives." Butthe research team kept pushing back, "No! There issomething consistently unusual about them. We can't ignore them." And I'd respond, "But the comparison companies also had leaders, even some great leaders. So, what's different?" Back and forth the debate raged. Finally—as should always be the case—the data won. The good-to-great executives were all cut from the same cloth. It didn't matter whether the company was consumer or industrial, in crisis or steady state, offered services or products. It didn't matter when the transi tion took place or howbig the company. All the good-to-great companies had Level

5 leadershipat the time oftransition. Furthermore, the absence ofLevel 5leadership showed up asa consistent pattern in the comparison companies. Given that Level 5 leadership cuts against the grain of con ventional wisdom, especially the beliefthat we need larger-than-life sav iors with big personalities to transform companies, it is importantto note that Level 5 isan empirical finding, not an ideological one. HUMILITY + WILL = LEVEL 5 Level 5 leaders are a study in duality: modest and willful, humble and fearless. To quickly grasp this concept, think of United States President AbrahamLincoln (one of the few Level 5 presidents in United Stateshis tory), who never let his ego get in the way of His primaryambition for the largercause of an enduring great nation.Yet those who mistook Mr. Lin coln's personal modesty, shy nature, and awkward manner as signs of weakness found themselves terribly mistaken, to the scaleof 250,000Con federate and 360,000 Unionlives, including Lincoln's own .

While it might be a bit ofa stretch to compare the good-to-great CEOs to Abraham Lincoln, theydid display the sameduality. Consider the case of Colman Mockler, CEO of Gillette from 1975 to 1991. During Mockler's tenure, Gillette faced three attacks that threatened to destroy the company's opportunity forgreatness. Twoattacks came ashostile takeover bids from Revlon, led by Ronald Perelman, a cigar-chomping raider with a reputation for breaking apart companies to pay down junk bonds and finance more hostile raids.15 The third attack came from Coniston Part ners, an investment group that bought 5.9 percent of Gillette stock and initiated a proxy battle to seize control of the board, hoping to sell the company to the highest bidder and pocket a quick gain on theirshares.16 Had Gillette been flipped to Perelman at the price he offered, shareowners would have reaped an instantaneous 44 percent gain on theirstock.17 Looking at a $2.3 billion short-term stock profit across 116 million shares, most executives would have capitulated, pocketing millions from flipping their own stock and cashing in on generous golden parachutes.18 Colman Mockler did not capitulate, choosing instead to fight for the future greatness of Gillette,eventhough he himselfwouldhave pocketed a substantial sum on his own shares. A quiet and reserved man, always courteous, Mocklerhad the reputation ofa gracious, almostpatriciangen tleman. Yet those who mistook Mockler's reserved nature for weakness found themselves beaten in the end. In the proxy fight, senior Gillette executives reached out to thousands of individual investors—person by person, phone call by phone call—and won the battle. Now, you might be thinking, "But that just sounds like self-serving entrenched management fighting for their interests at the expense of shareholder interests." On the surface, it mightlookthat way, but consider two keyfacts. First, Mocklerand his team staked the company's future on huge invest ments in radically new and technologically advanced systems (laterknown as Sensor and Mach3). Had the takeover been successful, these projects would almost certainly have been curtailed or eliminated, and none of us would be shaving with Sensor, Sensor forWomen,or the Mach3—leaving hundreds ofmillions ofpeople toa more painful daily battle with stubble.19 Second, at the time of the takeover battle, Sensor promised significant future profits that were not reflected in the stock price because it was in secret development. With Sensor in mind, the board and Mockler believed that the future value of the shares far exceeded the current price,even with the price premium offered by the raiders. To sell out would have made short-term shareflippers happy but would have been utterly irresponsible to long-term shareholders. In the end, Mockler andtheboard were proved right, stunningly so. Ifa shareflipper had accepted the 44 percent price premium offered by Ronald Perelman on October 31,1986, and then invested the full amount in the general market for ten years, through the end of 1996, he would have come out three times worse offthan a shareholder who had stayed with Mockler and Gillette.20 Indeed, the company, its customers, and the shareholders would have been illserved had Mockler capitulated to the raiders, pocketed his millions,and retired to a life of leisure. Sadly, Mockler was neverable to enjoy the full fruits of his effort. On January 25, 1991, the Gillette teamreceived an advance copy ofthe cover ofForbes magazine, which featuredan artist's rendition of Mockler stand ing atopa mountain holding a giantrazor above his head in a triumphal pose, while the vanquished languish on the hillsides below. The other executives razzed the publicity-shy Mockler, who had likely declined requests to be photographedforthe coverin the first place, amused at see ing him portrayed as a corporateversion ofConan the Triumphant. Walk ing back to his office, minutes afterseeingthis public acknowledgmentof his sixteenyears ofstruggle, Mocklercrumpled to the floor, struckdead by a massive heart attack.21 I do not know whether Mockler would have chosen to die in harness, but I am quite confident that he would not have changed his approach as chief executive. His placid persona hid an inner intensity,a dedication to making anything he touched the best it could possibly be—not just because of what he would get, but because he simply couldn't imagine doing it any other way. It wouldn't have been an option within Colman

Mockler'svalue system to takethe easy path and turn the company overto those who would milk it like a cow, destroying its potential to become great, any more than it would have been an option for Lincoln to sue for peace and loseforever the chance ofan enduring great nation.

Ambition for the Company: Setting Up Successors for Success When DavidMaxwell became CEO of Fannie Mae in 1981,the company was losing $1 million every single business day. Overthe next nine years, Maxwell transformed Fannie Mae into a high-performance culture that rivaled the best Wall Streetfirms, earning $4 million every business day and beatingthe generalstock market 3.8to 1.Maxwell retiredwhilestill at the top of his game, feeling that the company would be ill served if he stayed on too long,and turned the companyoverto an equallycapablesuc cessor, Jim Johnson. Shortly thereafter, Maxwell's retirement package, whichhad grown to be worth $20million based on Fannie Mae'sspectac ularperformance, becamea pointofcontroversy in Congress (FannieMae operates under a governmentcharter). Maxwell respondedbywritinga let ter to his successor, in which he expressed concern that the controversy wouldtrigger an adverse reaction in Washington that could jeopardize the future of the company. He then instructed Johnson not to pay him the remaining balance—$5.5 million—and asked that the entire amount be contributed to the Fannie Maefoundation for low-income housing.22 DavidMaxwell, like DarwinSmithand Colman Mockler, exemplified a key trait of Level 5 leaders: ambition first and foremost for the company and concern for itssuccess rather than for one's own riches and personal renown. Level 5 leaders wantto see the company even more successful in the nextgeneration, comfortable with the ideathat mostpeoplewon'teven know that the roots ofthat success trace back to their efforts. As one Level 5 leader said, "I want to look outfrom my porch at one ofthe great compa nies in the world someday and be ableto say, 1 usedto work there.' " In contrast, the comparison leaders, concerned more with their own reputation for personal greatness, often failed to set the company up for success in the nextgeneration. After all,whatbettertestamentto yourown personal greatness than that the placefalls apartafteryouleave? Some had the "biggest dog" syndrome—they didn't mind other dogs in the kennel, as long as they remained the biggest one. One comparison CEO was said to have treated successor candidates "the way Henry the VIII treated wives."23 Consider the case of Rubbermaid, an unsustained comparison com pany that grew from obscurity to number one on Fortune's annual list of America's Most

Admired Companies and then, just as quickly, disinte grated into such sorry shapethat it had to be acquired by Newell to save itself. The architect of this remarkable story, a charismatic and brilliant leader named StanleyGault, became synonymous in the late 1980s with the success of the company. In 312 articles collected on Rubbermaid, Gault comes through as a hard-driving, egocentric executive. In one article, he responds to the accusation of being a tyrant with the state ment, "Yes, but I'm a sincere tyrant."24 In another, drawn directly from his owncommentson leadingchange,the word I appearsforty-four times ("I could lead the charge"; "I wrote the twelve objectives"; "I presented and explained the objectives"), whereas the word we appears just sixteen times.25 Gault had every reason to be proud of his executive success. Rubbermaid generated forty consecutive quarters of earnings growth under his leadership—an impressive performance, and one that deserves respect. But—and this isthe keypoint—Gaultdid not leavebehind a company that would be great without him. His chosen successor lasted only one yearon the joband the nextin line faced a managementteam so shallow that he had to temporarily shoulderfour jobs whilescramblingto identify a new number two executive.26 Gault'ssuccessors found themselves strug gling not only with a management void, but also with strategic voids that would eventually bring the company to its knees.27 Of course, you mightsay, "Yes, Rubbermaid fell apart after Gault, but that just proves his personal greatness as a leader." Exactly! Gault was indeed a tremendous Level 4 leader, perhaps one of the best in the last fifty years. But he was not a Level 5 leader, and that isone key reason why Rubbermaid went from good to great for a brief shining moment and then, justas quickly, went from greatto irrelevant. A Compelling Modesty In contrast to the very/-centric style of the comparison leaders, we were struckby howthe good-to-great leaders didnttalkabout themselves. Dur ing interviews with the good-to-great leaders, they'd talk about the com pany and the contributions of other executives as long as we'd like but would deflect discussion about their own contributions. When pressed to talkabout themselves, they'dsay things like, "I hope I'm not soundinglike a big shot." Or, "If the board hadn't picked such great successors, you probably wouldn't be talking with me today." Or, "Did I have a lot to do with it? Oh, that sounds so self-serving. I don't think I can take much credit.We were blessed withmarvelous people." Or, "There are plenty of people in this companywho could do my jobbetter than I do." It wasn't justfalse modesty. Those whoworked with or wroteabout the good-to-great leaders continually used words like quiet, humble, modest, reserved, shy, gracious, mild-mannered, self-effacing, understated, did not believe his own clippings; and so forth. Board member Jim Hlavacek described Ken Iverson, the CEO who oversaw Nucor's transformation from near bankruptcyto one ofthe mostsuccessful steel companies in the world: Ken isa verymodest and humble man. I'veneverknown a person assuc cessful in doing what he's done that'sas modest. And, I work for a lot of CEOs of large companies.And that's true in his private life as well.The simplicity of him. I mean little thingslike he always gets his dogs at the local pound. He has a simple house that's he's lived in for ages. He only has a carport and he complained to me one dayabout how he had to use his credit card to scrapethe frost offhiswindows and he brokethe credit card. "You know, Ken, there's a solution for it; enclose your carport." And he said, "Ah, heck, it isn'tthatbigofa deal " He'sthat humble and simple.28 The eleven good-to-great CEOs are some of the most remarkable CEOsofthe century, given thatonly eleven companies from the Fortune 500 metthe exacting standards for entry into this study. Yet, despite their remarkable results, almost no one ever remarked about them! George Cain, Alan Wurtzel, David Maxwell, Colman Mockler, Darwin Smith, Jim Herring, Lyle Everingham, Joe Cullman, FredAllen, Cork Walgreen, Carl Reichardt—how many of these extraordinary executives had you heard of? The good-to-great leaders never wanted to become larger-than-life heroes. They never aspired to be put on a pedestal or become unreach able icons. They were seemingly ordinary people quietly producing extra ordinary results. Someofthe comparison leaders provide a striking contrast. ScottPaper, the comparison company to Kimberly-Clark, hired a CEO named Al Dunlap, a man cut from a very different cloth than Darwin Smith. Dunlap loudly beat on his own chest, telling anyone who would listen (and manywhowould prefer not to)aboutwhathe had accomplished. Quoted in Business Week abouthis nineteenmonths atop ScottPaper, he boasted, "The Scott story will go down in the annals ofAmerican business history as one ofthe most successful, quickest turnarounds ever, [making] other turnaroundspale by comparison."30 According to Business Week, Dunlap personally accrued $100 million for 603 days of work at Scott Paper (that's $165,000 per day), largely by slashing the workforce, cutting the R&D budget in half, and putting the company on growth steroids in preparation for sale.31 After selling off the company and pocketing his quick millions, Dunlap wrote a book about himself, in which he trumpeted his nickname Rambo in

Pinstripes. "I love the Rambomovies," he wrote. "Here's a guywho has zero chance of success and always wins. Rambo goes into situations against all odds, expecting togethisbrains blown out. Buthe doesn't. Atthe end ofthe day he succeeds, he gets rid of the bad guys. He creates peace out of war. That's what I do, too."32 Darwin Smith may have enjoyed the mindless Rambo movies aswell, but I suspect he never walked out ofa theater and said to his wife, "You know, I really relate to this Rambo character; he reminds me of me." We found this pattern particularly strong in the unsustained compar isons—cases where the company would show a leap in performance under a talented yet egocentric leader, only to decline in later years. Lee Iacocca, for example, saved Chrysler from the brink of catastrophe, per forming one of the most celebrated (and deservedly so) turnarounds in American business history. Chryslerrose to a height of 2.9 times the mar ket at a point about halfway through his tenure. Then, however, he divertedhis attention to makinghimselfone ofthe mostcelebrated CEOs in American business history. Investors Business Daily and the WallStreet Journal chronicled how Iacoccaappeared regularly on talk shows like the Today show and Larry King Live, personally starred in over eighty com mercials, entertained the idea of running for president of the United States (quotedat one point, "RunningChrysler hasbeen a biggerjobthan running the country. ... I could handle the national economy in six months"), and widely promoted his autobiography. The book, Iacocca, soldseven million copies and elevated him to rockstarstatus, leading him to be mobbed by thousands of cheering fans upon his arrival in Japan.34 Iacocca's personal stock soared, but in the second half of his tenure, Chrysler'sstockfell 31 percent behind the general market. Sadly, Iacocca had trouble leaving center stage and letting go of the perks of executive kingship. He postponed his retirement so many times that insiders at Chrysler began to joke thatIacocca stood for"I AmChair manofChrysler Corporation Always."35 And when he didfinally retire, he demanded that the board continue to provide a private jet and stock options.36 Later, he joined forces with noted takeover artist Kirk Kerkorian to launch a hostile takeover bidfor Chrysler.37 Chrysler experienced a brief return to glory in the five years after Iacocca's retirement, but the company's underlying weaknesses eventu ally led to a buyout by German carmaker Daimler-Benz.38 Certainly, the demise of Chrysler as a stand-alone company does not rest entirely on Iacocca's shoulders (thenextgeneration ofmanagement madethe fateful decision to sell the company to the Germans), but the fact remains: Iacocca's brilliant turnaround in the early 1980s did not prove to be sus tained andChrysler failed tobecome an enduring great company. Unwavering Resolve ... to Do What Must Be Done It is very important to grasp that Level 5 leadership is not just about humility and modesty. It is equally about ferocious resolve, an almost stoic determination to do whatever needs to be done to make the com pany great. Indeed, we debatedfora longtime on the research team about how to describe the good-to-great leaders. Initially, we penciled in terms like "selfless executive" and "servant leader." But members of the team vio lently objected to these characterizations. "Those labels don't ring true," saidAnthony Chirikos. "It makes them sound weak or meek,but that's not at all the way I think of Darwin Smith or Colman Mockler. They would do almost anything to make the com pany great." Then Eve Lisuggested, "Whydon't we justcall them Level 5 leaders? Ifweput a label like 'selfless' or'servant' on them, peoplewill get entirely the wrongidea.We need to get people to engagewith the whole concept, to seeboth sides ofthe coin. Ifyouonlygetthe humilityside,youmiss the whole idea." Level 5 leaders are fanatically driven, infected with an incurable need to produce results. They will sell the mills or fire their brother, if that's what it takes to makethe company great. When George Cain became CEO of AbbottLaboratories, it sat in the bottom quartile of the pharmaceutical industry, a drowsy enterprise that had lived for years off its cash cow, erythromycin. Cain didn't have an inspiring personality to galvanize the company, but he had something much more powerful: inspired standards. He could not stand mediocrity in any form and was utterly intolerant of anyone who would accept the idea thatgood isgood enough. Cain then setoutto destroy one ofthe key causes of Abbott's mediocrity: nepotism. Systematically rebuilding both the board and the executive team withthe bestpeople he could find, Cain made it clear that neither family tiesnor length oftenure would haveany thing to do with whether you held a key position in the company. If you didn't have the capacity to become the best executive in the industry in your span ofresponsibility, thenyou would lose your paycheck.39 Such rigorous rebuilding might be expected from an outsider brought in to turn the company around, but Cain was an eighteen-year veteran insider anda family member, the son of a previousAbbott pres ident. Holiday gatherings were probably tense for a few years in the Cain clan. ("SorryI had to fire you. Want another slice of turkey?") In the end, though, family members were quite pleased with the perfor mance of their stock, for Cain set in motion a profitable growth machine that, from its transition date in 1974 to 2000, created share holder returns that beat the market4.5 to 1,handilyoutperforming indus try superstars Merck and Pfizer. Upjohn, the direct comparison company to Abbott, also had family leadership during the same era as George Cain. Unlike George Cain, Upjohn's CEO never showed the same resolve to break the mediocrity of nepotism. By the timeAbbott had filled all key seats with the bestpeople, regardless offamily background, Upjohn still had Blevel family members holding key positions.40 Virtually identical companies with identical stock charts up to the point of transition, Upjohn then fell 89 percent behind Abbott over the next twenty-one years before capitulating in a merger to Pharmacia in 1995.A superb example of insider-driven change comes from Charles R. "Cork" Walgreen 3d, who transformed dowdy Walgreens into a company that outperformed the stock market byover fifteen times from the end of 1975 to January 1, 2000.42 After years ofdialogue and debate within his executive team about Walgreens' food-service operations, Cork sensed that the team had finally reached a watershed point ofclarity and under standing: Walgreens' brightest future lay in convenient drugstores, not food service. Dan Jorndt, who succeeded Walgreen as CEO in 1998, described whathappened next: Cork said atone ofourplanning committee meetings, "Okay, now I am going to draw the line in the sand. We aregoing to be out ofthe restau rant business completely in five years." At the time, we had over five hundred restaurants. You could have heard a pin drop. He said, "I want toleteverybody know theclock is ticking " Six months later, we were at our next planning committee meeting and someone mentioned just in passing thatweonly hadfive years tobe outofthe restaurant business. Cork was nota real vociferous fellow. Hesort oftapped onthe table and said, "Listen, you have four and a halfyears. Isaid you had five years six months ago. Now you've got four and a half years." Well, that next day, things really clicked into gear to winding down ourrestaurant business. He never wavered. He never doubted; he never second-guessed.43 Like Darwin Smith selling the mills at Kimberly-Clark, Cork Walgreen's decision required stoic resolve. Not that food service was the largest part ofthe business (although it did add substantial profits to the bottom line). The real problem was more emotional. Walgreens had, after all, invented the malted milkshake and food service was a long-standing family tradition dating back to hisgrandfather. Some food-service outlets were even named after the CEO himself—a restaurant chain named Corky's. But nomatter, ifWalgreens had to fly inthe face oflong-standing familytradition in order to focus itsresources where it could be the best in the world (convenient drugstores), Cork would do it. Quietly, doggedly, simply.44 The quiet, dogged nature of Level 5 leadersshowed up not only in big decisions, like selling off the food-service operations or fighting corpo rate raiders, but also in a personal style of sheer workmanlike diligence. Alan Wurtzel, a second-generation family member who took over his family's small company and turned it into Circuit City, perfectly cap tured the gestalt of this trait. When asked about differences between himself and his counterpart CEO at Circuit City's comparison company, Wurtzel summed up: "The showhorseand the plowhorse—hewas more ofa show horse, whereas I was more ofa plow horse."45 The Window and the Mirror Alan Wurtzel's plow horse comment is fascinating in light of two other facts. First,he holds a doctorof jurisprudence degree fromYale—clearly, his plow horse nature had nothing to do with a lack of intelligence. Sec ond, his plowhorse approachsetthe stage fortrulybest inshow results. Let me put it this way: If you had to choose between $1 invested in Circuit Cityor $1 invested in General Electric on the day that the legendary Jack Welch took overGE in 1981 and held to January 1, 2000,you would have been betteroffwith CircuitCity—by six times.46 Nota bad performance, for a plow horse. You might expect that extraordinary results like these would lead Alan Wurtzel to discuss the brilliant decisions he made. But when we asked him to list the top five factors in his company's transformation, ranked by importance, Wurtzel gave a surprising answer: The number one factor was luck. "We were in a great industry, with the wind at our backs." We pushed back, pointing out that we selected the good-to-great com panies based on performance that surpassed their industry's average. Fur thermore, the comparison company (Silo) was in the same industry, with the same wind and probablybiggersails! We debated the point for a few minutes, with Wurtzel continuing his preference for attributing much of hissuccess to just being in the right place at the right time. Later, when asked to discuss the factors behind the enduring nature ofthe transforma tion, he said,"The first thing that comesto mind isluck. ... I was luckyto find the rightsuccessor."47 Luck. What an odd factor to talk about. Yet the good-to-great execu tives talked a lot about luck in our interviews. In one interview with a Nucor executive, we asked why the company had such a remarkable track record of good decisions; he responded: "I guess we were just lucky."48 Joseph F. Cullman 3d, the Level 5 transition CEO of Philip Morris, flat-out refused to take creditfor his company's success, attribut inghisgood fortune to having great colleagues, successors, and predeces sors.49 Even thebook he wrote—a book he undertook atthe urging ofhis colleagues, which he never intended to distribute widely outside the company—had the unusual title Ym a Lucky Guy. The opening para graph reads: "I was a very lucky guy from the very beginning of mylife: marvelous parents, good genes, lucky in love, lucky in business, and lucky when a Yale classmate had myorders changed to report to Wash ington, D.C., in early 1941, instead of to a ship that was sunk with all hands lostin the North Atlantic, lucky to be in the Navy, and lucky to be alive at eighty-five."50 We were at first puzzled by this emphasis on good luck. After all, we found no evidence that the good-to-great companies were blessed with more good luck (or more bad luck, for that matter) than the comparison companies. Then we began to notice a contrasting pattern in the compar ison executives: They credited substantial blame to bad luck, frequendy bemoaning the difficulties ofthe environment theyfaced. Compare Bethlehem Steel to Nucor. Both companies operated in the steel industry and produced hard-to-differentiate products. Both compa niesfaced the competitive challenge of cheap imported steel. Yet execu tives at the two companies had completely different views of the same environment. Bethlehem Steel's CEO summed up the company's prob lems in 1983 byblaming imports: "Our first, second, and third problems are imports."51 Ken Iverson and his crewat Nucor considered the same challenge from imports a blessing, a stroke of good fortune ("Aren't we lucky; steel is heavy, and theyhave to shipit all the way across the ocean, giving us a huge advantage!"). Iverson saw the first, second, and third problems facing the American steel industry not to be imports, but man agement.52 He even went so far as to speak out publicly against govern ment protection against imports, telling a stunned gathering of fellow steel executives in 1977 that the real problems facing the American steel industry lay in the fact that management had failed to keep pace with innovation.53 The emphasis on luck turns out to be part ofa pattern that we came to call the window and the mirror .

The comparison leaders did justthe opposite. They'd lookout the win dow for something or someone outside themselves to blame for poor results, but would preen in frontoftlj,e mirrorand credit themselves when things went well. Strangely, the window and the mirror do not reflect objective reality. Everyone outside the window points inside, directly at the Level 5 leader, saying, "He was the key; without his guidance and leadership, wewould not have become a great company." Andthe Level 5 leader points right back out the window and says, "Look at all the great peopleand good fortune that madethis possible; I'm a lucky guy." They're both right, of course. Butthe Level 5s would never admitthatfact.

CULTIVATING LEVEL 5 LEADERSHIP Not longago, Ishared the Level 5finding with a gathering ofseniorexec utives. A woman who had recently become chief executive of her com pany raised her hand and said, "I believe what you say about the good-to-great leaders. But I'm disturbed because when I look in the mir ror, I know that I'm not Level 5, not yet anyway. Part of the reason I got this job is because of my ego drives. Are you telling me that I can't make this a greatcompanyif I'm not Level 5?" "I don't know forcertainthat youabsolutely mustbe a Level 5 leaderto make yourcompany great," I replied. "I will simply pointbackto the data: Of 1,435 companies that appeared on the Fortune 500 in our initial can didate list, only eleven made the very tough cut into our study. In those eleven, all of them had Level 5 leadership in key positions, including the CEO, at the pivotal time oftransition." She sat there, quiet for moment, and you could tell everyone in the roomwas mentally urgingher to ask the question. Finally, she said, "Can you learn to become Level 5?" My hypothesis is that there are two categories of people: thosewho do not have the seed ofLevel 5andthose who do. The first category consists of people who could never in a million years bring themselves to subju gate their egoistic needs to the greater ambition of building something larger and more lasting than themselves. For these people, work will always be first and foremost about what they get—fame, fortune, adula tion, power, whatever—not whattheybuild, create, and contribute.

The second category of people—and I suspect the larger group—con sists ofthose who have the potential to evolve to Level 5; the capability resides within them, perhaps buried or ignored, but there nonetheless. And under the right circumstances—self-reflection, conscious personal development, a mentor, a great teacher, loving parents, a significant life experience, a Level 5 boss, or anynumberofotherfactors—they beginto develop. In looking at the data, we noticed thatsome ofthe leaders in ourstudy had significant lifeexperiences that mighthave sparked orfurthered their maturation. Darwin Smith fully blossomed afterhis experience with can cer. Joe Cullman was profoundly affected by his World War II experi ences, particularly the last-minute change of orders that took him off a doomed ship on which he surely would have died.54 A strong religious beliefor conversion mightalso nurturedevelopment ofLevel 5traits. Colman Mockler, for example, converted to evangelical Christianity while getting his MBA at Harvard, and later, according to the book Cutting Edge, became a prime mover in a group of Boston business executives who metfrequently over breakfast todiscuss the carryover ofreligious val ues to corporate life.55 Otherleaders in ourstudy, however, had no obvi ous catalytic event; they just lednormal lives andsomehow endedup atop the Level 5 hierarchy. I believe—although I cannot prove—that potential Level 5 leaders are highly prevalent in our society. The problem is not, in my estimation, a dearth ofpotential Level 5 leaders. They exist all around us, ifwe just know what to look for. And what is that? Look for situations where extraordinary results exist but whereno individual steps forth to claimexcess credit.You will likely find a potentialLevel 5leader at work. Foryourowndevelopment, I would love to be able to give youa listof stepsfor becoming Level 5, but we have no solid research data that would supporta crediblelist. Our research exposed Level 5 as a key component inside the black box ofwhat ittakes toshift a company from good to great. Yet inside that black box is yet another black box—namely, the inner development ofa person toLevel 5. We could speculate on what might be inside that innerblack box, but itwould mostly be justthat—speculation. So, in short, Level 5 is a very satisfying idea,a powerful idea, and, to pro duce the best transitions from good to great, perhaps an essential idea. A "Ten-Step Listto Level 5" wouldtrivialize the concept. My best advice, based on the research, is to begin practicing the other good-to-great disciplines we discovered. We found a symbiotic relation shipbetweenLevel 5and the remainingfindings. On the one hand, Level 5 traits enable you to implement the other findings; on the other hand, practicingthe otherfindings helpsyouto becomeLevel 5.Think of it this way: This chapter isabout whatLevel 5sare; the restofthe bookdescribes whattheydo. Leadingwiththe otherdisciplines can help you movein the right direction. There is no guarantee that doing so will turn you into a full-fledged Level 5, but it gives you a tangibleplace to begin. We cannot sayforsure whatpercentageof people have the seed within, or how many of those can nurture it. Even those of us who discovered Level 5 on the research team do not know for ourselves whether we will succeed in fullyevolving to Level 5.And yet,all of us who worked on the finding have been deeply affected and inspired by the idea. Darwin Smith, Colman Mockler, Alan Wurtzel, and all the other Level 5s we learned about have become models for us, something worthy to aspire toward. Whether or not we make it all the way to Level 5, it is worth the effort. For like all basic truths about what is best in human beings, when we catch a glimpse of that truth, we know that our own lives and all that we touch will be the better for the effort.

When MBAs come to us we have to fundamentally retrain them—nothing they learned will help them succeed at innovation. —Scott Cook, Founder and Chairman of the Executive Committee, Intuit ABOVE, WE QUOTE Scott Cook criticizing traditional management training. Is he simply being inflammatory? Perhaps. But many other innovative leaders have also criticized traditional management training. For example, Elon Musk, founder of Tesla, SpaceX, and PayPal, argued that "As much as possible, avoid hiring MBAs. MBA programs don't teach people how to create companies . . . At my companies, our position is that we hire someone in spite of an MBA, not because of one." 1 While we all recognize that management training has immense value, why do some leaders of innovative companies offer such harsh criticisms? Here's our explanation of where we have made a wrong turn when it comes to innovation. In 1911 Frederick Taylor wrote the landmark book Principles of Scientific Management. It had such a powerful impact on the emerging industrial corporations of the twentieth century that it earned Taylor the title "father of scientific management." Taylor's management principles were taught at the new, emerging business schools of the day and applied at rising industrial powers such as Ford Motor Company and General Electric. Indeed, Henry Ford, Alfred Sloan, and other corporate legends looked to scientific management as their management textbook, and Taylor's influence is still felt in business schools worldwide. What were Taylor's principles of scientific management? First, he recommended that work be carefully planned and broken into separate tasks. The idea was that managers could analyze the tasks of production—for example, through time and motion studies—to determine the fastest and most costeffective way to complete them. Then the manager's job was to make sure the task was standardized as much as possible and that workers followed the prescribed process. Taylor argued that task specialization was critical because it offered numerous benefits—for example, allowing for clear responsibility and accountability. It also enabled managers to match worker skills with the task, thereby facilitating a division of labor. 2 These principles—task specialization, work standardization, accountability, and division of labor—quickly spread throughout US industry. Taylor's ideas greatly simplified the job of managing the complex tasks of the emerging industrial corporations. Moreover, his principles—when applied effectively— had a powerful positive impact on the performance of the large companies of his day. We see Taylor's handiwork everywhere. Every large company is broken into functions for task specialization—R&D, procurement, operations, marketing, HR, and finance. Every large organization seems to strive for division of labor, standardization of work, accountability, and the pursuit of best practices. But even though Taylor's principles have done much good, there's one problem: they're exactly the wrong prescription for managing innovation. They're great principles for efficiently performing tasks to sustain a customer, but they work poorly for guiding work to create a customer (Peter Drucker's "central purpose" of business and the clear focus of start-ups). 3 They turn individuals into good managers (of execution) but bad innovators. How does it happen? Consider task specialization and division of labor. Specialization makes sense when a problem is well defined and characterized by low uncertainty—the kinds of problems companies typically face as they move up the famous S-curve from growth to maturity (see figure 2-1). Let's say a company needs to produce a thousand widgets at the lowest possible cost, and to respond to five thousand daily service calls. The company knows roughly how many widgets to produce and how many calls to service; it needs to figure out the most efficient way to do it. Because these tasks are quite different, the company divides them into separate functions and hires experts in operations or service to perform the tasks. Managers are held accountable based on performance metrics—say, cost per unit produced or ratings of customer satisfaction with service calls. Managers quickly learn the value of hiring and developing specialists with deep expertise (as opposed to generalists with broad expertise), because the problems are well enough defined that it's easy to match a specialist with the problem. These tactics are in fact the right ones for many problems that managers face, and applying them is simply good management. FIGURE 2-1 The S-curve and the right style of management Unfortunately, this is the wrong approach when you're trying to solve highuncertainty problems, the kind a company or start-up faces at the introduction and growth stages of the S-curve (see "Sloan Versus Durant: A Contrast in Management Styles"). When you face high uncertainty about how to create a customer, you aren't sure what type of expertise will be most valuable. So you want people who have broad expertise, the kind of people who can see the problem, and possible solution, from various angles. That's why the practices that make someone a good manager can be roadblocks in efforts to ignite insights and bring new ideas to market. Sloan versus Durant: A Contrast in Management Styles Alfred Sloan is known as the father of the modern corporation, having transformed General Motors into the model corporation of his era by introducing principles such as specialized management roles, decentralized organization, and cost accounting. Sloan's ideas on dividing tasks into manageable chunks led him to break GM into divisions (Cadillac, Buick, Chevy, Pontiac), each focused on a different customer segment. 4 Sloan's management principles—along with those of contemporaries like Taylor as well as Henry Ford, who pioneered mass production techniques—contributed much to the early development of management theory and practice. Sloan's influence is evident today in the number of institutions that bear his name and the number of business schools that teach his ideas. But Sloan's success and influence on management overlook an interesting question: Where did General Motors come from? Indeed, Sloan took the reins of GM only after it was generating nearly $4 billion in inflation-adjusted revenues. In fact, GM was founded by Billy Durant, a creative entrepreneur who made millions in the horse-and-buggy industry before starting GM. Durant was an experimenter who pioneered products in both industries and grew GM until the board of directors, recognizing that he was a talented entrepreneur but a poor manager, replaced him. Durant then cofounded Chevrolet, eventually repurchased control of GM, and ran the firm until the board removed him a second time and replaced him with Sloan. 5 That Sloan is so well known, and Durant so little known, is intriguing. What were Durant's management theories? Why did they work in the early days but fail as GM became a large corporation? The answer is simple: management theory was developed to solve the large-company management problem and not the innovation problem. The former emerged during the Industrial Revolution, when the economy was transformed from small workshops to large businesses of unprecedented scale, producing things like oil, textiles, autos, and railways. To make the trains run on time and increase the production of autos, these large corporations required a new profession: management. They needed managers to plan, coordinate, rationalize, and optimize the operations of large, complex organizations. Business schools emerged to operations of large, complex organizations. Business schools emerged to train this new cadre of managers to be effective at resolving the problems faced by large corporations, such as "What new features should we add?" or "How can we lower costs by 5 percent?" These are low-uncertainty problems calling for incremental changes to existing products or processes. In contrast, most start-up or corporate entrepreneurs are trying to launch new products that have disruptive potential. They face highuncertainty problems such as "Will consumers want to use a personal computer (a demand problem faced by Apple), and can we make it easy enough for children to use (a technology problem)?" Or, "Will people buy products over the internet (a demand problem faced by Amazon.com), and can we provide fulfillment in a low-cost and reliable way (a technology problem faced by Amazon.com)?" "Will people make payments over the internet (a demand problem faced by PayPal), and can our technology provide them the ease of use and security they need?" Although these firms successfully solved some high-uncertainty problems, business history is littered with failures—in many cases, because they applied the wrong theory: they followed business-school management theory (designed for low-uncertainty problems), and not innovation-school management theory (necessary for high-uncertainty problems). Four Key Roles of the Leader To apply the innovator's method, established companies must make a critical transition from their natural tendency to rely exclusively on traditional management to applying entrepreneurial management when facing the uncertainty of innovation. We've identified four key roles that leaders must fulfill if they hope to turn their organizations into successful innovators, composed of teams that innovate like a network of start-ups. These roles are critical to ensure that the innovator's method is incorporated into the company's processes and the day-to-day behaviors of employees. First, and most important, the leader must become the chief experimenter and not the chief decision maker. As shown in figure 2-2, the other three roles support, and enable, the chief experimenter role. The second role is to set the grand challenge—not only to inspire others to pursue an opportunity but also to challenge the organization to break free of Taylor's principles of scientific management. Third, the leader must build broad and deep expertise in the innovator's method, which is needed to ensure that the organization has the capability to generate insights, discover problems worth solving, and rapidly prototype solutions. The fourth role of the leader is to remove barriers to change and install systems to facilitate the fast experiments required to test the team's hypotheses —and resolve the uncertainties—at each step. FIGURE 2-2 Be the chief experimenter Be the Chief Experimenter In traditional management, managers are decision makers. You analyze information and make decisions that will affect the future of your organization. In a way, you're trying to predict the future, and position the company to succeed. For many managers, decision making is the essence of what it means to be a manager. But when you're acting under uncertainty, the available information is too scarce, or even absent, for you to predict the future with any confidence. The best you can do is guess, and you may be wrong more often than you're right. But if you aren't making decisions, what is your role as a leader of innovative teams? The innovator's method enables you to make effective decisions about the future—but you must first define a new role for yourself. You must learn a new way to be right. For Intuit's Scott Cook and Brad Smith, it's often a matter of reprogramming new hires. "Unfortunately, you know how big companies and hierarchies make decisions," says Cook. "They tend to rely on politics, PowerPoint, and persuasion." So to fix that, you've got to change how and where decisions are made . . . enabling decisions to be made by the best idea you can validate in the market. This means moving decisions from bosses voting their opinions, to enabling and measuring customers voting with their feet. This goes against what people have been taught in business school. Most leaders in business have been successful because of analysis. They see themselves as decision makers and their job is to do great planning and analysis. That's the kind of change that we are trying to create at Intuit. 6 Rather than becoming great planners and power decision makers, the company's new leaders are taught to champion experiments. Similarly, at Google, founders Larry Page and Sergey Brin have always supported the notion that decisions should be made by rich data from experiments—so much so that in 2002 they experimented with a completely flat organization, eliminating engineering managers. That experiment lasted only a few months, until too many people went directly to Page with questions about expense reports and interpersonal and career issues. 7 But the philosophy that even top Google executives must back their ideas with data lives on. To illustrate, in one instance Larry Page and Marissa Mayer (former VP at Google who is now CEO at Yahoo!) supported the idea to develop a massive digital archive of books. But rather than simply use their positions to make the decision to proceed, the two went so far as to clamp a three-hundred-page book to a piece of plywood, manually photograph each of its pages, and run the images through character recognition software, all to establish that it would take only forty minutes to digitize a book. How do chief experimenters differ from decision-making managers? They focus on three things: Forming leap-of-faith assumptions with their team Rapidly testing those assumptions through experiments (mostly with customers) Letting the data (mostly from customers) make the decisions As a leader, you don't have to do everything yourself: instead, decisions move downward in the hierarchy to small teams, where data reveals what the decision should be—or what the next experiment should be. Says Cook, "[Intuit CEO] Brad Smith and I have changed the questions that we ask. We used to ask things like, 'Well, what's your answer, and what's your analysis behind it?' And now we ask, 'OK, what's the fastest way to get an experiment to test that idea?'" 8 Jeff Bezos of Amazon manages in a similar style using similar questions. A few years ago, Bezos charged a team with analyzing the supply chain to come up with recommendations for an overall design of the company's logistics. The goal was to ensure that fulfillment could be done fast and economically. As one team member recalls, "When we presented our analysis, while all other executives were happy with it, Jeff was not. He insisted on being more rigorous and envisioned everybody in the company making decisions based on simulation outputs. So a team was formed to build supporting supply chain simulations— simulations that allowed us to see the results of different kinds of decisions. These simulation tools are now currently used throughout the company to make decisions." 9 The simulations allowed Bezos to experiment under uncertainty before building solutions. This leadership style is working at Amazon, Google, and Intuit because the leader walks the talk. Says Cook, "Brad and I have to live by the same rules. So we end up asking ourselves questions like, 'I have got a fundamental belief of what we should do. Now, what are the leap-of-faith assumptions on which it is based? And how are we going to test the leap-of-faith assumptions that are crucial to my beliefs?' We need to do this just like we would do for anyone else . . . Experiments will be nothing but window dressing until you change who and how decisions are made." 10 So a key step in becoming a great leader of innovation is to change how decisions are made—and that starts with you. Set the Grand Challenge In a now famous 1979 visit to Xerox Palo Alto Research Center (PARC) in California, Steve Jobs recalled seeing a rough graphical user interface. "It was incomplete, some of it wasn't even right, but the germ of the idea was there," he said. "Within ten minutes, it was so obvious that every computer would work this way someday." 11 Jobs then took his engineering team on a tour of PARC— and returned to Apple focused on developing a personal computer that incorporated, and improved on, the PARC technologies. Jobs assembled a team of brilliant engineers, gave them the needed resources, and infused the Macintosh team with a vision of creating the world's easiest-touse personal computer. That's what an innovative leader does. In contrast, the executive team at Xerox lacked the discovery skills necessary to exploit technologies developed in their own company. As PARC scientist Larry Tesler observed, "After an hour looking at demos they [Jobs and Apple programmers] understood our technology and what it meant more than any Xerox executive understood after years of showing it to them." Jobs agreed with Tesler, saying, "Basically they were copier heads that just had no clue about a computer or what it could do. And so they just grabbed defeat from the greatest victory in the computer industry. Xerox could have owned the entire computer industry today." 12 Years later, when Apple was considering offering a portable music device, Jobs and his leadership team set the vision with the tagline "1,000 songs in your pocket." That's why the first iPod was the size it was—small enough to fit in a pocket. These examples illustrate one reason Steve Jobs was a great leader of innovation: he had a nose for opportunity, and he set the grand challenge. You don't have to be Steve Jobs in terms of identifying the right opportunity, but you do have to set the grand challenge for your team. To do that, says Intuit's Cook, "Leaders should ask questions like these: 'What is the most important problem, the biggest pain point, that we can solve? How does the customer measure the gain? How can we move the needle the most for the customer?'" 13 You don't necessarily have to articulate the solution (for example, the number of songs on a device), but you need to push people to search for opportunities. For example, when Intuit considered the Indian market as an opportunity, Alex Lintner, the executive overseeing Intuit's Indian operations, asked his team to "create new businesses that will improve the financial lives of Indians." This grand challenge led the Mobile Bazaar team to identify an opportunity for the 150 million farmers in India to improve their financial lives by getting better prices. The Intuit team then sought to create a product that would do that. Another dimension of setting the grand challenge may be even more important: giving the team and organization permission to break free of traditional management and use entrepreneurial management. This is extremely difficult. If you're like most people, when you started kindergarten you were assigned a desk and given clear instructions on what to do and how to do it. Most of us have been in those assigned desks ever since, completing our assigned tasks. To break that pattern, leaders must set a different grand challenge for the organization, saying something like, "I expect you to go figure out where your desk should be, and discover which assignments will create the most value for customers." At Valve Software, a multibillion-dollar company that has already revolutionized the video gaming industry, founder Gabe Newell sets a radical vision to ruthlessly pursue customer value. To enable employees to do that, he has torn down all the bureaucracy. 14 He instructs every new hire, "Your desk has wheels. Your job is to figure out where you create the most value for customers, and move it there." Valve's leaders argue that as a company Valve has "spent the last decade going out of its way to recruit the most intelligent, innovative, talented people on Earth; telling them to sit at a desk and do what they're told obliterates 99 percent of their value." 15 Recent innovations include creating the platform on which 80 percent of all PC games are sold and making the first foray into the video game console market by a new company in more than a decade. Similarly, Amazon's Bezos uses the slogan "It's Still Day One" to remind employees that Amazon is still a start-up—and there is lots of runway ahead. It's such a central motivating idea that Bezos named one of the company's buildings Day One. Asked when Amazon will reach "Day Two," Bezos responded, "Day Two will be when the rate of change slows . . . And that's the sense in which I believe it's still Day One, and that it's early in the day. If anything, the rate of change is accelerating." 16 A key role for Bezos is to set the grand challenge for Amazon: to behave like a start-up. Build Broad and Deep Expertise When Ricardo dos Santos joined Qualcomm, a Fortune 100 manufacturer of semiconductors used in wireless devices, he was confident he could transform the company's failing "idea management program" (effectively a suggestion box) into a corporation-wide innovation program. Dos Santos had the support of a visionary CEO, a mandate to create disruptive new products, and the freedom to design a sweeping program to kick-start new ideas. Because prior efforts had flailed, dos Santos searched for ways to teach people how to transform their ideas into experiments to test their validity but with the caveat that the program had to be integrated with existing business units where people continue working full-time on their current projects. Dos Santos built a three-phase program called Venture Fest. In the first phase, employees submitted ideas, which were then reduced to the twenty best ideas based on peer review. Then Venture Fest trainees took part in a three-month, part-time boot camp, where they tested their ideas with customers and developed prototypes. In the final phase, they presented their ideas to top executives in a competition for funding, after which they attempted to convince an existing business unit to adopt the new idea. Generally Venture Fest was a success, with ideas submitted increasing from eighty-two in the first year to more than five hundred five years later. Moreover, Venture Fest participants identified many potential breakthrough ideas. But although Venture Fest fostered some truly transformation ideas, a few organization members outside the program began to question, and even attack, the program. Some managers weren't happy releasing some of their best people to work on projects not under their control. And from a more traditional management perspective, the Venture Fest projects seemed too open, fluid, and flexible, clashing with Qualcomm's rational, deadline-driven culture. Perhaps more dangerously, some R&D managers, many of whom felt they owned innovation, argued that the emerging new ideas fell outside the scope of existing R&D programs or didn't have as much intellectual property as usual. Despite the best intentions of many inside Qualcomm, Venture Fest encountered the kind of allergic reaction to implementing innovation that we have observed at many other companies that excel at execution. After five turbulent and exciting years, Venture Fest was quietly folded into R&D. 17 Build Broad Expertise The Qualcomm experience is similar to those in many organizations that try to "do innovation" by creating pockets of entrepreneurial management and experimentation expertise without generating broad awareness of the processes and goals associated with successful programs. This lack of understanding and appreciation for goals and methods can lead outsiders to misinterpret the innovator's methods as well as its output. Dos Santos recalls that Qualcomm made great strides in igniting new ideas on the "sell" side (the innovators) and increased the start-up spirit in the company overall. But if he were to do it again, he would focus on one more crucial goal: educating the "buy side"—the rest of the organization—"so that we could all be using the same language and match discovery efforts." 18 The greater the awareness and appreciation in your organization that innovation requires a different set of management tools, the easier it will be to apply the innovator's method. We aren't saying that everyone needs deep expertise in these principles, but simply that everyone needs some training to understand that managing uncertainty requires a different approach. Of course, if your organization faces greater uncertainty, you may choose to extensively train everyone. At Intuit, Cook and Smith make sure all new hires are trained in design for delight principles, completing a weeklong design training program within the first three months. The goal is not to make everyone an expert but to make sure everyone understands lean experimentation principles and knows the steps for generating insights and nailing the problem and solution. Employees gain a common language to describe the efforts to bring new ideas to market. Having the language to explain your actions gives people immense power in overcoming the inertia that often impedes change. In our interviews with dozens of innovators, they often cited the common language as one of the most important reasons for training everyone. But there's another reason smart leaders want everyone to understand the innovator's method: it generates ideas. Almost every study shows that searching broadly is the best way to uncover novel ideas that are worth pursuing. Build Deep Expertise Building broad understanding is necessary but not sufficient. It's also critical to build deep expertise within your organization. We've seen it done effectively in a couple of ways. One option is to create a lab or SWAT team that applies the innovator's method to new ideas. In addition to relevant engineering and technology experts, the lab has experts in design thinking and lean experimentation. For example, AT&T—not known for innovation in the past twenty years—recently created five labs (AT&T calls them "foundries"), each employing forty to fifty interdisciplinary experts. Their task: testing new insights generated inside and outside AT&T. The foundries house marketing experts from the business units, experts in telecommunications technologies, and experts in design thinking. What's more, AT&T has invited start-ups and established companies from many industries to participate in rapidly developing and experimenting with new technologies. Each new idea is run through a twelve-week project, where a team applies the kinds of tools we describe in this book to produce virtual or physical prototypes. Where do the ideas originate? A team of senior leaders across AT&T selects ideas from three sources: An internal idea board called The Innovation Program (or TIP), where ideas are posted and voted on A "fast pitch" program, where individuals and companies, most of them from outside AT&T (suppliers, start-ups), make ten-minute pitches to key AT&T decision makers The business units, where lead marketing executives who are assigned to the foundry full-time are charged with polling their business units for new ideas Each of the most promising ideas is funneled to a team of experts—a SWAT team—that applies elements of the innovator's method to generate a prototype. Although AT&T has been at this for less than five years, the foundries are credited with developing ideas that have helped push the company's innovation premium from minus 13 percent in the mid-2000s to almost 10 percent today. "As the foundries have proved their value, we're now using the term foundry as a verb," says John Donovan, SEVP of AT&T technology and network operations. "We've proven we get from prototype to product three times faster." 19 Other companies have developed similar labs and credit them with increasing their innovation output, including Hyatt Hotels and Hallmark as well as lesser-known companies like Banco Davivienda, a leading bank in Latin America.

CHAPTER THREE

# First Who Then What

When we began the research project, we expected to find that the first step in taking a company from good to great would be to set a new direction, a new vision and strategy for the company, and then to get peo ple committed and alignedbehind that newdirection. We found something quite the opposite. The executives who ignited the transformations from good to great did not first figure out where to drive the bus and then get people to take it there. No, they first got the right people on the bus (and the wrongpeople offthe bus) and then figured out where to drive it. They said, in essence, "Look,I don't reallyknowwhere we should take this bus. But I know this much: If we get the right people on the bus, the right people in the right seats,and the wrong people offthe bus, then well figure out how to take it someplace great."

The good-to-great leaders understood three simple truths. First, if you begin with "who," rather than "what," you can more easily adapt to a changing world. If people join the bus primarily because of where it is going, what happens if you getten miles down the road and you need to change direction? You've got a problem. But if people are on the bus because ofwho else is on the bus, then it's much easier to change direc tion: "Hey, I got on this bus because of who else is on it; if we need to change direction to be more successful, fine with me." Second, if you have the right people on the bus, the problem of how to motivate and manage people largely goes away. The right people don't need to be tightly managed orfired up; they will be self-motivated bythe inner drive to produce the best results and to be part of creating something great. Third, if you have the wrong people, it doesn't matter whether you dis cover the right direction; you still won't have a great company. Great vision withoutgreatpeopleisirrelevant. Consider the case of Wells Fargo. Wells Fargo began its fifteen-year stint of spectacular performance in 1983,but the foundation for the shift dates back to the early 1970s, when then-CEO Dick Cooley began build ing one ofthe most talented management teams in the industry (the best team, according to investor Warren Buffett).2 Cooley foresaw that the banking industry would eventually undergo wrenching change, but he did not pretendto know whatform that change would take. So instead of mapping out a strategy for change, he and chairman Ernie Arbuckle focused on "injecting an endless stream oftalent" directly into the veins of the company. They hired outstanding people whenever and wherever they found them,often without any specific job in mind. "That's how you buildthe future," he said. "IfI'm notsmart enough toseethe changes that are coming, theywill. And they'll be flexible enough to dealwith them."3 Cooley's approach proved prescient. No one could predict all thechanges thatwould be wrought bybanking deregulation. Yet when these changes came,no bankhandledthose challenges betterthanWells Fargo. Ata time when itssector ofthe banking industry fell 59percentbehind the general stock market, Wells Fargo outperformed the market byoverthree times.4 Carl Reichardt, who became CEO in 1983, attributed the bank's suc cess largely to the people around him, most of whom he inherited from Cooley.5 As he listed members oftheWells Fargo executive team thathad joined the company during the Cooley-Reichardt era, we were stunned. Nearly every person had gone on to become CEO of a major company:

BillAldingerbecame the CEO of Household Finance, Jack Grundhofer became CEO of U.S. Bancorp,Frank Newman became CEO ofBankers Trust, Richard Rosenberg became CEO of Bank of America, Bob Joss became CEO ofWestpac Banking (one of the largest banks in Australia) and later became dean of the Graduate School of Business at Stanford University—not exactly your garden variety executive team! Arjay Miller, an active Wells Fargo board member forseventeen years, told us that the Wells Fargo team reminded him of the famed "Whiz Kids" recruited to Ford Motor Company in the late 1940s (of which Miller was a member, eventually becoming president ofFord).6 Wells Fargo's approach was sim ple:You get the bestpeople, youbuild them into the bestmanagers in the industry, and you accept the fact that some of them will be recruited to becomeCEOs of other companies.7 Bank of America took a very different approach. While Dick Cooley systematically recruited the bestpeoplehe could get his hands on, Bankof America, according to the bookBreaking the Bank, followed something called the "weak generals, strong lieutenants" model.8 If you pickstrong generals for key positions, their competitors will leave. But if you pick weak generals—placeholders, rather than highly capable executives—then the stronglieutenants are more likely to stickaround. The weakgenerals model produced a climate very differentat Bank of America than the one atWells Fargo. Whereas the Wells Fargo crewacted as a strongteam of equal partners, ferociously debating eyeball-to-eyeball in search of the best answers, the Bank ofAmerica weak generals would wait for directions from above. Sam Armacost, who inherited the weak generals model, described the management climate: "I came away quite distressed from my first couple of management meetings. Not only couldn't I get conflict, I couldn't even get comment. They were all wait ing to see whichway the wind blew."9 A retired Bank of America executive described senior managers in the 1970s as "Plastic People" who'd been trained to quietlysubmit to the dic tates ofa domineering CEO.10 Later, after losing over $1 billion in the mid1980s, Bank ofAmerica recruited a gang ofstrong generals to turn the bank around. Andwhere did it find those strong generals? From rightacross the street at Wells Fargo. In fact, Bank of America recruited so many Wells Fargo executives during its turnaround that people inside began to referto themselves as "Wells ofAmerica."11 At thatpoint, Bank ofAmerica began to climb upward again,but it was too littletoo late. From 1973 to 1998, while Wells Fargo went from buildup to breakthrough results, Bank ofAmerica's cumulative stock returns didn't even keep pace with the general market.

Now, you mightbe thinking, "That's justgood management—the idea of gettingthe right people around you. What's new about that?" On one level, we have to agree; it is just plain old-fashioned good management. Butwhat stands out with suchdistinction in the good-to-great companies are two key points that made them quite different.

"First who" is a very simple idea to grasp, and a very difficult idea to do—and most don't do it well. It's easy to talk about paying attention to Good to Great 45 people decisions, but how manyexecutives have the discipline of David Maxwell, who heldoffon developing a strategy until he gotthe right peo ple in place, while the company was losing $1 million every single business day with $56 billion of loans underwater? When Maxwell became CEO of Fannie Mae during its darkest days, the board desperately wanted to know how he was going to rescue the company. Despite the immense pressure to act, to do something dramatic, to seize the wheeland startdri ving, Maxwell focused first on getting the rightpeopleon the Fannie Mae management team. His first act was to interview all the officers. He sat them down and said, "Look, this is going to be a very hard challenge. I want you to think about how demanding this is going to be. If you don't think you're going to like it,that's fine. Nobody's going to hate you."12 Maxwell made it absolutely clear that there would only be seats for A players who were going toputforth anA+ effort, andifyou weren't upfor it, you had better get offthe bus, and get offnow.13 One executive who had justuprooted his lifeand career to join Fannie Mae came to Maxwell and said, "I listened to you very carefully, and I don't wantto do this." He left andwent back towhere he came from.14 In all, fourteen oftwenty-six executives left the company, replaced by some of the best, smartest, and hardest-working executives in the entire world of finance.15 The same standard applied up and down theFannie Mae ranks as managers at every level increased the caliber oftheir teams and putimmense peer pressure upon each other, creating high turnover at first, when some people just didn'tpanout.16 "We hada saying, *You can'tfake itatFannie Mae,' " said one executive team member. "Eitheryou knew your stuffor you didn't, and if you didn't, you'd justblowout of here."17 Wells Fargo and Fannie Mae both illustrate the idea that "who" ques tions come before "what" questions—before vision, before strategy, before tactics, before organizational structure, before technology. Dick Cooley and David Maxwell both exemplified a classic Level 5 style when they said, "Idon'tknow where we should take this company, but I doknow that if I start with the right people, ask them the right questions, and engage them invigorous debate, we will find a way to make this company great." NOT A "GENIUS WITH A THOUSAND HELPERS" In contrast to the good-to-great companies, which built deep and strong executive teams, many of thc comparison companies followed a "genius 46 Jim Collins with a thousand helpers" model. In this model,the companyis a platform for the talents of an extraordinary individual. In these cases, the towering genius, the primary driving force in the company's success, isa greatasset— as long as the genius sticks around. The geniuses seldom build greatman agement teams, for the simple reason that they don't need one, and often don't want one. If you're a genius, you don't need a Wells Fargo-caliber management team of people who could run their own shows elsewhere. No, you justneed an army ofgood soldiers who can help implementyour great ideas. However, when thegenius leaves, the helpers areoften lost. Or, worse, theytryto mimictheirpredecessor with bold,visionary moves (trying to actlike a genius, without being a genius) that prove unsuccessful. Eckerd Corporation suffered the liability of a leader who had an uncanny genius for figuring out "what" to do but little ability to assemble the right "who" on the executive team. Jack Eckerd, blessed with monu mental personal energy (he campaigned for governor of Florida while running his company) and a genetic gift for market insight and shrewd deal making, acquired his way from two little stores in Wilmington, Delaware, to a drugstore empire of over a thousand stores spread across the southeastern United States. By the late 1970s, Eckerd's revenues equaledWalgreens‘, and it looked like Eckerd mighttriumph asthe great company in the industry. Butthen Jack Eckerd leftto pursue his passion for politics, running for senator and joining the Ford administration in Washington. Without hisguiding genius, Eckerd's company began a long decline, eventually being acquired by J. C. Penney.18 The contrast between Jack Eckerd and Cork Walgreen is striking. Whereas Jack Eckerd had a genius for picking the rightstores to buy, Cork Walgreen had a genius for picking the right people to hire.19 Whereas Jack Eckerdhad a giftforseeing whichstores shouldgo in what locations, CorkWalgreen had a gift for seeing whichpeopleshouldgo in what seats. Whereas Jack Eckerd failed utterly at the single most impor tant decision facing any executive—the selection of a successor—Cork Walgreen developed multiple outstanding candidates and selected a superstar successor, who may prove to be even better than Cork him self.20 Whereas Jack Eckerd had no executive team, but instead a bunch of capable helpers assembled to assist the greatgenius, Cork Walgreen built the best executive team in the industry. Whereas the primaryguid ance mechanism for Eckerd Corporation's strategy lay inside Jack Eck erd's head, the primary guidance mechanism for Walgreens' corporate

Level 5 + Management Team Level 5 Leader First Who Get the right people on the bus. Builda superior executive team. * Then What Once you have the right people in place, figure out the best path to greatness. Good to Great 47 A "Genius with a Thousand Helpers" (Comparison Companies) Level 4 Leader \ First What Set a vision for where to drive the bus. Develop a road map for driving the bus. * Then Who Enlista crew of highly capable "helpers" to make the vision happen.

strategy lay in the group dialogue and shared insights of the talented executive team. The "genius with a thousand helpers" model isparticularly prevalent in the unsustained comparison companies. The most classic case comes from a man known as the Sphinx, Henry Singleton ofTeledyne. Single ton grew up on a Texas ranch, with the childhood dream of becoming a great businessman in the model ofthe rugged individualist. Armed with a

Ph.D. from MIT, he founded Teledyne.21 The name Teledyne derives from Greek andmeans "force applied ata distance"—an aptname, as the central force holding the far-flung empire together was Henry Singleton himself. Through acquisitions, Singleton builtthe company from a small enter prise to number 293 on the Fortune 500 list in six years.22 Within ten years, he'd completed more than 100 acquisitions, eventually creating a far-flung enterprise with 130 profit centers in everything from exotic met als to insurance.23 Amazingly, the whole system worked, with Singletonhimself acting asthe glue that connected allthe moving parts together. At one point, he said, "I define my job as having the freedom to do what seems to me to be in the best interest of the company at any time."24 A 1978 Forbes feature story maintained, "Singleton will win no awards for humility, but who can avoid standing in awe of his impressive record?" Singleton continued to run the company well into hisseventies, with no serious thought given to succession. After all,why worry aboutsuccession whenthe very pointofthe whole thingisto serve asa platform to leverage the talents ofyour remarkable genius? "Ifthere isa single weakness in this otherwise brilliantpicture/7 the article continued, "it isthis: Teledyne is not so much a system as it is the reflection of one man's singular disci pline."25 What a weakness it turned out to be. Once Singleton stepped away from day-to-day management in the mid-1980s, the far-flung empire began to crumble. From the endof 1986 until its merger with Allegheny in 1995, Teledyne's cumulative stock returns imploded, falling 66 percent behind the general stock market. Singleton achieved hischildhood dream ofbecoming a great businessman, buthe failed utterly at the task ofbuild ing a great company.

IT'S WHO YOU PAY, NOT HOW YOU PAY THEM We expected to find that changes in incentive systems, especially execu tive incentives, would be highly correlated with making the leap from good to great. With allthe attention paid to executive compensation—the shift to stock options and the huge packages that have become common place—surely, we thought, the amount and structure of compensation must play a key role in going from good togreat. How else doyou getpeo ple to do the rightthings that create great results? We weredead wrong in our expectations. We fojund, no systematic pattern linking executive compensation to We spent weeks inputting compensation data from proxy statements and performed 112 separate analyses looking for patterns and correla tions. We examined everything we could quantify for the top five offi cers—cash versus stock, long-term versus short-term incentives, salary versus bonus, and so forth.

Some companies used stock extensively; oth ers didn't. Some had high salaries; others didn't. Some made significant use of bonus incentives; others didn't. Most importantly, when we ana lyzed executive compensation patterns relative to comparison companies, we found no systematic differences on the use of stock (or not), high salaries (or not), bonus incentives (or not), or long-term compensation (or not). The only significant difference we found was that the good-togreat executives received slightly less total cash compensation ten years after the transition than their counterparts at the still-mediocre compari son companies!26 Not that executive compensation is irrelevant. You have to be basically rational and reasonable (I doubt that Colman Mockler, DavidMaxwell, or Darwin Smith would have worked for free), andthe good-to-great compa nies did spend time thinking about the issue. Butonce you've structured something thatmakes basic sense, executive compensation falls away as a distinguishing variable in moving an organization from good togreat. Why might that be? It issimply a manifestation of the "first who" prin ciple:It's nothow you compensate your executives, it's which executives you have to compensate in the first place. If you have the right executives on the bus, they will do everything within their power to build a great com pany, not because of what they will "get" for it, but because they simply cannot imagine settling for anything less. Their moral code requires buildingexcellence forits own sake, and you're no more likely to change that witha compensation package than you'relikely to affect whether they breathe. The good-to-great companies understood a simple truth: The right people will do the right things and deliver the best results they're capableof,regardless ofthe incentive system.We were not able to lookasrigorously at nonexecutive compensation; such data is not available in assystematic a format as proxy statements for top officers. Nonetheless, evidence from source documents and articles suggests thatthe same idea applies at all levels ofan organization.27 A particularly vivid example is Nucor. Nucor built its entire system on the ideathat you can teachfarmers how tomake steel, but youcan't teach a farmer work ethic to people who don't have it in the first place. So, instead ofsetting up mills in traditional steel towns like Pittsburgh and Gary, it located its plants in places like Crawfordsville, Indiana; Norfolk, Nebraska; and Plymouth, Utah—places full ofrealfarmers whogo to bed early, rise at dawn, and get rightto work without fanfare. "Gotta milk the cows" and "Gonna plow the northforty before noon"translated easily into "Gotta roll some sheet steel" and "Gonna cast forty tons before lunch." Nucor ejected people who did not share this work ethic, generating as high as 50 percent turnover in the first year ofa plant, followed byvery low turnover as the right people settled in for the long haul.28 To attract and keep the best workers, Nucor paid itssteelworkers more than any other steel company in the world. But it built its pay system around a high-pressure team-bonus mechanism, withover 50percent of a worker's compensation tieddirectly tothe productivity ofhiswork teamof twenty to forty people.29 Nucorteammembers would usually show up for work thirty minutes early to arrange theirtools and prepare to blast offthe starting linethe instant theshift gunfired.30 "We have the hardest working steel workers in the world," said one Nucor executive. "We hire five, work themlike ten, and pay themlike eight."31 The Nucor system did not aim to turn lazy people into hard workers, but to createan environment where hardworking peoplewouldthrive and lazy workers would either jump or get thrown right off the bus. In one extreme case,workers chased a lazy teammate right out of the plant with an angle iron.

Nucor illustrates a key point. In determining "the right people," the good-to-great companies placed greater weight on character attributes than on specific educational background, practical skills, specialized knowledge, or work experience. Not that specific knowledge or skills are unimportant, but they viewed these traits as more teachable (or at least learnable), whereas they believed dimensions like character, work ethic, basic intelligence, dedication to fulfilling commitments, and values are more ingrained. As Dave Nassefof PitneyBowes put it: I used to be in the Marines,and the Marinesget a lot of credit for build ing people's values. But that's not the way it really works. The Marine Corps recruits people who share the corps' values, then provides them with the training required to accomplish the organization's mission. We look at it the same wayat PitneyBowes. We have more people who want to do the right thing than mostcompanies. We don't justlookat experi ence. We want to know: Who are they? Why are they?We find out who they are by asking them why they made decisions in their life. The answers to thesequestions give usinsight intotheircorevalues.33 One good-to-great executive said that his best hiring decisions often came from people with no industry or business experience. In one case, 52 Jim Collins he hireda manager who'd been captured twice duringthe Second World War and escaped both times. "I thought that anyone who could do that shouldn't have trouble with business."34 RIGOROUS, NOT RUTHLESS

The good-to-great companies probably sound like tough places to work—and they are. Ifyou don'thave what it takes, you probably won'tlast long. But they're not ruthless cultures, they're rigorous cultures. And the dis tinction is crucial. To be ruthless means hacking and cutting, especially in difficult times, orwantonly firing people without anythoughtful consideration. To be rig orous meansconsistently applying exacting standards at all timesand at all levels, especially in upper management. To be rigorous, not ruthless, means that the best people need not worry about their positions and can concentrate fullyon their work. In 1986, Wells Fargo acquiredCrockerBankand planned to shed gobs of excess cost in the consolidation. There's nothing unusual about that— every bank mergerin the era of deregulation aimed to cut excess cost out ofa bloated and protected industry. However, what was unusual about the Wells-Crocker consolidation is the way Wells integrated management or, to be more accurate, the way it didn't even tryto integrate most Crocker managementinto the Wells culture. The Wells Fargo team concludedrightup frontthat the vast majority of Crockermanagers wouldbe the wrong peopleon the bus. Crocker people had long been steeped in the traditions and perks of old-style banker cul ture, complete with a marbled executive dining room with its own chef and $500,000 worth of china.35 Quite a contrast to the spartan culture at Wells Fargo, wheremanagementate food preparedbya collegedormitory food service.36 Wells Fargo made it clearto the Crocker managers: "Look, this is not a mergerof equals; it'san acquisition; webought your branches and your customers; we didn't acquire you/7 Wells Fargo terminated most ofthe Crocker management team—1,600 Crocker managers gone on day one—including nearly allthe topexecutives.37 A critic might say, "That's justthe Wells people protecting their own." But consider the following fact: Wells Fargo also sent some of its own managers packing in cases where the Crocker managers were judged as better qualified. When it came to management, the Wells Fargo stan- Good to Great 53 dardswere ferocious and consistent. Likea professional sports team, only the best made the annual cut, regardless of position or tenure. Summed up one Wells Fargo executive: "The only way to deliver to the people who are achieving is to not burden them with the people who are not achieving."38 On the surface, thislooks ruthless. But the evidence suggests that the average Crocker manager was just not the same caliber as the average Wells manager and would have failed in the Wells Fargo performance culture. If they weren'tgoing to make it on the bus in the long term, why let them suffer in the short term? One seniorWells Fargo executive told us: "We all agreed this was an acquisition, not a merger, and there's no sensebeatingaround the bush, not beingstraightforward with people.We decided it would be best to simply do it on day one. We planned our efforts so that we could say, right up front, 'Sorry, we don't see a role for you,' or Yes, we do see a role; you have a job,so stop worrying about it.' We were not going to subject our culture to a death by a thousand cuts.' "39 To let people languish in uncertaintyfor months or years, stealing pre cioustime in their lives that theycould use to move on to somethingelse, when in the end they aren't goingto makeit anyway—that wouldbe ruth less. To deal with it right up front and let people get on with their lives— that is rigorous. Not that the Crocker acquisition is easy to swallow. It's never pleasant to see thousands ofpeoplelose their jobs, but the era ofbank deregulation saw hundreds ofthousands of lost jobs. Given that, it'sinteresting to note two points. First, Wells Fargo did fewer big layoffs than its comparison company, Bank of America.40 Second, upper management, including someseniorWells Fargo upper management, suffered more on a percent age basis than lower-level workers in the consolidation.41 Rigor in a goodto-great company appliesfirst at the top, focused on those who hold the largestburden of responsibility. To be rigorous in people decisions meansfirst becoming rigorous about top management people decisions. Indeed, I fear that people might use "first who rigor" as an excuse for mindlessly chopping out people to improve performance. "It'shard to do, but we've gotto be rigorous," I can hear them say. And I cringe. For not onlywill a lot of hardworking, good people get hurt in the process, but the evidence suggests that such tactics are contrary to producing sustained great results. The good-to-great com panies rarelyused head-count loppingas a tactic and almost never used it 54 Jim Collins asa primary strategy. Even in the Wells Fargo case, the companyused lay offs halfas much asBank ofAmerica duringthe transition era. In contrast, we found layoffs used five times more frequently in the comparison companies than in the good-to-great companies. Some of the comparison companies had an almost chronic addiction to layoffs and restructurings. It would be a mistake—a tragic mistake, indeed—tothink that the way you ignite a transition from good to great is by wantonly swinging the ax on vast numbers of hardworking people. Endlessrestructuringand mind less hacking were neverpart ofthe good-to-great model. How to Be Rigorous We'veextracted three practicaldisciplines fromthe researchfor being rig orous rather than ruthless. Practical Discipline #1:When in doubt, don't hire—keep looking. One of the immutable laws of management physics is "Packard's Law." (So called because we first learned it in a previous research project from DavidPackard, cofounderof the Hewlett-Packard Company.) It goes like this: No company can grow revenues consistently faster than its ability to getenough ofthe rightpeople to implementthat growth and still become a great company. If your growth rate in revenues consistently outpaces yourgrowth rate in people, yousimply will not—indeed cannot—build a great company. Good to Great 55 The management team at Circuit City instinctively understood Packard's Law. Driving around Santa Barbara the day after Christmas a few years ago, I noticed something different about the CircuitCity store. Otherstores had signs and banners reaching outtocustomers: "Always the Best Prices" or "Great After-Holiday Deals" or "Best After-Christmas Selection," and so forth. But not Circuit City. It had a banner that read: "Always Looking forGreat People." The sign reminded meofourinterview with Walter Bruckart, vice pres ident during the good-to-great years. When asked to name the top five factors that led to the transition from mediocrity to excellence, Bruckart said, "One would be people. Two would be people. Three would be peo ple. Four would be people. And five would be people. Ahuge partofour transition can be attributed to our discipline in picking the rightpeople." Bruckart then recalled a conversation with CEO Alan Wurtzel during a growth spurt at Circuit City: " 'Alan, I'm really wearing down trying to find the exact right person to fill this position or that position. At what point do I compromise?' Without hesitation, Alan said, You don't com promise. We find another way to get through until we find the right people.' One ofthe key contrasts between Alan Wurtzel at Circuit City and Sid ney Cooper at Silo is that Wurtzel spent the bulk of his time in the early years focused on getting the right people on the bus, whereas Cooper spent 80 percent ofhis time focusing ontheright stores tobuy.44 Wurtzel's first goal was to buildthe best, most professional management teamin the industry; Cooper'sfirst goal was simply to grow asfast as possible. Circuit City put tremendous emphasis on getting the right people all up and down the line, from delivery drivers to vice presidents; Silo developed a reputation fornot beingableto dothe basics, like making home deliveries without damaging the products.45 According to Circuit City's Dan Rexinger, "We made the best home delivery drivers in the industry. We told them, Tou are the last contact the customer has with Circuit City. Wearegoing tosupply you with uniforms. Wewill require that you shave, that you don't have B.O. You're going to be professional people.' The change in the way we handled customers when making a delivery was absolutely incredible. We would getthank-you notes backon how courte ous the drivers were." Fiveyears intoWurtzel's tenure, Circuit City and Silo had essentially the same business strategy (the same answers to the "what" questions), yet Circuit City took offlikea rocket, beating the gen eral stockmarket 18.5 to 1 in the fifteen years afteritstransition,while Silo 56 Jim Collins bumped along until itwas finally acquired by a foreign company.47 Same strategy, different people,different results. Practical Discipline #2: When you know you need to make a people change, act. The moment you feel the need totightly manage someone, you've made a hiring mistake. The best people don't need to be managed. Guided, taught, led—yes. But not tightly managed. We've all experienced or observed the following scenario. We have a wrong person on the busand we know it. Yet we wait, we delay, we try alternatives, we give a third and fourth chance, we hope thatthe situation will improve, we invest time in trying to properly manage the person, we build little systems to compen sate for his shortcomings, andso forth. Butthe situation doesn't improve. When we go home, we find ourenergy diverted by thinking (or talking to ourspouses) about that person. Worse, all the time and energy we spend on that one person siphons energy away from developing and working with all the right people. We continue to stumble along until the person leaves on hisown (to ourgreatsense ofrelief) orwe finally act(also to our great sense of relief). Meanwhile, our best people wonder, "What took you so long?" Letting the wrong people hang around is unfair to allthe right people, as they inevitably find themselves compensating for the inadequacies of the wrong people. Worse, it can drive away the best people. Strong per formers are intrinsically motivated by performance, and when they see their efforts impeded by carrying extra weight, they eventually become frustrated. Waiting too long before acting is equally unfair to the people who need to get offthe bus. Forevery minute you allow a person to continue holding a seat when you know that person will not make it in the end, you're stealing a portion of his life, time that he could spend finding a better place where he could flourish. Indeed, if we're honest with our selves, the reason wewait too longoften has less to do with concern for that person and more to do with our own convenience. He's doing an okay job and it would be a huge hassle to replace him, so we avoid the issue. Or we find the wholeprocess of dealingwith the issue to be stress ful and distasteful.

So, to save ourselves stress and discomfort, we wait. And wait. And wait. Meanwhile, all the best people are still wondering, "When arethey going todosomething about this? How longisthis going to go on?" Good to Great 57 Using data from Moody's Company Information Reports, we were able to examine the pattern of turnover in the top management levels. We found no difference in the amount of"churn" (turnover withina period of time) between the good-to-great and the comparison companies. But we did find differences in the pattern of churn.48 $pe gdojKo-great companies showed the following bipolar pattern at =the fop management level: Peopleeither stayed on the bus for a long vitirne or got off the bus in a hurry. In other Words, the good-to-great •• ^eoniparSles did notehurn more,fheychurned defer. ; <\ The good-to-great leaders did not pursue an expedient "trya lot of peo ple and keep who works" model of management. Instead, they adopted the following approach: "Let's take the time to make rigorous A+ selec tions rightup front. If we get it right, we'll do everything we can to tryto keep them on boardfora longtime. Ifwemake a mistake, then we'llcon front thatfact sothatwe cangeton with ourwork and theycan geton with their lives." The good-to-great leaders, however, would not rush to judgment. Often, they invested substantial effort in determining whether they had someone in the wrong seat before concluding that they had the wrong person on the bus entirely. When Colman Mockler became CEO of Gillette, he didn'tgoon a rampage, wantonly throwing people outthe win dows ofa moving bus. Instead, he spent fully 55 percent ofhis timeduring hisfirst two years in office jiggering around with the management team, changing or moving thirty-eight of the top fifty people. Said Mockler, "Every minute devoted to putting the proper person in the proper slot is worth weeks oftime later."49 Similarly, Alan Wurtzel ofCircuitCity sentus a letterafterreading an early draft ofthischapter, wherein he commented: Your point about "getting the right people on the bus" as compared to othercompanies isdeadon.There isone corollary that isalso important. I spent a lot of time thinking and talking about who sits where on the bus. I called it "putting square pegs in square holes and round pegs in round holes." ... Instead of firing honest and able people who are not performingwell, it is important to tryto movethem once or even two or three times to other positions where theymightblossom. 58 Jim Collins But how do you know when you know? Two key questions can help. First,if it werea hiring decision (ratherthan a "should this person get off the bus?" decision), would you hire the personagain? Second, if the per son came to tell you that he or she isleaving to pursue an exciting new opportunity, would youfeel terribly disappointed orsecretiy relieved? Practical Discipline #3:Putyour best people onyour biggest opportunities, not your biggest problems. In the early 1960s, R.J.Reynolds and PhilipMorris derived the vast major ityoftheir revenues from the domestic arena. R.J. Reynolds' approachto international business was, "Ifsomebody out there in the world wants a Camel, let them call us."50 Joe Cullman at Philip Morris had a different view. He identified international markets asthe single bestopportunity for long-term growth, despite the fact that the company derived less than 1 percent of itsrevenues fromoverseas. Cullman puzzled overthe best "strategy" for developing international operations and eventually came up with a brilliant answer: It was not a "what"answer, but a "who." He pulled his number one executive, George Weissman, offthe primary domestic business, and put him in charge of international. At the time, international amounted to almost nothing—a tiny exportdepartment, a struggling investment in Venezuela, another in Australia, and a tiny operation in Canada. "When Joe put George in charge of international, a lot of people wondered what George had done wrong," quipped oneofWeissman's colleagues. "I didn'tknow whether I was beingthrown sideways, downstairs or out the window," said Weiss man. "Here I was running 99% of the company and the next day I'd be running 1% orless."52 Yet, asForbes magazine observed twenty years later, Cullman'sdecision to move Weissman to the smallest part of the business was a stroke of genius. Urbane and sophisticated, Weissman was the perfect person to develop markets like Europe, and he built international into the largest and fastest-growing part of the company. In fact, under Weissman's stew- Good to Great 59 ardship, Marlboro became the best-selling cigarette in the world three years before it became number onein the United States.53 The RJR versus Philip Morris case illustrates a common pattern. The good-to-great companies madea habitofputtingtheir bestpeopleon their best opportunities, not their biggest problems. The comparison compa nies had a penchant for doing just the opposite, failing to grasp the fact that managing your problems can onlymake you good, whereas building your opportunities is the onlyway to become great. .0f change. If you creates placewhere Ihe best ^han&esjrt direction. . „ For instance, when Kimberly-Clark sold the mills, Darwin Smith made it clear: The company might be getting rid of the paper business, but it would keep itsbest people. "Manyof our people had come up through the paper business. Then, all ofa sudden, the crown jewels are being sold off and they're asking, 'What is my future?' " explained Dick Auchter. "And Darwin would say, We need all the talented managers we can get. We keepthem.' "54 Despite the fact that theyhad little or no consumer expe rience, Smith moved all the best paper people to the consumer business. We interviewed DickAppert, a senior executive who spent the majority of his career in the papermaking division at Kimberly-Clark, the same division soldoffto createfunds forthe company's bigmoveinto consumer products. He talked with pride and excitement about the transformation of Kimberly-Clark, how it had the guts to sell the paper mills, how it had the foresight to exit the paper business and throw the proceeds into the consumer business, and how it had taken on Procter & Gamble. "I never had any argument with our decision to dissolve the paper division of the company," he said. "We did get rid of the paper mills at that time, and I was in absolute agreement with that."55 Stop and think about that for a moment. The right people want to be part of building something great, and Dick Appertsaw that Kimberly-Clark could become great by selling the part of the company where he had spent most of his working life. The Philip Morris and Kimberly-Clark cases illustrate a final point 60 Jim Collins about "the right people." We noticed a Level 5 atmosphere at the top executive level of every good-to-great company, especially duringthe key transition years. Not that every executive on the team became a fully evolved Level 5 leader to the same degree as Darwin Smith or Colman Mockler, but each coremember ofthe teamtransformed personal ambi tion into ambition forthe company. Thissuggests that the team members had Level 5 potential—or at least they were capable of operating in a manner consistent withthe Level 5 leadership style. You might be wondering, "What's the difference between a Level 5 executive team member and justbeing a good soldier?" A Level 5 execu tive team memberdoes not blindly acquiesce to authority and is a strong leader in her own right, so driven and talented that she builds her arena into one of the very best in the world. Yet each team member must also have the ability to meldthatstrength intodoing whatever it takes to make the company great. Anarticle on PhilipMorris said ofthe Cullman era, "These guys never agreed on anything and they would argue about everything, and they would kill each other and involve everyone, high and low, talented peo ple. But when they had to make a decision, the decision would emerge. This made Philip Morris."56 No matter how much they argued, said a Philip Morrisexecutive, "theywerealways in search of the best answer. In the end, everybody stood behind the decision. All of the debates were for the commongood ofthe company, not yourowninterests."57 FIRST WHO, GREAT COMPANIES, AN D A GREAT LI FE Whenever I teach the good-to-great findings, someone almost always raises the issue of the personal cost in making a transition from good to Good to Great 61 great. In otherwords, isitpossible tobuild a great company and also build a greatlife? Yes. The secretto doingso liesrightin this chapter. I spenta few short days with a senior Gillette executive and hiswife at an executive conference in HongKong. Duringthe course of our conver sations, I asked them if they thought Colman Mockler, the CEO most responsible for Gillette's transition from good to great, had a great life. Colman's life revolved around three great loves, they told me: hisfamily, Harvard, and Gillette. Even during the darkest and most intense times of the takeover crises of the 1980s and despite the increasingly global nature of Gillette's business, Mockler maintained remarkable balance in his life. He did notsignificantly reduce the amountoftime he spentwith hisfam ily, rarely working evenings or weekends. He maintained his disciplined worship practices. He continued his active work on the governing board ofHarvard College.58 When I asked how Mockler accomplished all of this, the executive said, "Oh, it really wasn't that hard for him. He was so good at assem bling the right people around him, and puttingthe right people in the rightslots, that he just didn't need to be there all hours of the day and night. That was Colman's whole secret to success and balance." The executive went on to explain that he was just as likely to meet Mockler in the hardware store as at the office. "He really enjoyed puttering around the house, fixing things up. He always seemed to find time to relaxthat way." Then the executive's wife added, "When Colman died and we all went to the funeral, I looked around and realized how much love was in the room. This was a man who spent nearly all his waking hours with people who loved him, who loved what they were doing, and who loved one another—at work, at home, in his charitable work, wherever." Andthe statementranga bell forme, asthere was somethingabout the good-tb-great executive teams that I couldn't quite describe, but that clearly set them apart. In wrappingup our interviewwith George Weiss man of Philip Morris, I commented, "When you talk about your time at the company, it's as ifyou are describing a love affair." He chuckled and said, "Yes. Other than my marriage, it was the passionate love affair of my life. I don't think many people would understand what I'm talking about, but I suspect my colleagues would." Weissman and many of his executive colleagues kept offices at Philip Morris, coming in on a regu- lar basis, long after retirement. A corridor at the Philip Morris world headquarters is called "the hall of the wizards of was."59 It's the corridor where Weissman, Cullman, Maxwell, and others continue to come into the office, in large part because they simply enjoy spending time together. Similarly, DickAppertofKimberly-Clark said in hisinterview, "I neverhad anyone in Kimberly-Clark in all myforty-one years say any thing unkind to me. I thank God the day I was hired because I've been associated with wonderful people. Good, good people who respected and admired one another."60 Members of the good-to-great teams tended to become and remain friends for life. In many cases, they are still in close contact with each otheryears or decades after working together. It was striking to hear them talk about the transition era, for no matter how dark the days or how big the tasks, these people had fun! They enjoyed each other's company and actually looked forward to meetings. A number of the executives charac terized their years on the good-to-great teams as the high point of their lives. Their experiences went beyond just mutual respect (which they cer tainly had),to lasting comradeship. Adherence to the ideaof"first who" mightbe the closest linkbetween a great companyand a greatlife.For no matter what we achieve, ifwe don't spend the vast majority of our time with people we love and respect, we cannot possibly have a greatlife. But if wespend the vast majority of our time with people we love andrespect—people we really enjoy being on the buswith and who will never disappoint us—then wewill almost certainly have a great life, no matter where the bus goes. The people we inter viewed from the good-to-great companies clearly loved what they did, largely becausetheyloved whotheydid it with.

CHAPTER FOUR

# Never Lose Faith

the early 1950s, the Great Atlantic and Pacific Tea Company, com monly known as A&P, stood as the largest retailing organization in the world and one of the largest corporations in the United States, at one pointranking behind only General Motors in annual sales.2 Kroger, in contrast, stood asan unspectacular grocery chain,less than halfthe sizeof A&P, with performance that barely keptpace with the general market. Then in the 1960s, A&P began to falter while Kroger began to lay the foundations for a transition into a great company. From 1959 to 1973, both companies lagged behind the market, with Kroger pulling just a bit ahead of A&P. After that, the two companies completely diverged, and over the next twenty-five years, Kroger generated cumulative returns ten times the market and eighty timesbetterthan A&P. Howdid such a dramatic reversal offortunes happen? Andhowcould a company as great as A&P become so awful? A&P had a perfect model for the first half of the twentieth century, when two world wars and a depression imposed frugality upon Ameri cans: cheap, plentiful groceries sold in utilitarian stores. But in the afflu ent second half of the twentieth century, Americans changed. They wanted nicer stores, biggerstores, more choices in stores. They wanted fresh-baked bread, flowers, health foods, cold medicines, fresh produce, forty-five choices of cereal, and ten types of milk. They wanted offbeat items, like five different types of expensive sprouts and various concoc tionsofprotein powder and Chinese healingherbs. Oh, and they wanted to be able to do their banking and get their annual flu shots while shop ping. In short,they no longerwanted grocery stores. They wanted Super stores, with a big block "S" on the chest—offering almost everything under one roof, with lots of parking, cheap prices, clean floors, and a gazillion checkout lines. Now, right off the bat, you might be thinking: "Okay, so the story of A&P is one ofan aging company that had a strategy that was rightfor the times, but the times changed andthe world passed itbyasyounger, betterattuned companies gave customers more of whatthey wanted. What's so interestingabout that?" Here's what's interesting: Both Kroger and A&P were old companies (Kroger at 82 years, A&P at 111 years) headinginto the 1970s; both com panies had nearly all their assets invested in traditional grocery stores; both companies had strongholds outside the majorgrowth areas of the United States; and both companies hadknowledge ofhow the world aroundthem was changing. Yet one ofthese two companies confronted the brutal facts of reality head-on and completely changed its entire system in response; the other stuck its head in the sand. In 1958, Forbes magazine described A&P as "the Hermit Kingdom," run asan absolute monarchy byan aging prince.3 Ralph Burger, the suc cessor to the Hartford brothers who had builttheA&P dynasty, sought to preserve two things above all else: cash dividends for the family founda tion and the past glory of the Hartford brothers. According to one A&P director, Burger"consideredhimselfthe reincarnation of old John Hart ford, even to the point of wearing a flower in his lapel every day from Hartford's greenhouse. He tried to carry out, against all opposition, what he thought Mr. John [Hartford] would have liked."4 Burger instilled a "whatwould Mr. Hartford do?" approach to decisions, living bythe motto "You can't argue with a hundred years of success."5 Indeed, through Burger, Mr. Hartford continued to be the dominant force on the board for nearly twenty years. Never mind the factthat he was already dead.6 As the brutal facts about the mismatchbetween its past model and the changingworld began to pile up, A&P mounted an increasingly spirited defense against those facts. In one series of events, the companyopened a new store called The Golden Key, a separate brand wherein it could experiment with new methods and models to learn what customers wanted.7 Itsold noA&P-branded products, it gave the store manager more freedom, it experimented with innovative newdepartments, and it began to evolve toward the modern superstore. Customers really liked it. Here, rightunder their noses, theybegan to discover the answer to the questions ofwhy theywere losing market share and whattheycould do about it. What did A&Pexecutives do withThe Golden Key? Theydidn'tlike the answers thatit gave, sothey closed it.8 A&P then began a pattern of lurching from one strategy to another, always looking for a single-stroke solution to its problems. It held pep ral lies, launched programs, grabbed fads, fired CEOs, hired CEOs, and fired them yetagain. It launchedwhat one industry observer called a "scorched earth policy," a radical price-cutting strategy to build market share, but never dealt with the basic fact that customerswanted not lower prices, but different stores.9 The price cutting led to cost cutting, which led to even drabber stores and poorerservice, which in turn drove customers away, further driving down margins, resulting in even dirtier stores and worse service. "After a while the crud kept mounting," said one former A&P manager. "We not only haddirt, we haddirty dirt."10 Meanwhile, overat Kroger, a completely different patternarose. Kroger also conducted experiments in the 1960s to test the superstore concept.11 By 1970, the Kroger executive team came to an inescapable conclusion: The old-model grocery store (which accounted for nearly 100 percent of Kroger's business) was going to become extinct. Unlike A&P, however, Kroger confronted this brutaltruth and actedon it. The rise of Kroger is remarkably simple and straightforward, almost maddeningly so. During theirinterviews, Lyle Everingham andhisprede cessor Jim Herring(CEOs duringthe pivotal transition years) were polite and helpful, but a bit exasperated by our questions. To them, it just seemed so clear. When we asked Everingham to allocate one hundred points across the top five factors in the transition, he said: "I find your question a bit perplexing. Basically, we did extensive research, and the data came back loud and clear: The supercombination stores were the Good to Great way ofthe future.We also learnedthat youhad to be number one or num bertwo in each market, or you had to exit.* Sure, there was some skepti cism at first. But once we looked at the facts, therewas really no question about what we had to do. So we just did it."12 Kroger decided to eliminate, change, or replace every single store and depart every region that did not fit the new realities. The whole system would be turned inside out,store by store, block by block, city by city, state bystate. By the early 1990s, Kroger had rebuilt its entire system on thenew model andwas well ontheway tobecoming thenumber onegro cery chain in America, a position it would attain in 1999.13 Meanwhile, A&P still had over halfi14 FACTS ARE BETTER THAN DREAMS One of the dominant themes from our research is that breakthrough results come about by a series ofgood decisions, diligently executed and accumulated one on topofanother. Of course, the good-to-great compa nies did not have a perfect track record. But on the whole, they made many more good decisions than bad ones, and they made many more good decisions thanthe comparison companies. Even more important, on the really bigchoices, such as Kroger's decision to throw all its resources into the task ofconverting its entire system tothesuperstore concept, they were remarkably on target. This, of course, begs a question.

Are we merely studying a setof com panies that just happened by luck to stumble into the right set of deci sions? Or was there something distinctive about their process that dramatically increased the likelihood ofbeing right? The answer, it turns out, is thatthere was something quite distinctive abouttheirprocess. The good-to-great companies displayed two distinctive forms of disci plined thought. The first, andthetopic ofthis chapter, is thatthey infused the entire process with the brutal facts ofreality. (The second, which we *Keepin mind, this was the early1970s, a full decade beforethe "number one, num bertwo, or exit" idea became mainstream. Kroger, like all good-to-great companies, developed its ideas by paying attention tothedata right infront ofit,notby following trends andfads setby others. Interestingly, over halfthegood-to-great companies had some version of the "number one, number two" concept in place years before it became a managementfad. 70 Jim Collins will discuss in the next chapter, isthatthey developed a simple, yetdeeply insightful, frame ofreference for all decisions.) When, as in the Kroger case, you start with an honest anddiligent effort to determine the truthof the situation, the right decisions often become self-evident. Notalways, of course, but often. And even if all decisions do not become self-evident, onething is certain: You absolutely cannot make a series ofgood decisions without first confronting the brutal facts. The good-to-great companies operated in accordance with this principle, and the comparison compa niesgenerally did not. Consider Pitney Bowes versus Addressograph. It would be hardto find two companies in more similar positions at a specific moment in history thatthen diverged sodramatically. Until 1973, they hadsimilar revenues, profits, numbers of employees, and stock charts. Both companies held near-monopoly market positions with virtually the same customer base— Pitney Bowes in postage meters and Addressograph in address-duplicating machines—and both faced the imminentreality oflosing their monopo lies.15 By 2000, however, Pitney Bowes had grown toover 30,000 employ ees and revenues in excess of $4 billion, comparedto the sorry remnants ofAddressograph, which had less than $100 million and only 670 employ ees.16 For the shareholder, Pitney Bowes outperformed Addressograph 3,581 to 1(yes, three thousand five hundred and eighty-one times better). In 1976, a charismatic visionary leader named Roy Ash became CEO ofAddressograph. Aself-described "conglomerates," Ash had previously built Litton by stacking acquisitions together that had since faltered. According to Fortune, he sought to use Addressograph as a platform to reestablish his leadership prowess in theeyes oftheworld.17 Ash set forth a vision to dominate the likes of IBM, Xerox, and Kodak in the emerging field ofoffice automation—a bold plan for a company that had previously only dominated the envelope-address-duplication busi ness.18 There is nothing wrong with a bold vision, butAsh became so wed ded to his quixotic quest that, according toBusiness Week, he refused to confront the mounting evidence that his plan was doomed to fail and might take down the rest ofthe company with it. He insisted onmilking cash from profitable arenas, eroding the core business while throwing money after a gambit that had little chance ofsuccess.20 Later, after Ash was thrown out ofoffice and the company had filed for bankruptcy (from which it did later emerge), he still refused to confront reality, saying: "We lostsome battles, butwe were winning the war.Addressograph was not even close to winning the war, and people through out the company knew it at the time. Yet the truth went unheard until it was too late.22 In fact, many ofAddressograph's key people bailed outof the company, dispirited by their inability to get top management to deal with the facts.23 Perhaps we should give Mr. Ash some credit for being a visionary who tried to push his company togreater heights. (And, tobe fair, theAddress ograph board fired Ash before he had a chance to fully carry out his plans.)24 But theevidence from a slew ofrespectable articles written atthe time suggests thatAsh turned a blind eye to any reality inconsistent with his own vision ofthe world."When you turn over rocks and look at all the squiggly things under neath,youcan eitherput the rock down, or youcan say, 'My jobisto turn over rocks and lookat the squiggly things/ even if whatyou see can scare the hell out ofyou."25 That quote, from Pitney Bowes executive Fred Pur due, could have come from any of the PitncyBowes executives we inter viewed. Theyallseemcd a bit,well, to be blunt, neurotic and compulsive aboutPitney's position in the world. "This isa culture that isvery hostile tocomplacency," said oneexecutive.26 "We have an itch thatwhat we just accomplished, no matter how great, is never going to be good enough to sustain us," said another.27 Pitney's first management meeting ofthe new year typically consisted of about fifteen minutes discussing the previous year (almost always superb results) andtwo hours talking about the"scary squiggly things" that might impede future results.28 Pitney Bowes sales meetings were quite dif ferent from the "aren'twe great" rah-rah sales conferences typical at most companies: The entire management team would lay itself opentosearing questions and challenges from salespeople who dealt directly with cus tomers.29 The company created a long-standing tradition offorums where people could stand up and tell senior executives what the company was doing wrong, shoving rocks with squiggly things in their faces, andsaying, "Look! You'd better pay attention tothis."30 The Addressograph case, especially in contrast to Pitney Bowes, illus trates a vital point. Strong, charismatic leaders like Roy Ash can all too easily become the de facto reality driving a company. Throughout the study, we found comparison companies where the top leader led with such force or instilled such fear that people worried more about the leader—what he would say, what he would think, what he would do— than they worried aboutexternal reality andwhat it coulddo to the com pany. Recall the climate at Bank ofAmerica, described in the previous chapter, wherein managers would not even make a comment until they knew how the CEO felt. We did not find this pattern at companies like Wells Fargo and Pitney Bowes, where people were much more worried about the scary squiggly things than about the feelings of top manage ment. The moment a leaderallows himselfto becomethe primary reality peo ple worry about, rather than reality being the primary reality, you have a recipe for mediocrity, or worse. This is one of the key reasons why less charismatic leaders often produce betterlong-term results than their more charismatic counterparts.

Winston Churchill understood the liabilities of his strong personality, and he compensatedfor them beautifully during the SecondWorld War. Churchill, as you know, maintained a bold and unwavering vision that Britain would not justsurvive, but prevail as a great nation—despite the wholeworld wondering not ifbut when Britain would sue for peace. Dur ing the darkest days, with nearly all of Europe and North Africa under Nazi control, the United States hoping to stay out of the conflict, and Hitler fighting a one-front war (he had not yet turned on Russia), Churchill said: "We are resolved to destroy Hitler and every vestige of the Naziregime. From this, nothingwill turn us.Nothing! We will neverpar ley. We will never negotiate with Hitleror any of his gang. We shallfight him by land. We shall fight him by sea. We shall fight him in the air. Until,with God's help, wehave rid the earth of hisshadow."31 Armed with this bold vision, Churchill never failed, however, to con front the most brutal facts. He feared that his towering, charismatic personality might deter bad news from reaching him in itsstarkest form. So, early in the war, he created an entirely separate department outside the normal chain of command, calledthe Statistical Office, with the prin cipal function of feeding him—continuously updated and completely unfiltered—the mostbrutalfacts ofreality.32 He reliedheavily on this spe cial unit throughout the war, repeatedly asking forfacts, just the facts. As the Nazi panzers swept across Europe, Churchill went to bed and slept soundly: "I. . . had no need for cheering dreams," he wrote. "Facts are better than dreams.

A CLIMATE WHERE THE TRUTH IS HEARD Now, you might be wondering, "How do you motivate people with brutal facts? Doesn't motivation flow chiefly from a compelling vision?" The answer, surprisingly, is, "No." Not because vision is unimportant, but because expending energy trying to motivate people islargely a waste of time. One of the dominant themesthat runs throughout this book is that ifyousuccessfully implement itsfindings, youwill not need to spend time and energy "motivating" people. If you have the right people on the bus, theywill be self-motivated. The real question then becomes: How doyou manage in such a way as not tode-motivate people? And one of the single mostde-motivating actions youcan take isto hold out false hopes, soonto be sweptaway by events.

How do you create a climate where the truth is heard? We offer four basicpractices: J. Lead with questions, notanswers. In 1973,one yearafter he assumedCEO responsibility from his father, Alan Wurtzel's company stood at the brink of bankruptcy, dangerously close to violation of its loan agreements. At the time, the company (then named Wards, not to be confused with MontgomeryWard) was a hodgepodge of appliance and hi-fi stores with no unifying concept. Over the nextten years, Wurtzeland his team not onlyturned the com pany around, but also created the Circuit City concept and laid the foundations fora stunning record ofresults, beatingthe markettwentytwo times from its transition date in 1982to January 1, 2000. When Alan Wurtzel started the long traverse from near bankruptcy to these stellarresults, he began with a remarkable answerto the ques tion ofwhere to take the company: I don't know. Unlike leaders such as Roy Ash of Addressograph, Wurtzel resisted the urge to walk in with "the answer." Instead, once he put the right people on the bus, he began not with answers, but with questions. "Alan was a real spark," said a board member. "He had an abilityto askquestions that were just marvelous. We had some wonderful debates in the boardroom. It was never just a dog and pony show, where you would just listen and then go to lunch."34 Indeed, Wurtzel stands as one of the few CEOs in a large corporation who put more questions to his board members than they put to him. He used the same approach with his executive team, constantly pushingand probing and prodding with questions. Each stepalongthe way, Wurtzel wouldkeep asking questions until he had a clear picture of reality and its implications. "They used to call me the prosecutor, becauseI wouldhome in on a question," saidWurtzel. "You know, like a bulldog, I wouldn'tlet go until I understood. Why,why, why?" Like Wurtzel, leaders in each of the good-to-great transitions oper ated with a somewhat Socratic style. Furthermore, they used questions for one and only one reason: to gain understanding. They didn't use questions as a form of manipulation ("Don't you agree with me on that? . . .")or asa way to blameor put down others ("Why did youmess this up? ..."). When we asked the executives abouttheirmanagement team meetings during the transition era, theysaidthat theyspent much ofthe time "justtrying to understand." The good-to-great leaders made particularly good use of informal meetings where they'd meet with groups of managers and employees with no script, agenda, or set of action items to discuss. Instead, they would startwith questions like: "So, what's on your mind?" "Can you tell me about that?" "Can you help me understand?" "What should we beworried about?" Thesenon-agenda meetings became a forum where current realities tended to bubble to the surface.

2. Engage in dialogue anddebate, notcoercion. In 1965, you could hardlyfind a company more awfiil than Nucor. It had onlyone division that mademoney. Everything else drained cash. It had no culture to be proud of. It had no consistent direction. It was on the verge of bankruptcy. Atthe time, Nucor was officially known as the Nuclear Corporation of America, reflecting its orientation to nuclear energy products, including the Scintillation Probe (yes, they really named it that), usedforradiation measurement. It had acquired a seriesof unrelated businesses in such arenasassemiconductor supplies, rare earth materials, electrostatic office copiers, and roof joists. At the start of its transformation in 1965, Nucor did not manufacture one ounce of steel. Nor did it make a penny of profit. Thirty years later, Nucor stood as the fourth-largest steelmaker in the world35 andby 1999 made greater annual profits than any other American steel company.36 How did Nucor transition from the utterly awful Nuclear Corpora tion ofAmerica into perhaps the best steel company in America? First, Nucor benefitedfrom the emergence of a Level 5 leader, Ken Iverson, promoted to CEO from general manager ofthe joist division. Second, Iverson got the rightpeople on the bus, buildinga remarkable team of peoplelike Sam Siegel (described by one of his colleagues as "the best money manager in the world, a magician") and David Aycock, an oper ations

genius.

And then what? Like Alan Wurtzel, Iverson dreamed of building a great company, but refused to beginwith"the answer" forhowto get there. Instead, he played the role ofSocratic moderator in a series ofraging debates. "We established an ongoing series ofgeneral manager meetings, and myrole was more as a mediator," commented Iverson. "They were chaos. We would stay there for hours, ironing out the issues, until we came to something.... Attimes, the meetings would get soviolent that people almost went across the table at each other.... People yelled. They waved their arms around and pounded on tables. Faces would get red and veins bulged out."38 Iverson's assistant tells of a scene repeated over the years, wherein colleagues would march into Iverson's office and yell and scream at each other, but then emerge with a conclusion.39 Argue and debate, then sell the nuclear business; argue and debate, then focus on steel joists; argue and debate, then begin to manufacture their own steel; argue and debate, then invest in their own mini-mill; argue and debate, then build a second mini-mill, and so forth. Nearly all the Nucor executives we spoke with described a climate of debate, wherein the company's strategy "evolved through many agonizing arguments and fights."Conduct autopsies, without blame. In 1978, PhilipMorris acquired the Seven-Up Company, only to sell it eight years later at a loss.The financial loss was relatively small compared to Philip Morris's total assets, but it was a highly visible black eye thatconsumed thousands ofhours ofprecious management time. In our interviews with the Philip Morris executives, we were struck by how they all brought up the debacle on their own and discussed it openly. Instead ofhiding their big, ugly mistake, they seemed tofeel an almost therapeutic need totalk about it. In his book, Ym a Lucky Guy, Joe Cullman dedicates five pages to dissecting the 7UP disaster. He doesn't hold back the embarrassing truth about how flawed the deci sion was. It is a five-page clinical analysis of the mistake, its implica tions, and its lessons. Hundreds, ifnotthousands, ofpeople hours had been spent inautop sies ofthe 7UP case. Yet, as much as they talked about this conspicuous failure, no one pointed fingers to single out blame. There is only one exception to this pattern: Joe Cullman, standing in front ofthe mirror, pointing the finger right at himself. "[It] ... became apparent thatthis was another Joe Cullman plan that didn't work," he writes.42 He goes even further, implying that if he'd only listened better to the people who challenged his idea at the time, the disaster might have been averted. He goes outofhis way to give credit tothose who were right in retrospect, naming those specific individuals who were more prescient than himself. In an era when leaders go to great lengths to preserve the image of their own track record—stepping forth to claim credit about how they were visionary when their colleagues were not, but finding others to blame when their decisions go awry—it is quite refreshing to come across Cullman. He set the tone: "J will take responsibility for this bad decision. Butwewill all take responsibility forextracting the maximum learningfrom the tuitionwe've paid." 4. Build "red flag" mechanisms. Welive in an information age, when those with more and betterinfor mation supposedly have an advantage. If you look across the rise and fall oforganizations, however, you will rarely find companies stumbling because they lacked information. Bethlehem Steel executives had known for years about the threat of mini-mill companies like Nucor. They paid little attention until they woke up one day to discover large chunks ofmarket share taken away.43 Upjohn had plenty of information that indicated some of its forth coming products would fail todeliver anticipated results or, worse, had potentially serious side effects. Yet itoften ignored those problems. With Halcion, for example, an insider was quoted in Newsweek saying, "dis missing safety concerns about Halcion had become virtual company policy." In another case when Upjohn found itself under fire, itframed its problems as "adverse publicity," rather than confronting the truth of its own shortcomings.44 Executives at Bank ofAmerica had plenty of information about the realities ofderegulation, yet they failed toconfront the onebigimplica tionofthose realities: In a deregulated world, banking would be a com modity, and the old perks and genteel traditions ofbanking would be gone forever. Not until ithad lost $1.8 billion did Bank ofAmerica fully accept this fact. In contrast, Carl Reichardt ofWells Fargo, called the ultimate realist by his predecessor, hit the brutal facts of deregulation head-on.45 Sorry, fellow bankers, but we can preserve the banker class no more. We've gotto be businessmen with asmuch attention to costs and effectiveness as McDonald's.

One particularly powerful way to accomplish this isthrough red flag mechanisms. Allow me to use a personal example to illustrate the idea. When teaching by the case method at Stanford Business School, I issued to each MBA student an 8.5" x 11" bright red sheet of paper, with the following instructions: "This is your red flag for the quarter. If you raise your hand with your red flag, the classroom will stop for you. There are no restrictions on when and how to use your red flag; the decision rests entirely in yourhands. You can use it to voice an observa tion, share a personal experience, present an analysis, disagree with the professor, challenge a CEO guest, respond to a fellow student, ask a question, make a suggestion, or whatever. There will be no penalty whatsoever for any use ofa red flag. Your red flag canbe used only once during the quarter. Your red flag is nontransferable; you cannot give or sell it to another student." With thered flag, I had noidea precisely what would happen each day in class. In one situation, a student used her red flag to state, "Professor Collins, I think you are doing a particularly ineffective job ofrunning class today. You are leading too much with your questions and stifling our independent thinking. Let us think for ourselves." The red flag con fronted mewith thebrutal fact thatmy own questioning style stood inthe way ofpeople's learning. Astudentsurvey attheendofthequarter would have given me thatsame information. But the red flag—real time, in frontof everyone in the classroom—turned information about the short comings ofthe class into information thatI absolutely could notignore. I got the idea for red flag mechanisms from Bruce Woolpert, who instituted a particularly powerful device called short pay at his company Graniterock. Short pay gives the customer full discretionary power to decide whether and how much to pay on an invoice based upon his own subjective evaluation ofhow satisfied he feels with a product orser vice. Short pay is not a refund policy. The customer does not need to return the product, nor does he need to call Graniterock for permis sion. He simply circles the offending item on the invoice, deducts it from the total, and sends a check for the balance. When I asked Woolpert hisreasons for short pay, he said, "You can geta lot ofinfor mation from customer surveys, but there are always ways of explaining away the data. With shortpay, you absolutely have to payattention to the data. You often don't know that a customer is upset until you lose that customer entirely. Shortpay acts as an early warning system that forces us to adjust quickly, longbefore we would lose that customer." To be clear, we did not generally find red flag mechanisms as vivid and dramatic asshort pay in the good-to-great companies. Nonetheless, I'vedecidedto includethisideahere,at the urging ofresearch assistant Lane Hornung. Hornung, who helped me systematically research and collate mechanisms across companies for a different research project, makes the compelling argument thatifyou're a fully developed Level 5 leader, you mightnot need redflag mechanisms. But ifyou are not yet a Level 5leader, or ifyou suffer the liability ofcharisma, redflag mech anisms give you a practical anduseful tool for turning information into information that cannot be ignored and for creating a climate where the truth is heard.* UNWAVERING FAITH AMID THE BRUTAL FACTS When Procter& Gamble invaded the paper-based consumer business in the late 1960s, Scott Paper (thenthe leader) simply resigned itselfto sec ond place without a fight and began looking for ways todiversify.46 "The company had a meeting for analysts in 1971 that was one of the most depressing I've ever attended," said oneanalyst. "Management essentially threw in the towel and said, We've been had.' "47 The once-proud com pany began to look at its competition and say, "Here's how we stack up against the best," and sigh, "Oh, well... at least there are people in the business worse than weare."48 Instead offiguring out howto get backon the offensive and win, Scott justtried to protectwhat it had. Conceding the top end of the market to P&G, Scott hoped that, by hiding away in the Bcategory, it would be leftalone bythe bigmonster that had invaded its turf.49 Kimberly-Clark, on the other hand, viewed competing against Procter & Gamble not as a liability, but as an asset. Darwin Smith and his team felt exhilarated by the idea of going up against the best, seeing it as an opportunity to make Kimberly-Clark better and stronger. They also viewed it as a way to stimulate the competitive juices ofKimberly people at alllevels. At one internal gathering, Darwin Smith stood up andstarted histalk bysaying, "Okay, I want everyone to rise in a momentofsilence." Everyone looked around, wondering what Darwin was up to. Did some onedie? And so, after a moment ofconfusion, they allstood up andstared at their shoes in reverent silence. After an appropriate pause, Smith looked out at the groupand said in a somber tone,"That was a moment of silence for P&G." The place went bananas. Blair White, a director who witnessed the incident, said, "Hehadeveryone wound up in this thing, allup anddown thecompany, right down totheplant floor. We were taking onGoliath!"50 Later, Wayne Sanders (Smith's successor) described to us the incredible benefit ofcompeting against the best: "Could we have a better adversary than P&G? Not a chance. I say that because we respect them so much. They are bigger than we are. They are very talented. They are great at marketing. They beat thehell outofevery one oftheir competitors, except one, Kimberly-Clark. Thatis oneofthe things thatmakes us so proud.

Robert Aders of Kroger summed this up nicely at the end of his inter view, describing the psychology ofthe Kroger team as itfaced the daunting twenty-year task of methodically turning over the entire Kroger system. "There was a certain Churchillian character towhat we were doing. We hada very strong will tolive, thesense that we are Kroger, Kroger was here before and will be here long after we are gone, and, by god, we are going to win thisthing. Itmight take us a hundred years, but we will persist for a hundred years, ifthat's what ittakes."52 Throughout ourresearch, we were continually reminded ofthe "hardi ness" research studies done bythe International Committee forthe Study ofVictimization. These studies looked at peoplewhohad suffered serious adversity—cancer patients, prisoners of war, accident victims, and so forth—and survived. Theyfound that people fell generally into three cat egories: those who were permanently dispirited by the event, those who got their life back to normal, and those who used the experience as a defining event that made them stronger.53 The good-to-great companies were likethose in the third group, with the "hardiness factor." When Fannie Mae began its transition in the early 1980s, almost no one gave it high odds for success, much less for greatness. Fannie Mae had $56 billion ofloans that were losing money. It received about 9 per cent interest on its mortgage portfolio but had to pay up to 15 percenton the debt it issued. Multiply that difference times $56billion, and youget a very large negative number! Furthermore, by charter, Fannie Mae could not diversify outside the mortgage finance business. Most people viewed Fannie Mae as totally beholden to shifts in the direction of interest rates—they go up and Fannie Mae loses, they go down and Fannie Mae wins—and many believed thatFannie Maecould succeed only ifthe gov ernment stepped in to clamp down on interest rates.54 "That's their only hope," said one analyst.55 But that's not the way David Maxwell and his newly assembled team viewed the situation. They never wavered in their faith, consistently emphasizing in their interviews with us that they never had the goal to merely survive but toprevail in the endasa great company. Yes, the inter estspread was a brutal fact thatwas notgoing tomagically disappear. Fan nie Mae had no choice but to become the best capital markets player in the world at managing mortgage interest risk. Maxwell and his team set out to create a new business model that woulddepend much less on inter estrates, involving the invention of very sophisticated mortgage finance instruments. Most analysts responded with derision. "When you've got $56billionworth ofloansin placeand underwater, talking about newpro grams is a joke," said one. "That's like Chrysler [then asking for federal loan guarantees to stave offbankruptcy] going into the aircraft business."56 After completing my interview with David Maxwell, I asked how he and histeam dealtwiththe naysayers duringthosedarkdays. "It was never an issue internally," he said. "Of course, wehad to stop doinga lot of stupid things,and we had to inventa completely new set offinancial devices. But we never entertained the possibility that wewouldfail. We weregoing to use the calamity as an opportunity to remake Fannie Mae into a great company."57 During a research meeting, a team member commented that Fannie Mae reminded her of an old television show, The Six Million Dollar Man withLee Majors. The pretextofthe series isthat an astronautsuffers a seri ous crash while testing a moon landing craft over a southwestern desert. Instead of just trying to save the patient, doctors completely redesign him into a superhuman cyborg, installing atomic-powered robotic devices such as a powerful left eye and mechanical limbs.58 Similarly, David Maxwell and his team didn't use the fact that Fannie Mae was bleeding and near death as a pretext to merely restructure the company. They used it as an opportunityto create something much stronger and more powerful. Step by step, day by day, month by month, the Fannie Mae team rebuilt the entire business model around risk managementand reshaped the corpo rate culture into a high-performance machine that rivaled anything on Wall Street, eventually generating stock returns nearly eight times the market over fifteen years. THE STOCKDALE PARADOX Of course, not all good-to-great companiesfaced a dire crisis like Fannie Mae; fewer than half did. But every good-to-great company faced signifi cant adversity along the way to greatness, of one sortor another—Gillette and the takeover battles, Nucor and imports, Wells Fargo and deregula tion, PitneyBowes losing its monopoly, Abbott Labs and a huge product recall, Kroger and the need to replace nearly 100percent of itsstores, and so forth. In every case,the managementteam responded with a powerful psychological duality. On the one hand, theystoically accepted the brutal facts of reality. On the other hand, they maintained an unwavering faith in the endgame,and a commitmentto prevail asa greatcompanydespite the brutal facts. We came to call this dualitythe Stockdale Paradox. The name refers to Admiral Jim Stockdale, who was the highestranking United States military officer in the "Hanoi Hilton" prisoner-ofwar camp during the height of the Vietnam War. Tortured over twenty times during his eight-year imprisonment from 1965 to 1973, Stockdale livedout the warwithoutany prisoner's rights, no set release date, and no certainty as to whether he would evensurvive to see hisfamily again. He shoulderedthe burden of command,doingeverything he could to create conditions that would increase the number of prisoners who would sur vive unbroken, whilefighting an internalwaragainst his captors and their attempts to usethe prisoners forpropaganda. Atone point,he beat himself with a stool and cut himselfwith a razor, deliberately disfiguring himself, so that he could not be put on videotape as an example of a "well-treated prisoner." He exchanged secret intelligence information with his wife through their letters, knowing that discovery would mean more torture and perhaps death. He instituted rules that would help people to deal with torture (no one can resist torture indefinitely, so he created a step wise system—after x minutes, you can say certain things—that gave the men milestones to survive toward). He instituted an elaborate internal communicationssystem to reduce the senseofisolation that their captors tried to create, which used a five-by-five matrix of tap codes for alpha characters. (Tap-tap equals the letter a, tap-pause-tap-tap equals the letter b, tap-tap-pause-tap equals the letterf, and so forth, for twenty-five letters, c doubling in for k.) Atone point, during an imposed silence, the prison ersmopped and swept the central yard using the code,swish-swashing out "We love you" to Stockdale, on the third anniversary of his being shot down. After his release, Stockdale became the first three-star officer in the history of the navy to wear both aviator wings and the Congressional Medal of Honor.59 You can understand, then, my anticipation at the prospect of spending part of an afternoon with Stockdale. One of my students had written his paperon Stockdale, whohappened to be a seniorresearch fellow studying the Stoic philosophers at the Hoover Institution rightacross the streetfrom my office, and Stockdale invited the twoof us for lunch. In preparation, I read In Loveand War, the book Stockdale and his wife had written in alter nating chapters, chroniclingtheir experiences during those eight years. As I moved through the book, I found myselfgetting depressed. It just seemed so bleak—the uncertainty of his fate, the brutality of his captors, and so forth. And then, it dawned on me: "Here I am sitting in my warm and comfortable office, looking out over the beautiful Stanford campus on a beautifulSaturday afternoon. I'm getting depressed readingthis, and I knowthe end ofthe story! I know that he gets out, reuniteswith his fam ily, becomes a national hero, and gets to spend the later years of his life studying philosophy on this same beautiful campus. If it feels depressing for me, how on earth did he deal with it when he was actually there and didnot know theendof thestory?" "I neverlostfaith in the end ofthe story," he said, when I asked him. "I never doubted not onlythat I would get out, but also that I would prevail in the end and turn the experience into the defining event of my life, which, in retrospect, I would not trade." I didn't say anything for manyminutes, and we continued the slow walk toward the faculty club, Stockdale limping and arc-swinging his stiffleg that had never fullyrecovered from repeatedtorture. Finally, after about a hundred meters of silence, I asked, "Who didn't make it out?" "Oh, that's easy," he said. "The optimists." "The optimists? I don't understand," I said, now completely confused, given what he'd saida hundred meters earlier. "The optimists. Oh, theywere the oneswhosaid,We're goingto be out by Christmas.' And Christmas would come, and Christmas would go. Then they'd say, 'We're going to be out by Easter.' And Easter would come, and Easterwouldgo.And then Thanksgiving, and then it would be Christmas again.And they died ofa broken heart." Anotherlong pause,and morewalking. Then he turned to me and said, "This is a very important lesson. You must never confuse faith that you willprevail in the end—whichyou can neverafford to lose—with the dis cipline to confront the most brutal facts of your current reality, whatever they might be." To this day, I carrya mental image of Stockdale admonishing the opti mists: "We're not getting out byChristmas; deal with it!" That conversation withAdmiral Stockdale stayed with me, and in fact had a profound influence on myowndevelopment. Lifeis unfair—sometimes to our advantage, sometimes to our disadvantage. We will all experience disappointments and crushing events somewhere along the way, setbacks for which there is no "reason," no one to blame. It might be disease; it might be injury; it might be an accident; it might be losinga lovedone; it might be getting swept away in a political shake-up; it might be getting shot down over Vietnam and thrown into a POW camp for eight years. What separates people, Stockdale taught me, is not the presence or absence of difficulty, but how they deal with the inevitable difficulties of life. In wresding with life's challenges, the Stockdale Paradox (you must retainfaith that youwill prevail in the end and youmust also confrontthe most brutalfacts of your currentreality) has proved powerful for coming backfrom difficulties notweakened, butstronger—not justforme, but for all those who've learned the lesson and triedto apply it. I neverreally considered mywalk withStockdale aspart of my research into great companies, categorizing it more as a personal rather than cor porate lesson. But as we unraveled the research evidence, I kept coming backto it in myownmind. Finally, one dayduring a research-team meet ing, I shared the Stockdale story. There was silence around the table when I finished, and I thought,"Theymustthink I'm really out in leftfield." Then Duane Duffy, a quiet and thoughtful team member who had done the A&P versus Kroger analysis, said, "That's exactly what I've been struggling with. I've been trying to get my hands around the essential dif ference between A&P and Kroger. And that's it. Kroger was like Stockdale, and A&P was likethe optimists whoalways thought they'd be out by Christmas." Then other team members began to chime in, noting the same differ ence betweentheir comparison sets—Wells Fargo versus BankofAmerica both facing deregulation, Kimberly-Clark versus Scott Paper both facing the terrible might of Procter & Gamble, Pitney Bowes versus Addresso graph both facing the loss of their monopolies, Nucor versus Bethlehem Steel both facing imports, and so forth. They all demonstrated this para doxical psychological pattern,and wedubbed it the Stockdale Paradox. The Stockdale Paradox is a signature of all those who create greatness, be it in leading their own lives or in leadingothers. Churchill had it dur ing the Second World War. Admiral Stockdale, like Viktor Frankl before him, lived it in a prison camp. And while our good-to-great companies cannot claim to have experienced either the grandeur of saving the free world or the depth ofpersonal experience ofliving in a POWcamp, they all embraced the Stockdale Paradox. It didn't matter how bleak the situa tion or how stultifying their mediocrity, they all maintained unwavering faith that theywould not justsurvive, but prevail asa great company. And yet, at the same time, they became relentlessly disciplined at confronting the most brutal facts of their current reality. Like much of what we found in our research,the keyelements of great ness aredeceptively simple andstraightforward. The good-to-great leaders were abletostrip away somuch noise andclutter and justfocus on the few things that would have the greatest impact. They were able to do so in large partbecause they operated from both sides ofthe Stockdale Paradox, never letting one side overshadow the other. Ifyou are able to adopt this dualpattern, you will dramatically increase the odds ofmaking a series of good decisions and ultimately discovering a simple, yetdeeply insightful, concept for making the really bigchoices. And onceyou have thatsimple, unifying concept, you will bevery close tomaking a sustained transition to breakthrough results. It istothe creation ofthatconcept thatwenow turn.

CHAPTER FIVE

# Simplicity within the Three Circles

Are you a hedgehog or a fox? In hisfamous essay "The Hedgehog and the Fox," IsaiahBerlin divided the world into hedgehogs and foxes, based upon an ancient Greek para ble: "The fox knows many things, but the hedgehog knows one big thing."2 The fox isa cunningcreature, able to devise a myriad ofcomplex strategies forsneakattacks upon the hedgehog. Dayin and dayout, the fox circles around the hedgehog's den, waiting for the perfect moment to pounce. Fast, sleek, beautiful, fleet offoot, and crafty—the fox looks like the sure winner. The hedgehog, on the other hand, isa dowdier creature, looking likea geneticmix-up between a porcupineand a smallarmadillo. He waddles along, going about his simple day, searching for lunch and takingcare of his home. The fox waits in cunningsilence at the juncturein the trail. The hedge hog, minding his own business, wanders right into the path of the fox.

"Aha, I've gotyou now!" thinks the fox. Heleaps out,bounding across the ground, lightning fast. The litde hedgehog, sensing danger, looks up and thinks, "Here we go again. Will he ever learn?" Rolling up into a perfect little ball, the hedgehog becomes a sphere ofsharp spikes, pointing out ward in all directions. The fox, bounding toward his prey, sees the hedge hogdefense and calls offthe attack. Retreating back to the forest, the fox begins tocalculate a new lineofattack. Each day, some version ofthis bat tle between the hedgehog and the fox takes place, and despite the greater cunning ofthe fox, the hedgehog always wins. Berlin extrapolated from this little parable to divide people into two basic groups: foxes and hedgehogs. Foxes pursue many ends at the same time and seethe world in allits complexity. Theyare "scattered or diffused, moving on many levels," says Berlin, never integrating theirthinking into one overall concept or unifying vision. Hedgehogs, on the other hand, simplify a complex world intoa single organizing idea, a basic principle or conceptthat unifies and guides everything. Itdoesn't matter howcomplex the world, a hedgehog reduces all challenges and dilemmas to simple— indeed almost simplistic—hedgehog ideas. Fora hedgehog, anything that doesnotsomehow relateto the hedgehog idea holdsno relevance. Princeton professor Marvin Bressler pointed out the power of the hedgehog during one ofourlong conversations: "You wantto know what separates those who make the biggest impact from all the others who are just as smart? They're hedgehogs." Freud and the unconscious, Darwin and natural selection, Marx and class struggle, Einstein and relativity, Adam Smith and division oflabor—they were all hedgehogs. They took a complex world and simplified it."Thosewholeave the biggest footprints," said Bressler, "have thousands calling after them, 'Good idea, but you went too far!'"3 To be clear, hedgehogs are notstupid. Quite the contrary. They under stand that the essence of profound insight is simplicity. What could be more simple than e = mc2? What could be simpler than the idea of the unconscious, organized into an id, ego, and superego? What could be more elegant than Adam Smith's pin factory and "invisible hand"? No, the hedgehogs aren'tsimpletons; they have a piercing insight that allows them to see through complexity and discern underlying patterns. Hedge hogs see what is essential, and ignore the rest. What does all this talk of hedgehogs and foxes have to do with good to great? Everything Consider the case ofWalgreens versus Eckerd. Recall how Walgreens generated cumulative stock returns from the end of 1975 to 2000 that exceeded the market by over fifteen times, handily beating such great companies as GE, Merck, Coca-Cola, and Intel. It was a remarkable per formance for such an anonymous—some might even say boring—com pany. When interviewing Cork Walgreen, I kept asking him to godeeper, to help us understand these extraordinary results. Finally, in exasperation, he said, "Look, it justwasn't that complicated! Once we understood the concept, we justmoved straight ahead."4 Whatwas theconcept? Simply this: thebest, most convenient drugstores, with high profit percustomer visit. That's it. That's thebreakthrough strat egy that Walgreens used to beat Intel, GE, Coca-Cola, and Merck. In classic hedgehog style, Walgreens took this simple concept and imple mented itwith fanatical consistency. It embarked on a systematic program to replace allinconvenient locations with more convenient ones, preferably corner lots where customers could easily enterandexit from multiple direc tions. Ifa great corner location would openup justhalfa block away from a profitable Walgreens store in a good location, the company would close the good store (even ata cost of$1 million toget outofthelease) toopen a great new store on the corner.5 Walgreens pioneered drive-through pharmacies, found customersliked the idea, and built hundreds of them. In urban areas, the company clustered its stores tightly together, on the preceptthat no one should have towalk more thana few blocks to reach aWalgreens.6 In down town San Francisco, for example, Walgreens clustered nine stores withina one-mile radius. Nine stores!7 If you look closely, you will see Walgreens stores asdensely packed in some cities asStarbucks coffee shops in Seattle. Walgreens then linked its convenience conceptto a simple economic idea, profit per customer visit. Tight clustering (nine stores per mile!) leads to local economies ofscale, which provides the cash for more clus tering, which in turn draws more customers. By adding high-margin ser-vices, like one-hour photo developing, Walgreens increased its profit per customer visit. More convenience led to more customer visits, which, when multiplied times increased profit per customer visit, threw cash back into the system to build even more convenientstores. Store by store, block byblock, city bycity, region byregion, Walgreens becamemoreand more ofa hedgehog withthisincredibly simple idea. In a world overrun by managementfaddists, brilliant visionaries, rant ing futurists, fearmongers, motivational gurus, and all the rest, it'srefresh ing to see a companysucceedso brilliantly bytaking one simple concept and justdoing it with excellence and imagination. Becoming the best in the worldat convenient drugstores, steadily increasingprofitper customer visit—what could be more obvious and straightforward? Yet, if it was so obvious and straightforward, why didn't Eckerd see it? WhileWalgreens stuck only to cities where it could implement the con venience/clustering concept, we found no evidence of a similarly coher ent concept for growth at Eckerd. Deal makers to the core, Eckerd's executives compulsively leapt at opportunities to acquire clumps of stores—forty-two units here, thirty-six units there—in hodgepodge fash ion, with no obvious unifying theme.

While Walgreens executives understood that profitable growth would come by pruning away all that did notfit with the Hedgehog Concept, Eckerd executives lurched after growth for growth's sake. In the early 1980s, just as Walgreens became religious about carrying out its conve nient drugstore concept, Eckerd threw itselfinto the home video market with its purchase ofAmerican Home Video Corporation. Eckerd's CEO toldForbes magazine in 1981, "Some feel the purerweare the betterwe'll be. But I want growth, and the home video industry is only emerging— unlike, say, drugstore chains."8 Eckerd's home video foray produced $31 million in losses before Eckerd sold it toTandy, which crowed thatit got the deal for $72 million below book value.9 In the precise year of Eckerd's American Home Video acquisition, Walgreens and Eckerdhad virtually identical revenues ($1.7 billion). Ten years later, Walgreens had grown to over twice the revenues of Eckerd, accumulating net profits $1 billion greater than Eckerd over the decade. Twenty years later, Walgreens was going strong, as one of the most sustained transformations in ourstudy. Meanwhile, Eckerd ceased to exist asan independent company .

THE THREE CIRCLES The notion of a Hedgehog Concept originated in our research team meetings when we were trying to make sense ofWalgreens' spectacular returns. "Aren't we justtalking aboutstrategy?" I asked. "Convenient drugstores, profit per customer visit—isn't that justbasic strategy? What's so interest ing about that?" "But Eckerd also had strategy," said Jenni Cooper, who analyzed the contrastbetweenthe two companies. "Wecan'tsay that it's justabout hav ing strategy. They both had strategy." Jenniwas correctin her observation. Strategy per se did not distinguish the good-to-great companies from the comparison companies. Both sets of companies had strategic plans, and there is absolutely no evidence that the good-to-great companies invested moretime and energy in strategy development and long-range planning. "Okay, soare we justtalking aboutgood strategy versus bad strategy?" The team sat there for a minute, thinking. Then Leigh Wilbanks observed, "ButwhatI find sostriking istheirincredible simplicity. I mean, look at Kroger with the superstore concept, or Kimberly-Clark with the move to paper-based consumer products, or Walgreens with convenient drugstores. Thesewere simple, simple, simple ideas." The research-team members all jumped into the fray, bantering about the companies they were studying. Itsoon became abundantly clear that all the good-to-great companies attained a very simple concept that they used as a frame of referencefor all their decisions, and this understanding coincided withbreakthrough results. Meanwhile, the comparison compa nies like Eckerd got all tripped up by theirsnazzy strategies for growth. "Okay," I pushed back, "but issimplicity enough? Just because it'ssimple doesn't mean it'sright. The world isfilled with failed companies that had simple but wrong ideas." Then we decided to undertake a systematic look at the concepts that guided the good-to-great companies in contrast tothe comparison compa nies. After a few months of sifting and sorting, considering possibilities and tossing them out, we finally cameto seethat the Hedgehog Concept in each good-to-great company wasn't just anyrandom simple idea.

More precisely, a Hedgehog Concept is a simple, crystalline concept that flows from deep understanding about the intersection ofthe following three circles: 1.What you can be the best in the world at (and, equallyimportant, what you cannot be the best in the world at). This discerningstandard goes far beyond core competence. Just because you possess a core compe tence doesn't necessarily mean you can be the best in the world at it. Conversely, whatyou can be the bestat might not even be something in which you are currently engaged. 2. What drives your economic engine. All the good-to-great companies attainedpiercinginsight into howto mosteffectively generate sustained and robust cash flow and profitability. Inparticular, they discovered the single denominator—profit per x—that had thegreatest impact ontheir economics. (Itwould be cash flow per x in the social sector.) 3. What you are deeply passionate about. The good-to-great companies focused on those activities that ignited their passion. The idea here is nottostimulate passion buttodiscover what makes you passionate.

Toquickly grasp the three circles, consider thefollowing personal anal ogy. Suppose you were able toconstruct awork life thatmeets thefollowing three tests. First, you are doing work for which you have a genetic orGodgiven talent, and perhapsyoucouldbecomeone ofthe bestin the worldin applying thattalent. ("I feel thatI was just born tobedoing this.") Second, you are well paid for what you do. ("I getpaid todothis? Am I dreaming?") Third, you aredoing work you are passionate about andabsolutely love to do, enjoying theactual process for its own sake. ("I look forward togetting upandthrowing myselfinto my daily work, andIreally believe inwhat I'm doing.") Ifyou could drivetoward the intersection ofthese three circlesand translate that intersection into a simple, crystalline concept that guided your life choices, thenyou'd have a Hedgehog Concept for yourself. To have a fully developed Hedgehog Concept, you need allthree circles. Ifyou make a lotofmoney doing things at which you could never be the best, you'll only build a successful company, nota great one. Ifyou become the best at something, you'll never remain on top ifyou don't have intrinsic ^^\ passion for what you are doing. Finally, you can be passionate all you want, / but ifyou can't be the best at it or it doesn't make economic sense, then you / might have a lotoffun, butyou won't produce great results. f UNDERSTANDING WHAT YOU CAN (AND CANNOT) BE THE BEST

AT "Theystick with whattheyunderstand andlettheirabilities, not their egos, determine what they attempt."11 Sowrote Warren Buffett abouthis $290 million investment in Wells Fargo despite hisserious reservations about the banking industry.12 Prior to clarifying its Hedgehog Concept, Wells Fargo had tried to be a global bank, operating like a mini-Citicorp, and a mediocre one at that. Then, at first under Dick Cooley and then under CarlReichardt, Wells Fargo executives began to ask themselves a piercing set of questions: What can we potentially do better than any other com pany, and, equally important, what can we not do better than any other company? And ifwe can't be the best at it,then why arewedoing it at all? Putting aside theiregos, theWells Fargo team pulled the plugon the vast majority ofits international operations, accepting the truththatit could not be better than Citicorp in global banking.13 Wells Fargo then turned its attentionto what it could be the bestin the world at: running a bank like a business, with a focus on the western United States. That's it. That was the essence ofthe Hedgehog ConceptthatturnedWells Fargo from a mediocre Citicorp wanna-be to one ofthe best-performing banks in the world. Carl Reichardt, CEO ofWells Fargo at the time oftransition, stands as a consummate hedgehog. While his counterparts at Bank of America went into a reaction-revolution panic mode in response to deregulation, hiringchange gurus who used sophisticated models and time-consuming encountergroups, Reichardt stripped everything down to its essential sim plicity.14 "It's not spacesciencestuff," he told us in our interview. "What we did was so simple, and wekept itsimple. It was so straightforward and obvious that it sounds almost ridiculousto talk about it. The average busi nessman coming from a highly competitive industry with no regulations would have jumped on this like a goose on a Junebug.

Reichardt kept people relentlessly focused on the simple hedgehog idea, continually reminding them that "there's more money tobemade in Modesto than Tokyo."16 Those who worked with Reichardt marveled at his genius for simplicity. "IfCarl were an Olympic diver," said oneofhis colleagues, "he would not do a five-flip twisting thing. Hewould do the best swan dive inthe world, and do itperfecdy over and over again."17 The Wells Fargo focus on its Hedgehog Concept was so intense that it became, in its executives' own words, "amantra." Throughout ourinter views, Wells Fargo people echoedthe same basic theme—"It wasn't that complicated. We just took a hard-nosed look at what we were doing and decided tofocus entirely on those few things we knew we could do better than anyone else, not getting distracted into arenas that would feed our egosand at which we could not be the best."

Every company would like tobethebest atsomething, butfew actually understand—with piercing insight and egoless clarity—what they actually have thepotential tobethebest atand, just as important, what they cannot bethe best at. And itis this distinction thatstands as one oftheprimary con trasts between thegood-to-great companies andthecomparison companies. Consider the contrast between Abbott Laboratories and Upjohn. In 1964, thetwo companies were almost identical in terms ofrevenues, prof its, and productlines. Both companies had the bulk of their business in pharmaceuticals, principally antibiotics. Both companies had family management. Both companies lagged behindthe rest ofthe pharmaceuti cal industry. But then, in 1974, Abbott had a breakthrough in perfor mance, producing cumulative returns of 4.0 times the market and 5.5 times Upjohn over the nextfifteen years. One crucialdifference between the two companies is thatAbbott developed a Hedgehog Concept based on what it could be the bestat and Upjohn did not. Abbott began by confronting the brutal facts. By 1964, Abbott had lost the opportunity to become the best pharmaceutical company. While Abbott haddrowsily lumbered along in the 1940s and 1950s, living offits cash cow, erythromycin, companies like Merck hadbuiltresearch engines that rivaled Harvard and Berkeley. By 1964, George Cain and hisAbbott team realized that Merck and others had such a huge research lead that trying tobethebest pharmaceutical company would belike a high school football teamtrying to take on the Dallas Cowboys. Even though Abbott's entire history lay in pharmaceuticals, becoming the best pharmaceutical company was no longer a viable option. So, guided by a Level 5leader and tapping into thefaith side ofthe Stockdale Paradox (Theremustbe a way for usto prevail asa greatcompany, and we will find it!), the Abbott team sought to understand what it could be the best at.Around 1967, a key insight emerged: We've lost the chanceto be the best pharmaceutical company, but we have anopportunity to excel at creating products thatcontribute to cost-effective health care. Abbott had experimented with hospital nutritional products, designed tohelppatients quickly regain theirstrength after surgery, and diagnostic devices (one of the primary ways to reduce health care costs isthrough proper diagnosis). Abbott eventually became the number one company in both ofthese are nas, which moved it far downthe path of becoming the best company in the world atcreating products that make health care more cost-effective.18

Upjohn never confronted the same brutal reality andcontinued tolive with the delusion that it could beat Merck.19 Later, when it fell even fur ther behind the pharmaceutical leaders, it diversified into arenas whereit definitely could not be the bestin the world, such as plastics and chemi cals. As Upjohn fell even further behind, itreturned to a focus on ethical drugs, yetnever confronted the fact thatitwas just toosmall towin in the big-stakes pharmaceutical game .Despite consistently spending nearly twice the percentage ofsales on R&D asAbbott, Upjohn saw its profits dwindle toless than halfthose ofAbbott before being acquired in 1995.

Clearly, a Hedgehog Concept is not the same as a core competence. You can have competence at something but not necessarily have the potential tobe the best in theworld at it. To use an analogy, consider the young person who gets straight A's inhigh school calculus and scores high onthemath part ofthe SAT, demonstrating a core competence atmathe matics. Doesthat mean the person shouldbecomea mathematician? Not necessarily. Suppose now that this young person goes off to college, enrolls in math courses, and continues toearn A's, yet encounters people who are genetically encoded for math. As one such student said after this experience, "It would take me three hours to finish the final. Then there were those who finished the same final in thirty minutes and earned an A+. Their brains are just wired differendy. I could be a very competent mathematician, but I soon realized I could never be one of the best." That young person mightstill getpressure from parents and friends to continue with math, saying, "But you're so good at it." Just like our young person, many people have beenpulled orhave fallen intocareers where theycan never attain complete mastery andfulfillment. Suffering from the curse of competence but lacking a clear Hedgehog Concept, they rarely become greatat whatthey do. The Hedgehog Conceptrequires a severe standard ofexcellence. It'snot just about building onstrength and competence, butabout understanding what your organization truly has the potential to be the very bestat and sticking to it.Like Upjohn, the comparison companies stuck to businesses at which theywere "good" but couldnever be the best, orworse, launched offin pursuit ofeasy growth andprofits in arenas where they had no hope ofbeing the best. They made money butnever became great. Every good-to-great company eventually gained deep understanding of this principle and pinned theirfutures on allocating resources to those few arenas where they could potentiallybe the best. (See the table below.) The comparison companies rarelyattained this understanding .

CHAPTER SIX

# INSIGHT INTO YOUR ECONOMIC ENGINE WHAT IS YOUR DENOMINATOR?

The good-to-great companies frequently produced spectacular returns in very unspectacular industries. The banking industry ranked in the bottom quartile of industries (in total returns) during the same period that Wells Fargo beat the market by fourtimes. Even more impressive, both Pitney Bowes and Nucor were in bottom 5 percent industries; yet both these companies beat the marketbywell overfive times. Only one of the good-to-great companies had the benefit of being in a great industry (defined as a top 10 percent industry); five were in good industries; five were in bad to terrible industries. This is not a book on microeconomics. Each company and each indus try had its own economic realities, and I'm not going to belabor them all here. The central point is that each good-to-great company attained a deep understanding ofthe key drivers in itseconomic engine and built its system in accordance withthis understanding. That said, however, we did notice one particularly provocative form of economic insightthat every good-to-great company attained,the notion of a single "economic denominator." Think about it in terms of the follow ing question:Ifyou could pick oneandonly one ratio—profit per x (or, in the socialsector, cash flow per x)—to systematically increase over time, what x would have the greatest and most sustainable impact on your economic engine? We learned that thissingle questionleadsto profound insightinto the inner workings of an organization's economics. Recall how Walgreens switched itsfocus from profit per store to profit per customer visit. Convenient locations are expensive, but by increasing profit per customer visit, Walgreens was able to increase convenience (nine stores in a mile!)andsimultaneously increaseprofitability across its entire system. The standard metric of profitper storewould have run con traryto the convenience concept. (The quickestway to increase profit per store is to decrease the number of stores and put them in less expensive locations. This would have destroyed the convenience concept.) Or considerWells Fargo. When the Wells team confronted the brutal fact that deregulation would transform banking into a commodity, they realized that standard banker metrics, like profit per loan and profit per deposit, would no longer be the key drivers. Instead, they grasped a new denominator: profit per employee. Following this logic, Wells Fargo became one of the first banksto change its distribution system to relypri marily on stripped-down branches and ATMs .

For example, Fannie Mae grasped the subtle denominator of profitper mortgage risk level, not per mortgage (which would be the "obvious" choice). It's a brilliant insight. The real driverin Fannie Mae's economics is the abilityto understand risk ofdefault in a package of mortgages better than anyone else. Then it makes money selling insurance and managing the spread on that risk. Simple, insightful, unobvious—and right. Nucor, for example, made its mark in the ferociously price competitive steel industrywith the denominator profitper ton of finished steel.Atfirst glance, you might think that per employee or per fixed cost might be the proper denominator. But the Nucor people understood that the driving force in its economic engine was a combination of a strong-work-ethic culture andthe application ofadvanced manufacturing technology. Profit per employee or per fixed cost would not capture this duality as well as profit per ton of finished steel. Do you need to have a single denominator? No, but pushing for a sin gle denominator tends to produce better insight than letting yourselfoff the hook with three or four denominators. The denominator question serves as a mechanism to force deeper understandingof the keydrivers in your economic engine. As the denominator question emerged from the research, we tested the question on a number of executive teams. We found that the question always stimulated intense dialogue and debate.

whilethe comparison companies usually did not. In fact, we found only one comparison case that attained a pro found insightinto its economics. Hasbro built its upswing on the insight that a portfolio ofclassic toys and games, suchasG.I.Joe and Monopoly, produces more sustainable cash flow thanbigonetime hits.23 In fact, Has bro isthe one comparison companythat understood all three circlesofthe Hedgehog Concept. It became the best in the world at acquiring and renewingtried-and-true toys, reintroducing and recycling them at justthe righttime to increaseprofitper classic brand.And itspeople had greatpas sion for the business. Systematically building from all three circles, Has bro became the best-performing comparison in ourstudy, lending further credence to the power ofthe Hedgehog Concept. Hasbrobecame an unsustained transition in part because it lost the dis cipline to stay within the three circles, afterthe unexpecteddeath ofCEO Stephen Hassenfeld. The Hasbro case reinforces a vitallesson. Ifyou suc cessfully apply these ideas, butthen stop doing them, you willslide back ward, from great togood, orworse. The only way to remain great is to keep applying the fundamental principles that made you great UNDERSTANDING YOUR PASSION When interviewing the Philip Morris executives, we encountered an intensityand passion thatsurprised us.Recall from chapter 3 how George Weissman described working at the company asthe greatloveaffair of his life, second only to his marriage. Even with a most sinful collection of consumerproducts (Marlboro cigarettes, Millerbeer, 67 percentfat-filled Velveeta, Maxwell House coffee for caffeine addicts, Toblerone for choco holics,and so forth),we found tremendouspassion for the business. Most of the top executives at Philip Morris were passionate consumers of their own products. In 1979,Ross Millhiser,then vice chairman of Philip Mor ris and a dedicated smoker, said, "I love cigarettes. It's one of the things that makes life really worth living."24 The Philip Morris people clearly loved their companyand had passion for what they were doing. It's as if they viewed themselves as the lone, fiercely independent cowboy depicted in the Marlboro billboards. "We have a right to smoke, and we will protect that right!" A board member told me during my research fora previous project, "I really love being on the board ofPhilip Morris. It's like being partofsomething really special." She said this as she proudly puffed away.25 Now, you might say, "But that is just the defensiveness of the tobacco industry. Ofcourse they'd feel that way. Otherwise, how could they sleep at night?" But keep in mind that R. J. Reynolds was also in the tobacco business and under siege from society. Yet, unlike Philip Morris, R. J. Reynolds executives began to diversify away from tobacco into any arena where it could get growth, regardless ofwhether they had passion for those acquisitions or whether the company could be the best in the world at them. The Philip Morris people stuck much closer to the tobacco busi ness, in large part because they loved that business. In contrast, the R. J. Reynolds people saw tobacco as just a way to make money.

As vividly portrayed in the book Barbarians at the Gate, R. J. Reynolds executives eventually lost passion for anything except making themselves rich through a leveraged buyout.26 Itmay seem odd totalk aboutsomething as soft andfuzzy as "passion" as an integral part of a strategic framework. But throughout the good-togreat companies, passion became a key part of the Hedgehog Concept. You can'tmanufacture passion or"motivate" people tofeel passionate. You can only discover what ignites your passion and the passions of those around you.

When Gillette executives made the choice to build sophisticated, rela tively expensive shaving systems rather than fight a low-margin battle with disposables, they did so inlarge part because they just couldn't get excited about cheap disposable razors. "Zeien talks about shaving systems with the sort oftechnical gusto one expects from a Boeing or Hughes engi neer," wrote one journalist about Gillette's CEO in 1996.28 Gillette has always been at its best when itsticks to businesses that fit its Hedgehog Concept. "People who aren't passionate aboutGillette need not apply," wrote a Wall Street Journal reporter, who went on to describe how a top business school graduate wasn't hired because she didn't show enough passion for deodorant.29 Perhaps you, too, can't get passionate about deodorant. Perhaps you might find it hardto imagine being passionate aboutpharmacies, grocery stores, tobacco, or postage meters. You might wonder about what type of person gets all jazzed upabout making a bank as efficient as McDonald's, or who considers a diaper charismatic. In the end, it doesn'treally matter. The point is thatthey felt passionate about what they were doing and the passion was deep and genuine. This doesn't mean, however, that you have to be passionate about the mechanics of the business per se (although you might be). The passion circle can be focused equally on what the company stands for. For exam ple, the Fannie Mae people were not passionate about the mechanical process of packaging mortgages into market securities. But they were terrifically motivated by the whole idea of helping people of all classes, backgrounds, and races realize the American dream ofowning their home. Linda Knight, who joined Fannie Mae in 1983, just as thecompany faced its darkest days, told us: "This wasn't justany old company getting into trouble; thiswas a company at the core ofmaking homeownership a real ity for thousands ofAmericans. It's a role thatis far more important than just making money, andthat's why we felt such depth ofcommitment to preserve, protect, and enhance the company."30 As another Fannie Mae executive summed up,"Isee usas a key mechanism for strengthening the whole social fabric ofAmerica. Whenever I drive throughdifficult neigh borhoods thatarecoming back because more families own theirhomes, I return to work reenergized." THE TRIUMPH OF UNDERSTANDING OVER BRAVADO On the research team, we frequently found ourselves talking aboutthe dif ference between "prehedgehog" and "posthedgehog" states. In the prehedgehog state, it's like groping through the fog. You're making progress on a long march, but you can't see all that well. At each juncture in the trail, you can only see a little bit ahead and must move at a deliberate, slow crawl. Then, with the Hedgehog Concept, you break intoa clearing, the fog lifts, and you can see for miles. From then on, each juncture requiresless deliberation, and you can shiftfrom crawl to walk, and from walk to run. In the posthedgehog state, miles oftrail move swiftly beneath your feet, forks in the road fly past asyou quickly make decisions that you couldnot have seensoclearly in the fog. What's so striking about thecomparison companies is that—for all their change programs, frantic gesticulations, and charismatic leaders—they rarely emerged from thefog. They would try torun,making bad decisions atforks in the road, and then have to reverse course later. Or they would veer off the trail entirely, banging into trees and tumbling down ravines.(Oh, butthey were sure doing it with speed and panache!) Nowhere is this more evident than in the comparison companies' mindless pursuit ofgrowth: Over two thirds ofthe comparison companies displayed an obsession with growth without the benefit of a Hedgehog Concept.31 Statements such as "We've been a growth at any price com pany" and "Betting thatsize equals success" pepper the materials on the comparison companies. In contrast, not one of the good-to-great compa nies focused obsessively on growth. Yet they created sustained, profitable growth far greater thanthecomparison companies thatmade growth their mantra. Consider the case ofGreat Western and Fannie Mae. "Great Western is a mite unwieldy," wrote the Wall Street Transcript "It wants to grow everyway it can."32 The company found itself in finance, leasing, insur ance, and manufactured houses, continually acquiring companies in an expansion binge.33 Bigger! More! In 1985, GreatWestern's CEO told a gathering of analysts, "Don't worry about what you call us—a bank, an S&L, or a Zebra .Quite a contrastto Fannie Mae,whichhad a simple, crystalline under standing that it could be the best capital markets player in anything related tomortgages, better even thanGoldman Sachs or Salomon Broth ers in opening up the full capital markets tothemortgage process. It built a powerful economic machine by reframing its business model on risk management, rather than mortgage selling. And it drove the machine with great passion, the Fannie Mae people inspired by its vital role in democratizing home ownership. Until 1984, the stock charts tracked each otherlikemirrorimages. Then in 1984, one year after it clarified its Hedgehog Concept, Fannie Mae exploded upward, while Great Western kept lollygagging along until just before its acquisition in 1997. By focusing on its simple, elegant concep tion—and not just focusing on "growth"—Fannie Mae grew revenues nearly threefold from its transition year in 1984 through 1996. GreatWest ern,for all ofits gobbling ofgrowth steroids, grew revenues and earnings only 25 percent over the same period, thenlost its independence in 1997 .

The Hedgehog Concept is a turning point in the journey from good to great. In most cases, the transition date follows within a few years of the Hedgehog Concept. Furthermore, everything from here on out in the book hinges upon having the Hedgehog Concept. As will become abundantly clear in the following chapters, disciplined action—the third big chunk in the framework after disciplined people and disci plined thought—only makes sense in the context of the Hedgehog Concept. Despite its vital importance (or, rather, because ofits vital importance), it would be a terrible mistake to thoughtlessly attempt to jump rightto a Hedgehog Concept. You can't just go off-site for two days, pull out a bunch offlip charts, do breakout discussions, and come up with a deep understanding. Well, you can do that, butyou probably won't getitright. It would be likeEinsteinsaying, "I think it'stime to become a greatscien tist, so I'm going to go off to the Four Seasons this weekend, pull out the flip charts, and unlock the secrets of the universe." Insight just doesn't happen that way. It took Einstein ten years of groping through the fog to getthe theory ofspecial relativity, andhe was a bright guy.35 It took about four years on average for the good-to-great companies to clarify their Hedgehog Concepts. Like scientific insight, a Hedgehog Concept simplifies a complex world and makes decisions much easier. But whileit has crystalline clarity and elegantsimplicity once you haveit, getting the concept can be devilishly difficult and takes time. Recognize that getting a Hedgehog Conceptisan inherently iterative process, not an event. The essence ofthe process istogetthe rightpeople engaged in vigorous dialogue anddebate, infused with thebrutal facts andguided byquestions formed bythe three circles. Dowe really understand what we can be the best in the world at, as distinct from what we can just be successfulat? Do we really understand the drivers in our economic engine, including our economic denominator? Do we really understand what best ignites our passion? One particularly useful mechanism for moving the process along is a device that we came to call the Council. The Council consistsof a group of the right people who participate in dialogue and debate guided by the three circles,iteratively and overtime, about vitalissues and decisionsfac ing the organization. (See "Characteristics of the Council," below.) In response to the question, "How should we go about getting our Hedgehog Concept?" I would point to the diagram on page 114and say: "Build the Council, and use that as a model. Ask the right questions, engage in vigorous debate, make decisions, autopsy the results, and learn—all guided within the context of the three circles. Just keep going through that cycle of understanding." When asked, "Howdo weaccelerate the process ofgettinga Hedgehog Concept?"I wouldrespond: "Increase the number oftimesyougoaround that full cycle in a given period of time." If you go through this cycle enough times, guided resolutely by the three circles, you will eventually gainthe depth ofunderstanding required for a Hedgehog Concept. It will not happen overnight, but it will eventually happen.

Does every organization have a Hedgehog Concept to discover? What if you wake up, look around with brutal honesty, and conclude: "We're not the best at anything,and we neverhavebeen." Therein lies one of the mostexciting aspects ofthe entirestudy. In the majority ofcases, the goodto-great companies were not the bestin the world at anything and showed no prospects of becoming so.Infused with the Stockdale Paradox ("There must be something we can become the best at, and we willfind it! We must also confront the brutal facts of what we cannot be the best at, and we will not delude ourselves!"), every good-to-great company, no matter howawful at the startofthe process, prevailed in itssearchfora Hedgehog Concept. As you search for your own concept, keep in mind that when the goodto-great companies finally grasped their Hedgehog Concept, it had none ofthe tiresome, irritating blasts ofmindless bravado typical ofthe compar ison companies. "Yep, we could be the best at that" was stated as the recognition of a fact, no more startling than observing that the sky is blue or the grass is green. When you get yourHedgehog Concept right, it has the quiet pingoftruth, likea single, clear, perfectly strucknote hangingin the air in the hushed silence of a full auditorium at the end of a quiet movement of a Mozart piano concerto. There is no need to saymuch of anything;the quiet truth speaks foritself. Fm reminded ofa personal experience in myownfamily that illustrates the vital difference betweenbravado and understanding. Mywife, Joanne, began racing marathons and triathlons in the early 1980s. As she accumu latedexperience—track times, swim splits, raceresults—she beganto feel the momentum of success. One day, she entered a race with many of the best woman triathletes in the world,and—despite a weakswim where she came out of the water hundreds of places behind the top swimmers and having to push a heavy, nonaerodynamic bike up a long hill—she man aged to cross the finish line in the top ten. Then, a few weeks later while sitting at breakfast, Joanne looked up from her morning newspaper and calmly, quietly said, "I think I could win the Ironman." The Ironman, the worldchampionship of triathlons, involves 2.4 miles of ocean swimming and 112 miles of cycling, capped offwith a 26.2-mile marathon footrace on the hot, lava-baked Kona coast of Hawaii. "Of course, I'd have to quit my job, turn down my offers to graduate school(shehad been admittedto graduate business schoolat a number of the top schools), and commit to full-time training. But..." Her words had no bravado in them, no hype, no agitation, no pleading. She didn't tryto convinceme. She simply observed whatshe had come to understand was a fact,a truth no more shocking than statingthat the walls were painted white. She had the passion. She had the genetics.And if she wonraces, she'd havethe economics. The goal to winthe Ironman flowed from early understanding ofher Hedgehog Concept. And, so, she decided to go for it. She quit her job. She turned down graduate schools. She sold the mills! (But she did keep me on her bus.) And three years later, on a hot October dayin 1985, she crossed the finish line at the Hawaii Ironman in first place,world champion. When Joanne set out to win the Ironman, she did not know if she would become the world's best triathlete. But she understood that she could, that it was in the realm of possibility, that she was not living in a delusion. And that distinc tion makes all the difference. It isa distinction that thosewho wantto go from good to great must grasp, and one that those who fail to become great so often never do.

CHAPTER SEVEN

# Culture of discipline

George Rathmann cofounded the biotechnology company Amgen. Over the next twenty years, Amgen grew from a struggling entre preneurial enterprise into a $3.2 billion company with 6,400 employees, creating blood products to improve the lives of people suffering through chemotherapy and kidney dialysis.2 Under Rathmann, Amgen became one of the few biotechnology companies that delivered consistent prof itability and growth. It became so consistently profitable, in fact, that its stock pricemultiplied over 150 times from its public offering in June 1983 toJanuary 2000. Aninvestor who bought as little as$7,000 ofAmgen stock would have realized a capital gainofover $1 million, thirteen timesbetter than the same investment in the general stock market. Few successful start-ups become great companies, in large part because they respond to growth and success in the wrong way. Entrepreneurial success is fueled by creativity, imagination, bold moves into uncharted waters, and visionary zeal. As a company grows and becomes more com plex, it begins to trip over its own success—too many new people, too many new customers, too many new orders, too many new products. Whatwas once great fun becomes an unwieldy ballofdisorganized stuff. Lack of planning, lack of accounting, lack ofsystems, and lack of hiring constraints create friction. Problems surface—with customers, with cash flow, with schedules. In response, someone (often a board member) says, "It'stimeto grow up. Thisplaceneeds some professional management." The company begins to hire MBAs and seasoned executives from blue-chip companies. Processes, procedures, checklists, and allthe rest begin tosprout up like weeds. What was once an egalitarian environment gets replaced with a hierarchy. Chains of command appear for the first time. Reporting relationships become clear, and an executive class with special perks begins to appear. "We" and "they" segmentations appear—just like in a real company. The professional managers finally rein in the mess. They create order out of chaos, but theyalso kill the entrepreneurial spirit. Members ofthe founding team begin to grumble, "This isn't fun anymore. I used to be able to justgetthings done. Now I have to fill out these stupid forms and follow these stupid rules. Worst of all, I have to spend a horrendous amount of time in useless meetings." The creative magic begins to wane assome ofthe most innovative people leave, disgusted bythe burgeoning bureaucracy and hierarchy. The exciting start-up transforms into just another company, with nothing special to recommend it. The cancer of mediocrity begins to grow in earnest. George Rathmannavoided thisentrepreneurial death spiral. He under stood that the purpose ofbureaucracy isto compensate for incompetence and lack of discipline—a problem thatlargely goes away if you have the right people in the first place. Most companies build their bureaucratic rules to manage the small percentage ofwrong people on the bus,which in turn drives away the right people on the bus, which then increases the percentage of wrong people on the bus, which increases the need for more bureaucracy to compensate for incompetence and lack of disci-* pline,which then further drives the right people away, and soforth. Rath mann also understood an alternative exists: Avoid bureaucracy and hierarchy and instead create a culture ofdiscipline. When you put these two complementary forces together—a culture ofdiscipline withan ethic of entrepreneurship—you get a magical alchemyofsuperiorperformance and sustained results.

Why start this chapter with a biotechnology entrepreneur rather than one of our good-to-great companies? Because Rathmanncredits much of his entrepreneurial success to what he learned while working at Abbott Laboratories before founding Amgen: WhatI gotfrom Abbott was the idea thatwhen you setyour objectives for the year, you record them in concrete. You can change your plans through the year, but you never change what you measure yourself against. You are rigorous at the end ofthe year, adhering exactly to what yousaidwas going to happen. You don't geta chance to editorialize. You don'tgeta chanceto adjust and finagle, and decide thatyoureally didn't intend to do that anyway, and readjust your objectives to make yourself look better. You never just focus on what you've accomplished for the year; youfocus on whatyou've accomplished relative to exactly whatyou saidyou weregoingto accomplish—no matterhow tough the measure. Thatwas a discipline learned atAbbott, andthatwe carried intoAmgen.

Many of the Abbott disciplines trace back to 1968, when it hired a remarkable financial officer named Bernard H. Semler. Semler did not see his job as a traditional financial controller or accountant Rather, he set out to inventmechanismsthat woulddrive culturalchange. He createda whole new framework of accounting that he called Responsibility Accounting, whereinevery item ofcost, income,and investment would be clearly identi fied with a single individual responsible for thatitem.4 The idea, radical for the 1960s, was to createa system whereinevery Abbott managerin every type of job was responsible for his or her return on investment, with the same rigor that an investor holds an entrepreneur responsible. There would be no hiding behind traditional accounting allocations, no slopping funds about to cover up ineffective management, no opportunities for finger-pointing.5 But the beautyof the Abbott system laynot justin itsrigor, but in how it used rigor and discipline to enable creativity and entrepreneurship. "Abbott developed a very disciplined organization, but not in a linear way of thinking," said George Rathmann. "[It] was exemplary at having both financial discipline and the divergent thinking of creative work. We used financial discipline as a way to provide resources for the really creative work."6 Abbott reduced its administrative costs as a percentage ofsales to the lowest in the industry (by a significant margin) and at the same time became a new product innovation machine like 3M,deriving up to 65 per cent ofrevenues from newproducts introduced in the previous fouryears.7 This creativedualityran through every aspectofAbbottduring the tran sition era, woven into the veryfabric of the corporate culture. On the one hand, Abbottrecruited entrepreneurial leadersand gave them freedom to determine the best path to achieving their objectives. On the other hand, individuals had to commit fully to the Abbottsystem and were held rigor ously accountable for their objectives. They had freedom, but freedom within a framework. Abbott instilled the entrepreneur's zeal for oppor tunistic flexibility. ("We recognized that planning is priceless, but plans are useless," said one Abbott executive.)8 But Abbott also had the disci pline to say no to opportunities that failed the three circles test. While encouraging wide-ranging innovationwithin its divisions, Abbottsimulta neouslymaintained fanatical adherence to its HedgehogConcept of con tributing to cost-effective health care. Abbott Laboratories exemplifies a key finding ofour study: a culture of 1 discipline. Byitsnature, "culture" isa somewhatunwieldytopic to discuss, less prone to clean frameworks like the three circles. The main points of this chapter, however,boil down to one central idea:Buildа culture full of people who take disciplined action within the three circles, fanatically con sistent with the Hedgehog Concept More precisely, this meansthe following: 1. Builda culture around the idea offreedom and responsibility, within a framework. 2. Fill that culture with self-disciplined people who are willing to go to extreme lengths to fulfill their responsibilities. They will "rinse their cottage cheese." 3. Don't confusea culture ofdiscipline with a tyrannical disciplinarian. 4. Adhere withgreatconsistency to the Hedgehog Concept, exercising an almostreligious focus on the intersection of the three circles. Equally important, createa "stop doinglist" and systematically unplug anything extraneous. FREEDOM (AND RESPONSIBILITY) WITHIN A FRAMEWORK Picturean airlinepilot. She settles intothe cockpit, surroundedby dozens of complicated switches and sophisticated gauges, sitting atop a massive $84million pieceofmachinery. As passengers thump and stufftheir bags into overhead bins and flight attendants scurry about trying to get every one settledin, she beginsher preflight checklist. Step by methodical step, she systematically moves through every requireditem. Cleared for departure, she begins working with air traffic control, fol lowing precise instructions-—which direction to takeout ofthe gate, which way to taxi, which runway to use, which direction to take off. She doesn't throttle up and hurtle the jet into the air until she's cleared for takeoff. Once aloft, she communicates continuallywith flight-control centers and stays within the tight boundaries ofthe commercialair traffic system. On approach,however, she hitsa ferocious thunder-and-hail storm. Blast ingwinds, crossways and unpredictable, tilt the wings downto the left, then down tothe right. Looking outthewindows, passengers can'tseethe ground, onlythe thinningand thickening globs ofgray clouds and the spatter ofrain on the windows. The flight attendants announce, "Ladies and gentlemen, we've been asked to remainseated forthe remainder ofthe flight. Please put yourseats in the upright and locked position and placeallyourcarry-on bag gage under the seatin frontofyou. Weshouldbe on the groundshortly."

"Not tooshortly, I hope," think the lessexperienced travelers,unnerved by the roiling wind and momentary flashes of lightning. But the experi enced travelers justgo on readingmagazines, chatting with seatmates, and preparing for their meetings on the ground. "I've been through all this before," they think. "She'll only land if it's safe." Sure enough, on final approach—wheels down as a quarter of a million pounds of steel glides down at 130miles per hour—passengers suddenly hear the engines whine and feel themselves thrust back into their seats. The plane accelerates back into the sky. It banks around in a big arc back toward the airport. The pilot takes a moment to click on the intercom: "Sorry, folks. We weregettingsome bad crosswinds there. We're going to give it another try." On the next go, the winds calm just enough and she bringsthe plane down,safely. Now take a step back and think about the model here. The pilot oper ates within a very strictsystem, and she does not have freedom to go out side of that system. (You don't wantairline pilots saying, "Hey, I just read in a management bookabout the value ofbeing empowered—freedom to experiment, to be creative, to be entrepreneurial, to try a lot of stuff and keep what works!") Yetat the same time, the crucial decisions—whether to take off, whether to land, whether to abort, whether to land else where—rest with the pilot Regardless of the strictures of the system, one central factstands out above all others: The pilot has ultimate responsibil ityfor the airplane and the lives of the people on it. The point here is not that a companyshould have a system as strictand inflexible as the airtraffic system. After all, ifa corporate system fails, peo ple don't die by the hundreds in burning, twisted hunks of steel. Cus tomer service at the airlines might be terrible, but you are almost certain to get whereyou are going in one piece. The point of this analogy is that when we looked insidethe good-to-great companies, wewerereminded of the best part of the airline pilot model: freedom and responsibility within the framework of a highly developed system.

"Thiswas the secret to how we were able to run stores from a great dis tance, by remote control," saidBill Rivas of Circuit City. "It was the com bination of greatstore managers who had ultimate responsibility for their individual stores, operating within a greatsystem. You've gotto have man agement and people who believe in the system and who do whatever is necessary to make the system work. But within the boundaries of that sys tem,store managers had a lot ofleeway, to coincidewith their responsibil ity."9 In a sense, Circuit City became to consumer electronics retailing what McDonald's became to restaurants—not the most exquisite experi ence, but an enormously consistent one. The system evolved overtime as Circuit City experimentedbyadding new itemslike computers and video players (justlike McDonald'sadded breakfast EggMcMuffins). But at any given moment, everyone operated within the framework of the system. "That's one of the major differences between us and all the others who were in this same business in the early 1980s," said Bill Zierden. "They justcouldn't roll it out further,and wecould.We could stamp these stores out all over the country, with great consistency."10 Therein liesone ofthe keyreasons whyCircuit City tookoffin the early 1980s and beat the gen eral stockmarket by more than eighteen times overthe nextfifteen years. In a sense,much ofthis bookisabout creatinga culture of discipline. It allstarts withdisciplined people. The transition begins not bytryingto dis cipline the wrong people into the right behaviors, but by getting selfdisciplined people on the bus in the first place. Next we have disciplined thought. You need the discipline to confront the brutal facts of reality, while retainingresolute faith that you can and will create a path to great ness. Most importantly, you need the disciplineto persistin the search for understanding until you get your Hedgehog Concept. Finally, we have disciplined action, the primary subject of this chapter. This order is important.The comparison companies often tried to jump right to disci plined action. But disciplined action without self-disciplined people is impossible to sustain, and disciplined action withoutdisciplined thought is a recipe for disaster. Indeed, discipline by itself will not produce great results. We find plentyof organizations in history that had tremendous discipline and that marched rightinto disaster, withprecision and in nicelyformedlines. No, the point is to first getself-disciplined people who engage in very rigorous thinking, who then take disciplined action within the framework ofa con sistentsystem designed around the Hedgehog Concept.

Throughout our research, we were struck by the continual use ofwords like disciplined, rigorous, dogged, determined, diligent, precise, fastidious, systematic, methodical, workmanlike, demanding, consistent, focused, accountable, and responsible. They peppered articles, interviews, and source materials on the good-to-great companies, and were strikingly absentfrom the materials on the direct comparison companies. People in thegood-to-great companies became somewhat extreme inthefulfillment oftheir responsibilities, bordering in some cases on fanaticism. Wecameto callthisthe "rinsing your cottage cheese" factor. The anal ogy comes from a disciplined world-class athlete named Dave Scott, who wonthe Hawaii IronmanTriathlonsix times. In training, Scottwouldride his bike 75 miles, swim 20,000 meters, and run 17 miles—on average, every single day. Dave Scott did not have a weight problem! Yet he believed that a low-fat, high-carbohydrate diet would give him an extra edge. So, Dave Scott—a man who burned at least 5,000 calories a day in training—would literally rinse his cottage cheese to get the extra fat off. Now, there is no evidence that he absolutely needed to rinse his cottage cheese to win the Ironman; that's not the pointofthe story. The point is that rinsing his cottage cheese was simply one more small step that he believed would make him just that much better, one more small step added to all the other small steps to create a consistent program ofsuperdiscipline. I've always pictured Dave Scott running the 26 miles ofthe marathon—hammering away in hundred-degree heat on the black, baked lavafields of the Kona coastafterswimming 2.4 miles in the ocean and cycling 112 miles against ferocious crosswinds—and thinking to himself: "Compared to rinsing my cottage cheese every day, this just isn't that bad." Irealize thatit's a bizarre analogy. But ina sense, thegood-to-great com panies became like Dave Scott. Much of the answer to the question of "good to great" liesin the discipline to dowhatever it takes to becomethe best within carefully selected arenas and then toseek continual improve mentfrom there. It's really just thatsimple. And it's really just thatdifficult. ConsiderWells Fargo in contrast to Bank of America. Carl Reichardt never doubted thatWells Fargo could emerge from bank deregulation as a stronger company, not a weaker one. He saw that the key to becoming a greatcompany rested not with brilliant newstrategies but with the sheer determination to rip a hundred years of banker mentality out of the sys tem. "There's too much waste inbanking," said Reichardt. "Getting ridof it takes tenacity, not brilliance."11 Reichardtseta clear tone atthetop: We're notgoing toask everyone else tosuffer while we sit onhigh. We will start by rinsing ourown cottage cheese, right here in the executive suite. He froze executive salaries for two years (despite thefact thatWells Fargo was enjoying some ofthemost profitable years in its history).12 He shut the executive dining room and replaced it witha college dormfood-service caterer.13 He closed the executive elevator, sold the corporate jets, andbanned green plants from the executive suite as too expensive to water.14 He removed free coffee from the executive suite. Heeliminated Christmas trees for management.15 Hethrew reports back at peoplewho'd submitted them in fancy binders, with the admonishment: "Would you spend your own money this way? Whatdoes a binder add to anything?"16 Reichardt would sit through meetings with fellow executives, in a beat-up old chairwith the stuffing hanging out. Sometimes he would justsitthere and pickat the stuffing while listening to proposals to spend money, said onearticle, "[and] a lotofmust-do projects just melted away."17 Across the street atBank ofAmerica, executives also faced deregulation andrecognized theneed toeliminate waste. However, unlike Wells Fargo, B of A executives didn't have the discipline to rinse their own cottage cheese. Theypreserved theirposh executive kingdom in its imposing tower in downtown San Francisco, the CEO's office described in the book Breaking the Bank as"a northeast cornersuite with a large attached confer ence room, oriental rugs, and floor-to-ceiling windows thatoffered a sweep ing panorama of the San Francisco Bay from the Golden Gate to the Bay Bridge."18 (We found no evidence of executive chairs with the stuffing hanging out.) The elevator made its last stop at the executive floor and descended all the way to the ground in one quiet whoosh, unfettered by the intrusions oflesser beings. The vast open space in the executive suite made the windows look even taller than they actually were, creating a sense offloating above the fog in an elevated cityofalien elites who ruled theworld from above.19 Why rinse ourcottage cheese when life is so good? After losing $1.8 billion across threeyears in the mid-1980s, BofAeven tually made the necessary changes in response to deregulation (largely by hiring ex-Wells executives). Buteven in thedarkest days, BofAcould not bring itselfto get rid of the perks thatshielded its executives from the real world. Atone board meeting during Bank ofAmerica's crisis period, one member made sensible suggestions like "Sell the corporate jet." Other directors listened to the recommendations, then passed themby. A CULTURE, NOT A TYRANT We almostdidn't include this chapter in the book. On the one hand, the good-to-great companies became more disciplined than the direct com parison companies, as with Wells Fargo in contrastto Bank of America. On the otherhand, the unsustained comparisons showed themselves to be justasdisciplined asthe good-to-great companies. "Based on my analysis, I don'tthink we can put discipline in the book as a finding," said Eric Hagen, after he completed a special analysis unit looking at the leadership cultures across the companies. "It is absolutely clear that the unsustained comparison CEOs brought tremendous disci pline totheircompanies, andthatis why they gotsuch great initial results. So, discipline just doesn't pass muster as a distinguishing variable." Curious, we decided to look further into the issue, and Eric undertook a more in-depth analysis. As we further examined the evidence, it became clear that—despite surface appearances—there was indeed a huge differ ence between the two sets ofcompanies in theirapproach to discipline.

Consider Ray MacDonald, whotookcommand of Burroughsin 1964. A brilliant but abrasive man, MacDonald controlled the conversations, told all the jokes, and criticized those not as smart as he (which was pretty much everyone around him). He got things done through sheer force of personality, using a form of pressure that came to be known as "The MacDonald Vise."22 MacDonald produced remarkable results during hisreign. Every dollarinvested in 1964, the yearhe became pres ident, and taken out at the end of 1977, when he retired, produced returns 6.6 times better than the general market.23 However, the com pany had no culture of discipline to endure beyond him. After he retired, his helper minions were frozen by indecision, leavingthe com pany, according to Business Week, "with an inability to do anything."24 Burroughs then began a long slide, with cumulative returnsfalling 93 percent belowthe marketfrom the end of the MacDonald era to 2000. We found a similar story at Rubbermaid under Stanley Gault. Recall from the Level 5 chapterthat Gault quippedin response to the accusation ofbeing a tyrant, "Yes, but I'm a sincere tyrant." Gault brought strict dis ciplines to Rubbermaid—rigorous planning and competitor analysis, sys tematic market research, profit analysis, hard-nosed cost control, and so on. "This is an incredibly disciplined organization," wrote one analyst. "Thereis an incredible thoroughness inRubbermaid's approach tolife."25 Precise and methodical, Gault arrived at work by 6:30 and routinely worked eighty-hour weeks, expecting his managers to do the same.26 As chiefdisciplinarian, Gaultpersonally acted as the company's number one quality control mechanism. Walking down the street in Manhattan, he noticed a doorman muttering and swearing as he swept dirt intoa Rubber maid dustpan. "Stan whirled around and starting grilling the man on why he was unhappy," said Richard Gates, who told the story toFortune. Gault, convinced that the lip ofthe dustpan was too thick, promptly issued a dic tate to his engineers to redesign the product. "On quality, I'm a sonofabitch," said Gault. His chiefoperating officer concurred: "Hegets livid."27 Rubbermaid rose dramatically under the tyranny ofthis singularly dis ciplined leader but then just as dramatically declined when he departed. Under Gault, Rubbermaid beat the market 3.6 to 1. AfterGault, Rubber maid lost 59 percent of its value relative to the market, before being bought out by Newell. One particularly fascinating example of the disciplinarian syndrome was Chrysler under Lee Iacocca, whom Business Week described simply as, "The Man. The Dictator. Lee."28 Iacocca became president of Chrysler in 1979 and imposed his towering personality to discipline the organization into shape. "Right away I knew the place was in a state of anarchy [and] needed a dose oforder and discipline—and quick," wrote Iacocca of his early days.29 In his first year, he entirely overhauled the management structure, instituted strict financial controls, improved qual ity control measures, rationalized the production schedule, and con ducted mass layoffs to preserve cash.30 "I felt like an Army Surgeon. . . . We hadtodoradical surgery, saving what we could."31 In dealing with the unions, he said, "Ifyou don't help me out, I'm going to blow your brains out. I'll declare bankruptcy in the morning, and you'll all be out of work."32 Iacocca produced spectacular results and Chrysler became one ofthe most celebrated turnarounds in industrial history. About midway through his tenure, however, Iacocca seemed to lose focus and the company began todecline once again. The Wall Street Jour nalwrote: "Mr. Iacocca headed the Statue ofLiberty renovation, joined a congressional commission on budget reduction and wrote a secondbook. He began a syndicated newspaper column, bought an Italian villa where he started bottling hisownwine and olive oil.... Critics contend it all dis tracted him, and was a root cause ofChrysler's current problems.... Dis tracting ornot, it's clear thatbeing a folk hero is a demanding sideline."33 Worse than his moonlight career as a national hero, his lack of disci pline to stay within the arenas in whichChrysler could be the best in the world led to a binge of highly undisciplined diversifications. In 1985, he was lured into the sexy aerospace business. Whereas mostCEOs wouldbe content with a single Gulfstream jet, Iacocca decided to buy the whole Gulfstream company!34 Also in the mid-1980s, he embarked on a costly and ultimately unsuccessful joint venture with Italian sports car maker Maserati. "Iacocca had a softspot for Italians," said one retired Chrysler executive. "Iacocca, who owns a modest estate in Tuscany, was so intent on an Italian alliance that commercial realities were ignored, suggest industry insiders," wrote Business Week.35 Some estimates put the loss of the failed Maserati venture at $200 million, which, according to Forbes, was "an enormous sum to lose on a high-price, low-volume roadster. After all, no more than a few thousandwill everbe built."36 Duringthe first halfofhistenure, Iacocca produced remarkable results, taking the company from near bankruptcy to nearly three times the gen eral market. During the second half of Iacocca's tenure, the company slid 31 percent behind the market and faced another potential bankruptcy.37 "Like so many patients with a heart condition," wrote a Chrysler execu tive, "we'd survived surgery several years before only to revert to our unhealthylifestyle."38 The above cases illustrate a pattern we found inevery unsustained com parison: a spectacular rise under a tyrannical disciplinarian, followed by an equally spectacular decline when the disciplinarian stepped away, leaving behind noenduring culture ofdiscipline, orwhen thedisciplinar ian himself became undisciplined andstrayed wantonly outside the three circles. Yes, discipline is essential for great results, but disciplined action without disciplined understanding ofthe three circles cannot produce sustained great results. FANATICAL ADHERENCE TO THE HEDGEHOG CONCEPT For nearly forty years, Pitney Bowes lived inside the warm and protective cocoon ofa monopoly. With its close relationship to the U.S. Postal Ser vice and its patents on postage meter machines, Pitney attained 100 per centofthemetered mail market.39 By the end ofthe 1950s, nearly halfof allU.S. mail passed through Pitney Bowes machines.40 With gross profit margins in excess of 80 percent, no competition, a huge market, and a recession-proofbusiness, Pitney Bowes wasn'tso much a great company as it was a company with a great monopoly. Then, as almost always happens to monopolies when the protective cocoon is ripped away, Pitney Bowes began a long slide. First came a con sent decree that required Pitney Bowes to license its patents tocompetitors, royalty free.41 Within six years, Pitney Bowes had sixteen competitors.42 Pit ney fell into a reactionary "Chicken Little/the sky is falling" diversification frenzy, throwing cash after ill-fated acquisitions and joint ventures, including a $70 million bloodbath (54 percent ofnet stockholders' equity at the time) from a computer retail foray. In 1973, the company lost money for the first time in its history. Itwas shaping up tobe just another typical case of a monopoly-protected company gradually falling apart onceconfronted with the harsh reality ofcompetition. Fortunately, a Level 5 leader named Fred Allen stepped in and asked hard questions that led to deeper understanding of Pitney's role in the world. Instead of viewing itself as a "postage meter" company, Pitney came to see that it could be the best in the world at servicing the back rooms of businesses within the broader concept of "messaging." It also came to see that sophisticated back-office products, like high-end faxes andspecialized copiers, played right into its economic engine ofprofit per customer, building offits extensive sales andservice network. Allen andhis successor, George Harvey, instituted a model ofdisciplined diversification. For example, Pitney eventually attained 45 percent of the high-end fax marketfor large companies, ahugely profitable cash machine.43 Harvey began a systematic process ofinvestment in new technologies and products, such as the Paragon mail processor thatseals and sends letters, and by the late 1980s, Pitney consistently derived over halfits revenues from products introduced in the previous three years.44 Later, Pitney Bowes became a pioneer at linking backroom machines to the Internet, yet another opportunity for disciplined diversification. The key point is that every step ofdiversification and innovation stayed within the three circles. After falling 77percent behind the market from the consent decree to its darkest days in 1973, Pitney Bowes reversed course, eventually rising to over eleven timesthe market bythe start of 1999. From 1973 to 2000, Pit ney Bowes outperformed Coca-Cola, 3M, Johnson & Johnson, Merck, Motorola, Procter & Gamble, Hewlett-Packard, Walt Disney, and even General Electric. Can you think ofany othercompany that emerged from the protective comfort of a monopoly cocoon to deliver this level of results? AT&T didn't. Xerox didn't. Even IBM didn't. Pitney Bowes illustrates what can happen when a company lacks the discipline to stay within the three circles and, conversely, what can hap pen whenit regains that discipline.

In contrast, wefound a lackofdiscipline to stay withinthe three circles as a key factor in the demise of nearly all the comparison companies. Every comparison either (1) lacked the discipline to understand its three circles or (2) lacked the discipline to stay within the three circles. R.J. Reynolds is a classic case. Until the 1960s, R.J. Reynolds had a simple and clear concept, built around beingthe besttobacco company in the UnitedStates—a position it had heldfor at least twenty-five years.45 Then in 1964, the Surgeon General's Office issued its report that linked cigarettes with cancer, and R. J. Reynolds began to diversify away from tobacco as a defensive measure. Of course, all tobacco companies began to diversify at thattime for the same reason, including Philip Morris. But R. J. Reynolds' wanderings outside its three circles defied alllogic. R. J. Reynolds spent nearly a third oftotal corporate assets in 1970 to buy a shipping container company and an oil company (Sea-Land and Aminoil), the idea being to make money by shipping its own oil.46 Okay, nota terrible ideaon its own. Butwhat on earthdid it have to dowith R. J. Reynolds' Hedgehog Concept? It was a wholly undisciplined acquisition that came about in part because Sea-Land's founder was a close friend of R. J. Reynolds' chairman.47 After pouring more than $2 billion into Sea-Land, the total investment nearly equaled the entire amount of netstockholders' equity.48 Finally, after years ofstarving the tobacco business to funnel funds into the sink ing ship business, RJR acknowledged failure and sold Sea-Land.49 One Reynolds grandson complained: "Look, these guys are the world's best at making and selling tobacco products, butwhat do they know about ships oroil? I'mnotworried about them going broke, butthey look like country boys with toomuch cash in theirpockets."50 To be fair, Philip Morris did not have a perfect diversification record either, as evidenced byits failed purchase of7UP. However, in stark con trast to R.J. Reynolds, Philip Morris displayed greater discipline in response to the 1964 surgeon general's report. Instead of abandoning its Hedgehog Concept, Philip Morris redefined its Hedgehog Concept in terms of building global brands in not-so-healthy consumables (tobacco, beer, soft drinks, coffee, chocolate, processed cheese, etc.). Philip Morris' superior discipline to stay within the three circles is one key reason why the results of the two companies diverged so dramatically after the 1964 report, despite thefact that they both faced theexact same industry oppor tunities andthreats. From 1964 to 1989 (when R. J. Reynolds disappeared from public trading in a leveraged buyout), $1 invested in Philip Morris beat$1 invested in R. J. Reynolds by over four times. Few companies have the discipline to discover their Hedgehog Con cept, much less the discipline to build consistently within it. Theyfail to grasp a simple paradox: The more an organization has the discipline to stay within its three circles, the more it will have attractive opportuni ties for growth. Indeed, a great company is much more likely to die of indigestion from too much opportunity than starvation from too little. The challenge becomes not opportunity creation, but opportunity selec tion. This notion offanatical consistency relative to the Hedgehog Concept doesn't justconcern the portfolio ofstrategic activities. It can relate to the entire way you manage andbuild an organization. Nucor builtits success around the Hedgehog Concept ofharnessing culture and technology to produce steel. Central to the Nucor concept was the idea of aligning worker interests with management and shareholder interests through an egalitarian meritocracy largely devoid of class distinctions. Wrote Ken Iverson, in his 1998 book PlainTalk: Inequality still runs rampant in most business corporations. I'mreferring now to hierarchical inequality which legitimizes and institutionalizes the principle of"We" vs. "They." ... The people atthetopofthe corpo rate hierarchy grant themselves privilege after privilege, flaunt those privileges before the menandwomen who dothe real work, thenwon der why employees are unmoved by management's invocations to cut costs and boost profitability When I think ofthe millions ofdollars spent by people at the top of the management hierarchy on efforts to motivate people who are continually put down by that hierarchy, I can only shake my headin wonder.51 When weinterviewed KenIverson, he toldus that nearly100percent of the success of Nucor was due to its ability to translate itssimple concept into disciplined action consistent with thatconcept. Itgrew into a $3.5 bil lion Fortune 500 company with only four layers of management and a corporate headquarters staff offewer than twenty-five people—executive, financial, secretarial, the whole shebang—crammed into a rented office the size ofa small dental practice.52 Cheap veneer furniture adorned the obby, which itself was not much larger than a closet. Instead of a corpo rate dining room, executives hosted visiting dignitaries at Phil's Diner, a stripmallsandwich shop across the street.53 Executivesdid not receive better benefits than frontline workers. In fact, executives had fewer perks. For example, all workers (but not executives) were eligible to receive $2,000 peryear for each child for up tofour years of post-high school education.54 In one incident, a man came to Marvin Pohlman and said, "I have ninekids. Are you telling me thatyou'll pay for four years ofschool—college, trade school, whatever—for every single one of my kids?" Pohlman acknowledged that, yes, that's exactly what would happen. "Themanjustsat there and cried," said Pohlman. "I'll never forget it.It justcaptures in one momentsomuch ofwhatwewere trying to do."55 When Nucor had a highly profitable year, everyone in the company would have a very profitable year. Nucor workers became sowell paid that one woman told her husband, "If you get fired from Nucor, I'll divorce you."56 Butwhen Nucor faced difficult times, everyone from top to bot tom suffered. But people at the top suffered more. In the 1982 recession, forexample, worker paywentdown 25 percent, officer paywent down 60 percent, and the CEO's paywentdown 75 percent.Nucor tookextraordinary steps to keepat baythe class distinctions that eventually encroach on most organizations. All 7,000 employees' names appeared in the annual report, not just officers' and executives'.58 Every one exceptsafety supervisors and visitors wore the same color hard hats. The colorofhard hatsmightsoundtrivial, but it causedquite a stir. Some foremen complained that special-colored hard hats identified them as higher in the chain,an importantstatus symbol thattheycouldput on the back shelves of their cars or trucks. Nucor responded by organizing a series of forums to address the point that your status and authority in Nucor come from your leadership capabilities, not your position. If you don't likeit-—if youreally feel you need that class distinction—well, then, Nucor is just notthe right place for you.59 In contrast to Nucor's dental suite-sized headquarters, Bethlehem Steelbuilt a twenty-one-story office complex to house itsexecutive staff. At extra expense, it designed the building more like a cross than a rectan gle—a design that accommodated the large number of vice presidents who needed corner offices. "The vice presidents... [had to have] win dows in two directions, so it was out of that desire that we came up with the design," explained a Bethlehem executive.60 In his book Crisis in Bethlehem, John Strohmeyer details a cultureasfarto the other end ofthe continuum from Nucor asyoucan imagine. He describes a fleetofcorpo rate aircraft, used even fortaking executives' children to college and flit tingaway toweekend hideaways. Hedescribes a world-class eighteen-hole executive golf course, an executive country club renovated with Bethle hem corporate funds, and even how executive rank determined shower priority at the club.61 We came to the conclusion that Bethlehem executives saw the very purpose of their activities as the perpetuation of a class system that ele vated them to elite status. Bethlehem did not decline in the 1970s and 1980s primarily because of imports or technology—Bethlehem declined first and foremost because it was a culture wherein people focused their efforts on negotiating the nuances of an intricate social hierarchy, not on customers, competitors, or changes in the external world. From 1966 (atthe startof itsbuildup)to 1999, Nucor posted thirty-four consecutive years ofpositive profitability, while over those same thirty-four years, Bethlehem lost money twelve times and its cumulative profitability added up to less than zero. By the 1990s, Nucor's profitability beat Beth lehem's every single year, and at the end of the century, Nucor—which had been less than a third the size ofBethlehem onlya decade earlier— finally surpassed Bethlehem in total revenues.62 Even more astounding, Nucor's average five-year profit per employee exceeded Bethlehem by almost ten times.63 And for the investor, $1 invested in Nucor beat $1 invested in Bethlehem Steel byover 200times. To be fair, Bethlehem had one giant problem not faced by Nucor: adversarial labor relations and entrenched unions. Nucor had no union and enjoyed remarkably good relations with its workers. In fact, when union organizers visited one plant, workers felt so ferociously loyal to Nucorthatmanagement hadto protect the unionorganizers from workers who began shouting and throwing sand at them.64 But the union argument begs a crucial question: Why did Nucor have sucha better relationship with its workers in the first place? Because Ken Iverson and his team had a simple, crystalline Hedgehog Concept about aligning worker interests with management interests and—most impor tantly—because they were willing togo toalmost extreme lengths tobuild the entire enterprise consistent with that concept. Call them a bit fanati cal ifyou want, but to create great results requires a nearly fanatical dedi cation to the ideaofconsistency within the Hedgehog Concept. START A "STOP DOING" LIST Do you have a "to do" list? Do youalso have a "stop doing" list? Most of uslead busy but undisciplined lives. We have ever-expanding "to do" lists, trying tobuild momentum by doing, doing, doing—and doing more. And it rarely works. Those who built the good-to-great companies, however, made as much use of"stop doing" lists as "todo" lists. Theydis played a remarkable discipline to unplug all sorts ofextraneous junk. When Darwin Smith became CEO ofKimberly-Clark, he made great use of "stop doing" lists. He saw that playing the annual forecast game with Wall Streetfocused people too much on the short term, so he just stopped doing it. "On balance, Isee no net advantage to ourstockholders when we annually forecast future earnings," said Smith. "We will not do it"65 Hesaw "title creep" as a sign ofclass-consciousness andbureaucratic layering, so he simply unplugged titles. No one at the company would havea title, unless it was fora position where the outside world demanded a title. He saw increasing layers as the natural result of empire building.

So he simply unplugged a huge stack of layers with a simple elegant mechanism: If you couldn't justify to your peers the need for at least fif teen people reporting to you to fulfill your responsibilities, then you would have zero people reporting toyou.66 (Keep in mindthathe didthis in the 1970s, long before it became fashionable.) To reinforce the idea that Kimberly-Clark should begin thinking of itselfas a consutner com pany, not a papercompany, he unplugged Kimberly from all paper indus trytrade associations.67 The good-to-great companies institutionalized the discipline of "stop doing" through the useofa uniquebudget mechanism. Stop and thinkfor a moment: What isthe purpose ofbudgeting? Mostanswer that budgeting exists to decide howmuch to apportion to each activity, or to manage costs, or both. From a good-to-great perspective, both oftheseanswers are wrong.

Kimberly-Clark didn't justreallocate resources from the paper business to the consumer business. It completely eliminated the paper business, sold the mills, and invested all the money into the emerging consumer business. I had an interesting conversation withsomeexecutives froma company in the paper business. It's a good company, not yet a great one, and they had competeddirectly withKimberly-Clark before Kimberly transformed itselfinto a consumer company. Out of curiosity, I asked them what they thought ofKimberly-Clark. "What Kimberly did isnotfair," theysaid. "Not fair?" I looked quizzical. "Oh, sure,they've becomea much more successful company. But,you know, if we'd sold our paper business and become a powerful consumer company, we could have been great, too. But we just have too much invested in it, and we couldn't havebrought ourselves to do it." If you look back on the good-to-great companies, they displayed remarkable courage to channel their resources into onlyone or a few arenas. Once they understood their three circles, they rarely hedged their bets. Recall Kroger's commitment to overturn its entire system to create superstores, while A&P clung to the "safety" of its older stores. Recall Abbott's commitment to putthe bulk ofits resources into becoming num ber one indiagnostics and hospital nutritionals, while Upjohn clung to its core pharmaceutical business (where it could never be the best in the world). Recall how Walgreens exited the profitable food-service business and focused all its might into one idea: the best, most convenient drug stores. Recall Gillette and Sensor, Nucor and the mini-mills, KimberlyClark and selling the mills to channel all itsresources into the consumer business. They all had the guts to make huge investments, once they understood theirHedgehog Concept. The most effective investment strategy is a highly undiversified port folio when you are right. As facetious as that sounds, that's essentially the approach the good-to-great companies took. "Being right" means getting the Hedgehog Concept; "highly undiversified" means investing fully in those things that fit squarely within the three circles and getting rid of everything else. Ofcourse, the key here is the little caveat, "When you are right." But how do you know when you re right? In studying the companies, we learned that "being right" just isn't that hard ifyou have all the pieces in place. Ifyou have Level 5leaders who get the right people on the bus, if you confront the brutal facts ofreality, if you create a climate where the truth is heard, ifyou have aCouncil andwork within the three circles, ifyou frame all decisions in the context ofa crystalline Hedgehog Con cept, if you act from understanding, not bravado—if you do all these things, then you are likely to be right on the big decisions. The real ques tion is, once you know theright thing, do you have thediscipline todo the right thing and, equally important, to stop doing the wrong things.

CHAPTER EIGHT

# Technology Accelerators

July 28, 1999, drugstore.com—one ofthe first Internet pharma cies—sold shares ofits stock to the public. Withinseconds ofthe opening bell, the stock multiplied nearly threefold to $65 pershare. Four weeks later, the stock closed as high as $69, creating a market valuation ofover $3.5 billion. Notbadfor an enterprise thathadsold products for less than nine months, had fewer than 500 employees, offered no hope ofinvestor dividends,for years (ifnotdecades), and deliberately planned tolose hun dreds ofmillions ofdollars before turning a single dollar ofprofit.2 Whatrationale did people use tojustify these rather extraordinary num bers? "New technology will change everything," the logic went. "The Internet is going to completely revolutionize all businesses," the gurus chanted. "It's the great Internet landgrab: Be there first, be there fast, build market share—no matter how expensive—and you win," yelled the entrepreneurs. We entered a remarkable moment in history when the whole idea of trying to build a great company seemed quaint and outdated. "Built to Good to Great 145 Flip" became the mantra ofthe day. Just tell people you were doing some thing, anything, connected to the Internet, and—presto!—you became rich by flipping shares tothe public, even ifyou had no profits (or even a real company). Why take all the hard steps to go from buildup to break through, creating amodel that actually works, when you could yell, "New technology!" or "New economy!" and convince people to give you hun dreds of millions of dollars? Some entrepreneurs didn't even bother tosuggest thatthey would build a real company at all, much less a great one. One even filed to go public in March of2000 with an enterprise that consisted solely ofan informa tional Web site and a business plan, nothing more. The entrepreneur admitted to the Industry Standard that it seemed strange to go public before starting a business, but that didn't stop him from trying to persuade investors to buy 1.1 million shares at$7 to $9 per share, despite having no revenues, no employees, no customers, no company.3 With the new tech nology of the Internet, who needs all those archaic relics of the old econ omy? Or so the logic went. At the high point ofthis frenzy, drugstore.com issued its challenge to Walgreens. Atfirst, Walgreens‘ stock suffered from the invasion ofthe dot coms, losing over 40 percent ofits price in the months leading up to the drugstore.com public offering. Wrote Forbes in October 1999: "Investors seem to think thattheWeb race will be won by competitors who hit the ground running—companies like drugstore.com, which trades at 398 times revenue, rather thanWalgreen, trading at 1.4 times revenue."4 Ana lysts downgraded Walgreens' stock, and the pressure on Walgreens to react to the Internet threat increased as nearly $15 billion in market value evap orated.5 Walgreens‘ response in themidst ofthis frenzy? "We're a crawl, walk, run company," DanJorndt told Forbes in describ ing his deliberate, methodical approach to the Internet. Instead ofreacting like Chicken Little, Walgreens executives did something quite unusual for the times. They decided to pause and reflect. They decided to use their brains. They decided to think! Slow at first (crawl), Walgreens began experimenting with a Web site while engaging inintense internal dialogue and debate about its implica tions, within the context ofits own peculiar Hedgehog Concept. "How will the Internet connect toour convenience concept? How can we tie it to our economic denominator of cash flow per customer visit? How can we use the Web to enhance what we do better than any other company in 146 ]im Collins the world and in a way thatwe're passionate about?" Throughout, Wal greens executives embraced the Stockdale Paradox: "We have complete faith that wecan prevail in an Internet world asa great company; yet, we must also confront the brutal facts ofreality aboutthe Internet." OneWal greens executive told us afun little story about this remarkable moment in history. An Internet leader made a statement about Walgreens along the lines of, "Oh, Walgreens. They're too old and stodgy for the Internet world. They'll beleft behind." TheWalgreens people, while irked by this arrogant comment from the Internet elite, never seriously considered a public response. Said one executive, "Let's quietly go about doing what we need to do, and it'll become clear soon enough that they justpulled the tail of the wrongdog." Then a little faster (walk), Walgreens began tofind ways totiethe Inter net directly to its sophisticated inventory-and-distribution model and— ultimately—its convenience concept. Fill your prescription on-line, pop into your car and go to your local Walgreens drive-through (in whatever city you happen to be in at the moment), zoom past the window with hardly a moment's pause picking up your bottle ofwhatever. Or have it shipped to you, ifthat's more convenient. There was no manic lurching about, no hype, no bravado—just calm, deliberate pursuit ofunderstand ing, followed by calm, deliberate steps forward. Then, finally (run!), Walgreens bet big, launching an Internet site as sophisticated and well designed as most pure dot-coms. Just before writing this chapter, inOctober 2000, we went on-line touse Walgreens.com. We found it as easy to use and the system of delivery as reliable and well thought out as Amazon.com (the reigning champion of e-commerce at the time). Precisely one year after the Forbes article, Walgreens had fig ured out how to harnessthe Internet to accelerate momentum, making it just that much more unstoppable. Itannounced (on its Web site) a signif icant increase in job openings, to support its sustained growth. From its low point in 1999 at the depths ofthe dot-com scare, Walgreens' stock pricenearly doubled within a year. And what ofdrugstore.com? Continuing to accumulate massive losses, itannounced a layofftoconserve cash. At its high point, little more than a year earlier, drugstore.com traded ata price twenty-six times higher than atthe time ofthis writing. Ithad lost nearly all ofits initial value.6 While Walgreens went from crawl to walk to run, drugstore.com went from run to walk to crawl.

Perhaps drugstore.com will figure out a sustainable model that works and become a great company. But it will not become great because of snazzy technology, hype, and an irrational stock market. It will only become a great company if it figures out how to apply technology to a coherentconceptthat reflects understanding ofthe three circles. TECHNOLOGY AND THE HEDGEHOG CONCEPT Now, you mightbe thinking: "Butthe Internetfrenzy is justa speculative bubble that burst. So what? Everybody knew that the bubble was unsus tainable, that it just couldn't last. Whatdoes that teach us aboutgood to great?" To be clear: The pointofthis chapter has little to do with the specifics ofthe Internet bubble, perse. Bubbles come andbubbles go. It happened with the railroads. It happened with electricity. It happened with radio. It happened with the personal computer. It happened with the Internet. And itwill happen again with unforeseen new technologies. Yet through all of this change, great companies have adapted and endured. Indeed, most of the truly great companies of the last hundred years—from Wal-Mart toWalgreens, from Procter &Gamble to KimberlyClark, from Merck toAbbott—trace their roots back through multiple gen erations of technology change, be it electricity, the television, or the Internet. They've adapted before and emerged great. The best ones will adapt again. We could have predicted that Walgreens would eventually figure out the Internet. The company had a history ofmaking huge investments in technology long before other companies in its industry became tech savvy. In the early 1980s, it pioneered a massive network system called Intercom. The idea was simple: By linking all Walgreens stores electroni cally and sending customer data to a central source, it turned every Wal- greens outlet in the country intoa customer's localpharmacy. You live in Florida, but you're visiting Phoenix and need a prescription refill. No problem, the Phoenixstore islinked to the centralsystem, and it's justlike going down to yourhometown Walgreens store. This mightseem mundane by today's standards. But whenWalgreens made the investment in Intercom in the late 1970s, no one else in the industry had anything like it. Eventually, Walgreens invested over $400 million in Intercom, including $100 million for its own satellite system.7 Touring the Intercom headquarters—dubbed "EarthStation Walgreen"— "is like taking a trip through a NASA space center with itsstunning array ofsophisticated electronic gadgetry," wrote a trade journal.8 Walgreens' technicalstaff became skilled at maintaining every piece of technology, rather than relying on outside specialists.9 It didn'tstop there. Walgreens pioneered the application ofscanners, robotics, computerized inventory control, and advanced warehouse tracking systems. The Internet is just one more step in a continuous pattern. Walgreens didn'tadopt allofthis advanced technology just for the sake ofadvanced technology orin fearful reaction tofalling behind. No,it used technology asa tool to accelerate momentum after hitting breakthrough, and tied technology directly to its Hedgehog Concept of convenient drugstores increasing profit per customer visit. As an interesting aside, as technology became increasingly sophisticated in the late 1990s, Wal greens' CIO (chief information officer) was a registered pharmacist by training, nota technology guru.10 Walgreens remained resolutely clear: Its Hedgehog Concept would drive its use oftechnology, not the otherway around. The Walgreens case reflects a general pattern. In every good-to-great case, we found technological sophistication. However, it was never tech nology perse, butthepioneering application ofcarefully selected technolo gies. Every good-to-great company became a pioneer in the application of technology, but the technologies themselves varied greatly. (See the table on page 150.) Kroger, for example, was an early pioneer inthe application ofbarcode scanners, which helped it accelerate past A&P by linking frontline pur chases to backroom inventory management. This might not sound very exciting (inventory management is notsomething thattends to rivet read ers), but thinkofitthisway: Imagine walking back intothe warehouse and instead ofseeing boxes of cereal and crates of apples, you see stacks and stacks of dollar bills—hundreds of thousands and millions of freshly minted, crisp and crinkly dollar bills just sitting there on pallets, piled high to the ceiling. That's exactly how you should think of inventory. Every single case of canned carrots is not justa case of canned carrots, it's cash. And it's cash just sitting there useless, until you sell that case of canned carrots. Now recall how Kroger systematically shed its dreary old and small grocery stores, replacing them with nice,big, shiny superstores. To accom plish this task ultimately required more than $9 billion of investmentcash thatwould somehow have tobe pulled outofthe low-margin grocery business. To put this in perspective, Kroger put more than twice its total annual profits into capital expenditures on average every year for thirty years.11 Even more impressive, despite taking on$5.5 billion ofjunk bond debt to pay a onetime $40-per-share cash dividend plus an $8 junior debenture to fight off corporate raiders in 1988, Kroger continued its cash-intensive revamping throughout the 1980s and 1990s.12 Kroger modernized and turned over all its stores, improved the customer's shop ping experience, radically expanded the variety of products offered, and paid offbillions ofdollars ofdebt. Kroger's use ofscanning technology to takehundreds ofmillions of crisp and crinkly dollarbillsout ofthe ware house and put them to better use became a key element in its ability to pull offitsmagic trick—pulling not one, not two, but three rabbits out of a hat. Gillette also became a pioneer in the application oftechnology. But Gillette's technology accelerators lay largely in manufacturing technol ogy. Think about the technology required to make billions—literally bil lions—oflow-cost, high-tolerance razor blades. When you andI.pick up a Gillette razor, we expect the blade to be perfect and we expect it to be inexpensive pershave. Forexample, to createthe Sensor, Gillette invested over $200 million in design anddevelopment, most ofitfocused on man ufacturing breakthroughs, and earned twenty-nine patents.13 It pioneered the application of laser welding on a mass scale to shaving systems—a technology normally used for expensive and sophisticated products like heart pacemakers.14 The whole key to Gillette's shaving systems lay in manufacturing technology so unique and proprietary that Gillette pro tected it the way Coca-Cola protects its secret formula, complete with armed guardsand security clearances.

Technology as an Accelerator, Not a Creator, of Momentum When Jim Johnson became CEO of Fannie Mae, following David Maxwell, he and hisleadership team hireda consulting firm to conducta technologyaudit. The lead consultant, BillKelvie, used a four-level rank ing,with four being cutting edge and one being StoneAge. Fannie Mae ranked only a two. So,following the principle of "first who," Kelvie was hired to move the company ahead.16 When Kelvie came to Fannie Mae in 1990, the company lagged aboutten years behindWall Streetin the use of technology. Over the nextfive years, Kelvie systematically took Fannie Mae from a 2 to a 3.8 on the four-point ranking.17 He and his teamcreated over 300 computer applications, including sophisticated analytical programs to control the $600 billion mortgage portfolio, on-line data warehouses covering 60 million properties and streamlined workflows, significantly reducing paperand clerical effort. "We moved technology out ofthe back office and harnessed it to transform every part of the business," said Kelvie. "We created an expert system that lowers the cost of becoming a home owner. Lenders using our technology reduced the loan-approval time from thirtydays to thirty minutes and lowered the associated costs by over $1,000 perloan." To date, the system has saved home buyers nearly $4 billion.18 Noticethat the FannieMae transition beganin 1981, withthe arrival of David Maxwell, yet the company lagged behind in the application of technology until the early 1990s. Yes, technology became ofprime impor tance to Fannie Mae, but after it discovered its Hedgehog Concept and after it reached breakthrough. Technology was a key part of what Fannie Mae leaders called "the second wind" of the transformation and acted as an accelerating factor.19 The same pattern holds for Kroger, Gillette, Walgreens, and all the good-to-great companies—the pioneeringapplication oftechnology usually came late in the transition and neverat the start.

To make technology productive in a transformation from good to great means asking the following questions. Does the technology fit directly with yourHedgehog Concept? Ifyes, then you need to become a pioneer in the application ofthat technology. If no, then ask, do you need this tech nology at all? Ifyes, then allyou needisparity. (You don't necessarily need the world's most advanced phone system to be a great company.) If no, then the technology isirrelevant, and you can ignore it. We came to see the pioneering application of technology as just one more way in which the good-to-great companies remained disciplined within the frame oftheirHedgehog Concept. Conceptually, theirrelation ship totechnology is nodifferent from their relationship toany other category of decisions: disciplined people, who engage in disciplined thought, and who then take disciplined action. Ifa technology doesn't fitsquarely within theirthree circles, they ignore all the hype andfear and just go about their business with a remarkable degree of equanimity. However, once they understand which technologies are relevant, they become fanatical and creative in the application ofthose technologies. In the comparison companies, bycontrast, wefoundonlythree cases of pioneering in the application oftechnology. Those three cases—Chrysler (computer-aided design), Harris (electronics applied to printing), and Rubbermaid (advanced manufacturing)—were all unsustained compar isons, which demonstrates that technology alone cannot create sus tained greatresults. Chrysler, for instance, made superb use of advanced computer-aided and otherdesign technologies butfailed to linkthose tech nologies to a consistent Hedgehog Concept. As Chrysler strayed outside the three circles in the mid-1980s, from Gulfstream jets to Maserati sports cars, no advanced technology by itself could save the company from another massive downturn. Technology without a clear Hedgehog Con cept, and without the discipline to stay within the three circles, cannot make a company great.

CHAPTER NINE

# Built To Last

webeganthe Good to Great research project, we confronted a dilemma: How should we think about the ideas in Built to Last while doing the Good toGreat research? Briefly, Built toLast, based on a six-year research project conducted at Stanford Business School in the early 1990s, answered the question, What does it take to startand buildan enduringgreatcompany from the ground up? My research mentor and coauthor Jerry I. Porras and I studied eigh teen enduring great companies—institutions that stood the test of time, tracing their founding in some cases back to the 1800s, while becoming the iconic great companies of the late twentieth century. We examined companies like Procter& Gamble (founded in 1837), AmericanExpress (founded in 1850), Johnson & Johnson (founded in 1886), and GE (founded in 1892). One of the companies, Citicorp (nowCitigroup), was founded in 1812, the same year Napoleon marched into Moscow! The "youngest" companies in the studywereWal-Mart and Sony,which trace their origins backto 1945. Similarto thisbook, we used direct comparison companies—3M versus Norton, Walt Disney versus Columbia Pictures, Marriott versus Howard Johnson, and so forth—for eighteen paired com parisons. In short, we sought to identify the essential distinctions between great companies and good companies as they endure over decades, even centuries. When I had the first summer research team assembled for the good-togreat project, I asked, "What should be the role oi Built toLast in doing this study?" "I don't think it should playany role," said Brian Bagley. "I didn't join this team to do a derivative piece of work." "Neither did I," added Alyson Sinclair. "I‘m excited about a new pro ject and a new question. It wouldn't be very fulfilling to just fill in the pieces of your other book." "But wait a minute," I responded. "We spent six years on the previous study. It might be helpful to build on our previous work." "I seem to recall that you got the idea for this studywhen a McKinsey partner saidthat BuilttoLast didn't answer the question of how to change a good company into a great one," noted Paul Weissman. "What if the answers aredifferent?" Back and forth, to and fro, the debate continued for a few weeks. Then Stefanie Judd weighed in with the argument that swayed me. "I love the ideas in Built to Last and that's what worries me," she said. "I'm afraid that if we startwith BTL as the frame of reference, we'll just go around in cir cles, proving our own biases." It became clear that there would be sub stantially less risk in starting from scratch, setting out to discover what we would, whether it matched previous work or not.Now, five years later, with this book complete, we can stand back to look at the two works in the context of each other. Surveying across the twostudies, I offer the following four conclusions:

1.When I consider the enduring great companies from Built to Last, I now see substantial evidence that their early leaders followed the good-to-great framework. The onlyreal difference is that they did so as entrepreneurs in small, early-stage enterprises trying to get off the ground,ratherthan asCEOstrying to transform established companies from good to great. 2. In an ironic twist, I now see Good to Great not as a sequel to Built to Last, but asa prequel. Apply the findings in thisbookto createsustained greatresults, asa start-up or an established organization, and then apply the findings inBuilt to Last togofrom great results to an enduringgreat company. Established Good to Sustained Built to Enduring Company + Great -» Great + Last —> Great orStart-up Concepts Results Concepts Company 3.To make the shiftfrom a company with sustained great results to an enduring great company of iconic stature, apply the central concept fromBuilt toLast: Discover yourcore values and purpose beyond just making money (core ideology) and combine this with the dynamic of preserve the core/stimulate progress. 4. A tremendous resonance existsbetween the two studies; the ideas from each enrich and inform the ideas in the other. In particular, Good to Great answers a fundamental question raised, but not answered, in Built to Last: What is the difference between a "good" BHAG (Big HairyAudacious Goal) and a "bad" BHAG?

Looking backon the Built toLast study, it appears that the enduring great companies did in fact go through a process of buildup to breakthrough, following the good-to-great framework during their formative years. Consider, for example, the buildup-breakthrough flywheel pattern in the evolution of Wal-Mart. Most people think that Sam Walton just exploded onto the scene with his visionary idea for rural discount retail ing, hitting breakthrough almostasa start-up company. But nothing could be further from the truth .

SamWalton began in 1945 with a single dimestore. He didn't openhis second store until seven years later. Walton built incrementally, step by step, turn by turn of the flywheel, until the Hedgehog Concept of large discount marts popped out as a natural evolutionary step in the mid1960s. It took Walton a quarter ofa century to grow from thatsingle dime store to a chain of 38 Wal-Marts. Then, from 1970 to 2000, Wal-Mart hit breakthrough momentum and exploded to over 3,000 stores with over $150 billion (yes, billion) in revenues.2 Just like the story of the chicken jumping out of the egg that we discussed in the flywheel chapter, WalMart had been incubating for decades before the egg cracked open. As Sam Walton himself wrote: Somehow over the years people have gotten the impression that WalMart was . . . just this great idea that turned into an overnight success. But... it was an outgrowth of everything we'd been doing since [1945]... . And like most overnight successes, it was about twenty years in the making.3 If there everwas a classic case of buildup leading to a Hedgehog Con cept, followed by breakthrough momentum in the flywheel, Wal-Mart is it. The only difference is that Sam Walton followed the model as an entrepreneur buildinga great company from the ground up, rather than as a CEO transforming an established company from good to great. But it's the same basic idea.4 Hewlett-Packard provides another excellent example of the good-togreatideas at work in the formative stages ofa Built toLast company. For instance, Bill Hewlett and David Packard's entire founding concept for HP was not what, but who—starting with each other. They'd been best friends in graduate school and simply wanted to build a great company togetherthat wouldattractother peoplewithsimilar values and standards. The foundingminutes oftheir first meetingon August 23, 1937, begin by statingthat they woulddesign, manufacture, and sellproductsin the elec tricalengineeringfields, very broadly defined. But then thosesame found ing minutes go on to say, "The question of what to manufacture was postponed. . . ."5 Hewlett and Packard stumbled around for months trying to come up with something, anything, that would get the company out of the garage. They consideredyacht transmitters, air-conditioning control devices, med ical devices, phonograph amplifiers, you name it. They built electronic bowling alley sensors, a clock-drive for a telescope, andan electronic shock jiggle machine tohelp overweight people lose weight. Itdidn't really mat ter what the company made in the very early days, as long as it made a technical contribution and would enable Hewlett and Packard to build a company together andwith other like-minded people.6 Itwas the ultimate "first who ... then what" start-up. Later, as Hewlett and Packard scaled up, they stayed true totheguiding principle of "firstwho."After WorldWar II, even as revenues shrank with the end of their wartime contracts, they hired a whole batch offabulous people streaming outofgovernment labs, with nothing specific inmind for them to do. Recall Packard's Law, which we cited in chapter 3: "No com pany can grow revenues consistently faster than its ability to get enough of the right people to implement that growth and still become a great com pany." Hewlett and Packard lived andbreathed this concept and obtained a surplus ofgreat people whenever theopportunity presented itself. Hewlett and Packard were themselves consummate Level 5 leaders, first as entrepreneurs and later as company builders. Years after HP had established itself as one of the most important technology companies in the world, Hewlett maintained a remarkable personal humility. In 1972, HP vice president BarneyOliver wrote in a recommendation letter to the IEEE Awards Board for the Founders Award: While our success has been gratifying, it has not spoiled our founders. Only recently, at an executive council meeting, Hewlett remarked: "Look, weVe grown because the industry grew. We were lucky enough to be sitting on the nose when the rocket took off. We don't deserve a damn bit of credit."After a moment'ssilence, while everyone digested this humbling comment, Packard said: "Well, Bill, at least we didn't louse it up completely."7 Shortly before his death, I had the opportunity to meet Dave Packard. Despite being one of Silicon Valley's first self-made billionaires, he lived in the same small house that he and his wife built for themselves in 1957, overlooking a simple orchard. The tiny kitchen, with its dated linoleum, and the simply furnished living room bespoke a man who needed no materialsymbols to proclaim "I'm a billionaire. I'm important. I'm suc cessful." "His idea of a good time," said Bill Terry, who worked with Packard for thirty-six years, "was to get some of his friends together to string some barbed wire/'8 Packard bequeathed his$5.6 billion estate to a charitable foundation and, upon his death, his family created a eulogy pamphlet,witha photo ofhim sitting on a tractor in farming clothes. The caption made no reference to his stature as one of the great industrialists of the twentieth century.9 It simply read: "David Packard, 1912-1996, Rancher, etc." Level 5, indeed.

CORE IDEOLOGY: THE EXTRA DIMENSION OF ENDURING GREATNESS During our interview with Bill Hewlett, we asked him what he was most proud of in his long career. "As I look back on my life's work," he said, "I'm probably most proud of having helped create a company that by virtueof itsvalues, practices, and success has had a tremendous impact on the way companies are managed around the world."10 The "HP Way," as it became known, reflected a deeply held set of core values that distin guished the company more than any of its products. These values included technical contribution, respect for the individual, responsibility to the communities in which the company operates, and a deeply held beliefthat profit isnotthe fundamental goal ofa company. These princi ples,while fairly standardtoday, wereradicaland progressive in the 1950s. David Packard said of businessmen from those days, "While they were reasonably polite in their disagreement, it was quite evident that they firmly believed that I was not one ofthem, and obviously not qualified to manage an important enterprise."11 Hewlett and Packard exemplify a key "extra dimension" that helped elevate their company to the elite status of an enduringgreatcompany, a vital dimension for making the transition from good to great to built to last. That extra dimension is a guiding philosophy or a "core ideology," which consists ofcore values anda core purpose (reason for beingbeyond just makingmoney). These resemble the principles in the Declaration of Independence ("We hold these truths to be self-evident")—never per fectly followed, but always present asan inspiring standard and an answer to the question ofwhy it is importantthat we exist. Wewrote inBuilt to Last aboutMerck's decision to develop and distrib ute a drug that cured river blindness. This painful disease afflicted overa million people with parasitic worms thatswarm through the eyes to cause blindness. Because those who had the disease—tribal people in remote places liketheAmazon—had no money, Merckinitiated the creationofan independent distribution system togetthedrug toremote villages andgave the drugaway free to millions ofpeople aroundthe world.12 To be clear, Merck is not a charity organization, nor does it view itself assuch. Indeed, it has consistently outperformed the market as a highly profitable company, growing tonearly $6billion in profits andbeating the market by over ten timesfrom 1946 to 2000. Yet, despite its remarkable financial performance, Merck does not view its ultimate reason for being asmaking money. In 1950, George Merck 2d,sonofthe founder, setforth his company's philosophy: An important caveat to the concept of core values is that there are no specific "right" core values for becoming an enduring great company. No matter what core value you propose, we found an enduring great company that does not have that specific core value. A company need not have passion for its customers (Sonydidn't), or respect for the indi vidual (Disney didn't), or quality (Wal-Mart didn't), or social responsi bility (Ford didn't) in order to become enduring and great. This was one of the most paradoxical findings fromBuilttoLast—core values are essential for enduring greatness, but it doesntseem to matter whatthose core values are. The point is not what core values you have, but thatyou have core values at all, that you know what they are, that you build them explicitly into the organization, and that you preserve them over time. This notion of preserving your core ideology is a central feature of enduring greatcompanies. The obvious question is,Howdo you preserve the coreand yetadaptto a changing world? The answer: Embracethe key conceptof preserve the core/stimulate progress. The story ofWalt Disney exemplifies this duality. In 1923, an energetic twenty-one-year-old animatormoved from Kansas Cityto Los Angeles and triedto geta jobin the movie business. No film company would hire him, so he used his meager savings to rent a camera, set up a studio in his uncle'sgarage, and beginmaking animated cartoons. In 1934, Mr. Disney took the boldstep, never before taken, to create successful full-length ani mated feature films, including Snow White, Pinocchio, Fantasia, and Bambi. In the 1950s, Disney moved into television with the Mickey Mouse Club. Also in the 1950s, Walt Disney paid a fateful visit to a num ber of amusement parks and came away disgusted, calling them "dirty, phony places, run by tough-looking people."14 He decided that Disney could build something much better, perhaps even the best in the world, and the company launched a whole new business in theme parks, first with Disneyland and later with WaltDisney World and EPCOT Center.

Over time, Disneytheme parks havebecome a cornerstoneexperience for many families from all overthe world. Throughout all these dramatic changes—from cartoons to full-length feature animation, from the Mickey Mouse Club to Disney World-—the companyheld firmly to a consistent set of core values that included pas sionate belief in creative imagination, fanatic attention to detail, abhor rence of cynicism, and preservation of the "Disney Magic." Mr. Disney alsoinstilleda remarkableconstancy ofpurposethat permeated everynew Disney venture—namely, to bring happiness to millions, especially chil dren. This purpose cut across national borders and has endured through time. When my wife and I visited Israel in 1995, we met the man who broughtDisneyproducts to the MiddleEast. "The wholeidea,"he told us with pride, "is to bring a smile to a child'sface. That's really important here, wherethere aren't enoughsmiles on the children."WaltDisney pro vides a classic case of preserve the core and stimulate progress, holding a core ideology fixed while changingstrategies and practices overtime, and its adherence to this principle is the fundamental reason why it has endured as a great company .

GOOD BHAGS, BAD BHAGS, AND OTHER CONCEPTUAL LINKS In the table on page 198, IVe outlined a sketch of conceptual links between the two studies. As a general pattern, the Good-to-Great ideas appear to lay the groundwork for the ultimate success of the Built toLast ideas. Ilike to think ofGood to Great as providing the core ideas for getting a flywheel turning from buildup through breakthrough, while Built to Last outlines the core ideas for keeping a flywheel accelerating long into the future and elevating a company to iconic stature. You will notice in exam ining the table thateach ofthe Good-to-Great findings enables all four of the key ideas from Built to Last. To briefly review, those four key ideas are: 1. Clock Building, Not Time Telling. Build an organization that can endure and adapt through multiple generations ofleaders and multiple product life cycles; the exact opposite of being built around a single greatleader or a single great idea. 2. Genius ofAND. Embrace both extremes on a number of dimensions at the same time. Instead of choosing A OR B,figure out how to have A AND B—purpose ANDprofit, continuityAND change,freedom AND responsibility, etc. - 3. Core Ideology. Instill core values (essential and enduring tenets) and core purpose (fundamental reason for being beyond just making money) asprinciples to guide decisions and inspire people throughout the organization over a longperiod oftime. 4. Preserve the Core/ Stimulate Progress. Preserve the core ideology as an anchor pointwhile stimulating change, improvement, innovation, and renewal in everything else. Change practices and strategies while hold ing core values and purpose fixed. Setand achieve BHAGs consistent with the core ideology.

CHAPTER TEN

# The Innovator Method

IN 2008, INTUIT celebrated its twenty-fifth anniversary and named Brad Smith as CEO. Founded by Scott Cook, Intuit—maker of successful financial software packages like Quicken, QuickBooks, and TurboTax—had achieved remarkable success, growing revenues to more than $3 billion and creating a market value of $10.2 billion. But Cook and Smith were worried. Intuit had seemingly reached a performance plateau, and its market value had begun to fall. Annual revenue growth had dropped in half, from 15 percent (1998–2003) to 8 percent (2004– 2008), and annual income growth had slowed even more dramatically, from 31 percent to 6 percent. Not surprisingly, Intuit's annual market value growth had taken a hit as well, dropping from 14 percent to 5 percent. Worse, after studying Intuit's new product launches over the prior decade, Cook discovered that fewer than 10 percent could be called successful from a revenue and profit perspective. Meanwhile, Intuit's net promoter score (NPS), a measure of whether customers like a product enough to promote it to friends and colleagues, had flattened. 1 Finally, the company's innovation premium (IP), a measure of stock price premium paid by investors because of expectations of future growth through innovation, had dropped from 57 percent in 2000 to 20 percent in 2008. 2 After twenty-five years, by every measure, it seemed as if the company had reached the telltale limit of the S-curve: Intuit was moving from growth to maturity, with the threat of failure not far behind. Cook and Smith didn't want that to happen. But what could they do? Intuit was experiencing what happens to most successful start-ups as they grow into large, established corporations: execution becomes the highest priority as they scale the business to meet the demands of existing customers. Over time, the focus on execution crowds out innovation. Intuit was losing the ability to perform what Peter Drucker called management's fundamental task: "to create a customer." 3 Ironically, as companies focus on capturing value from customers, they often lose the ability to create customers. And something more had changed. It's a cliché to say that the world is more uncertain than ever before, but few people realize the extent of the increase in uncertainty over the past thirty years. More important, they don't understand that greater uncertainty has created the need to change the way most organizations are managed. The challenge of creating a customer is more complex and uncertain than ever before. Here's why. There are two types of uncertainty that influence a firm's ability to create a customer: demand uncertainty (will customers buy it?) and technological uncertainty (can we make a desirable solution?). * Uncertainty arises from the unknowns associated with solving any problem, which are sometimes called "unknown unknowns," such as hidden customer preferences or undiscovered elements of a technical solution. The more unknowns there are about customer preferences and behavior, the greater the demand uncertainty. For example, when Jenn Hyman of Rent the Runway came up with the idea to rent designer dresses over the internet, demand uncertainty was high because no one else was offering this service. 4 In contrast, when Samsung and Sony were deciding whether to launch LED TVs, which offered better picture quality at roughly the same price as plasma TVs, there was lower uncertainty about demand because customers were already buying TVs. Technological uncertainty results from uncertainty regarding the technologies that might emerge or need to be created for a new solution to emerge. For example, a wide variety of clean technologies (including wind, solar, and hydrogen) are vying to power vehicles and cities at the same time that a wide variety of medical technologies (chemical, biotechnological, genomic, and robotic) are being developed to treat diseases. As the overall rate of invention across industries increases, so does technological uncertainty.To better understand the uncertainty facing firms like Intuit, we studied the depth and degree of the shift in demand and technological uncertainty. First, we looked at multiple measures of the rate of technological change. One measure is the rate of invention patenting,This is an imperfect measure, but clearly it reflects a striking increase in the rate of invention in the past twenty years. 5 Not surprisingly, there has been a similarly dramatic increase in total R&D spending. As new technologies emerge, companies are rising, and falling, at a much faster pace than ever before. This phenomenon is amplified by increasingly faster changes in customers' demands for a new mix of products and services. For example, consider how quickly entertainment preferences have changed.

For more than three decades—between 1950 and 1980—we accessed TV shows and movies primarily through three networks (ABC, NBC, CBS) or at movie theaters. Then with the advent of the VCR, we've progressed to watching movies on our home TV screens via videocassettes and then DVDs, to watching them on our computers, then on our laptops, then on tablets, and now on our phones, mostly via internet streaming. When the DVD emerged, it was adopted more quickly than any previous consumer electronic device selling just over three hundred thousand units in the first year—until the iPad, which sold three million units in its first eighty days. 6 In short, customer preferences are not only changing but also changing at an accelerating pace.

It's not an exaggeration to say that a second Industrial Revolution has occurred, a revolution fueled by new technologies and customers and accompanied by radical uncertainty. Companies don't hold on to customers as long as they used to, and new technologies and competitors are emerging faster than ever before. What drives these dramatic increases in uncertainty? There are many reasons, but two disruptive technologies have played a crucial role: personal computing and the internet. Another key is the emergence of capitalism in countries such as China, India, Russia, and Brazil. Personal computing has placed powerful analytical tools into the hands of everyone having the motivation to master them. It has democratized and decentralized complex problem solving. Similarly, the internet has had a profound effect as a low-cost marketing and distribution channel for anyone wanting to sell a product. This means that more new products can be launched to a larger audience, and faster, than ever before. Finally, as China, India, Russia, and Brazil have joined the global economy, they have expanded the pool of potential entrepreneurs by 2.5 billion people.

These new entrepreneurs enjoy lower technical barriers to entry (with open source software, programming platforms, and cloud technologies), lower capital barriers (with the growth of venture capital, angel funding, and crowd-funding), lower production barriers (with the adoption of 3-D printers and global suppliers), and lower distribution and marketing barriers (with the internet and the emergence of direct shipping and social media). As a result, there are simply more competitors than ever before.

These changes have increased uncertainty to a tipping point—a threshold where the traditional ways we organized and managed corporations will no longer work to sustain growth in the future. This is especially true of companies in the industries having the highest uncertainty, such as computer software and medical equipment .In fact, the computer software industry—where Intuit competes—is at the high end of the uncertainty spectrum, with volatile revenues, heavy R&D spending, and new entrants emerging at an unprecedented rate. Intuit's Scott Cook was aware of the difficulty of predicting and meeting customer demand. That's why many of the company's new products had flopped. He had also seen new competitors come along to attack Intuit in new ways, with different technologies and business models. He realized that he needed to figure out a new way to manage in the highly volatile computer software industry if he hoped to compete with the startups. Here's where the Intuit story gets interesting.

Not everyone faces the same levels of uncertainty. Some industries have greater inherent demand or technological uncertainty. Consider the 2×2 matrix.

The horizontal axis plots each industry based on technological uncertainty, measured as the average R&D expenditures as a percentage of sales in the industry over the past ten years. The vertical axis plots each industry's demand uncertainty, measured as an equal weighting of industry revenue volatility, or change, over the past ten years and percentage of firms in the industry that entered or exited over the past ten years. Although these are imperfect measures, they identify the industries facing the highest, and lowest baseline levels of uncertainty.

Where does your industry sit? Do you face high or low uncertainty? As you can see, some industries face low uncertainty; examples include providers of personal services, such as hair styling and dry cleaning, who have used similar technologies to provide solutions for well-known .

demands. By contrast, in the lower-right quadrant are industries that face lower demand uncertainty but high technological uncertainty. For example, aircraft makers can generally predict the demand for aircraft production. The challenge they face is technological uncertainty; Boeing and Airbus spend large sums developing advanced new aircraft like the Boeing 787 and the Airbus A350.

Finally, industries in the upper-right quadrant—such as software, pharmaceuticals, and medical equipment—face high uncertainty in both demand and technology. For example, who would have predicted that medical robots would perform surgeries? When Intuitive Surgical launched the Da Vinci System medical robot—which allows surgeons to operate using

3-D visualization and four robotic arms—the company faced significant technical as well as demand uncertainty. Our analysis suggests that, on average, the top ten most uncertain industries require greater innovation management skills than the bottom ten. However, even if your industry provides clues about average uncertainty, every problem is characterized by its own level of uncertainty. For example, although Webvan was a food retailer in an industry with relatively low uncertainty, its online platform of home delivery faced both high demand uncertainty (will customers buy groceries online?) and high technological uncertainty (can we fulfill orders in a cost-effective way?). Demand uncertainty was high, because the company had few facts about demand and many assumptions. The same was true of technological uncertainty; it had many assumptions about which fulfillment technologies would work best. The ratio of assumptions to facts equals your uncertainty ratio. If your problem is characterized by a low uncertainty ratio, you can probably apply traditional management. If you have a high uncertainty ratio, then The Innovator's Method should guide you. Unfortunately for Webvan's investors, the company was not successful in experimenting to resolve its high-uncertainty problems before a full-scale launch—$500 million— that proved disastrous.The story of Intuit's journey gives managers an archetype for a new way of managing in a high-uncertainty industry. Intuit's transformation arguably began in 2004 with its adoption of the net promoter score. NPS is based on a single question posed to customers: How likely are you, on a scale of 0 (not at all likely) to 10 (extremely likely), to recommend this product or service to a colleague or friend? A product's NPS is the percentage of promoters (those who score themselves 9 or 10) minus the percentage of detractors (scores 0–6). 8 Net promoter score = % promoters minus % detractors Historically, Intuit products had dominated their markets by being significantly easier to use than competitors'. But soon competitors were catching up, so Intuit launched an effort to improve ease of use and NPS. It spent even more time with customers, observed detractors, and redesigned products. "We put a big focus on making our products easier to use," says Kaaren Hanson, design vice-president. "And when this company decides to go after something, we do it. So we pulled the lever." But these traditional management moves failed to move the meter. "Our net promoter scores didn't budge," Hanson says. "And it didn't result in a big jump in sales, which is what we expected. We pulled the damn lever, and nothing happened." 9 In other areas of the company, customer response to new products was especially disappointing.

"We were humbled when we looked back at ten years of innovation," says CEO Brad Smith, who took over for Steve Bennett in 2008. "We'd launched fifty-four products, and fewer than five had achieved any commercial success, measured by revenue or profit. And we were bad at shutting down the failures. When we did, we got labeled as not being patient enough .

Intuit's leaders knew they needed to figure out what would move customers and discover how to improve the success rate of new products. So a team was pulled together. "We went out to understand what was beyond ease," says Hanson. "And we looked at a lot of the usual suspects. We looked at Nike, we looked at the W Hotels, we looked at Harley-Davidson, and we looked at Apple. You name it, we probably looked at them." 11 The Intuit team realized that the most successful companies didn't just offer products that were easier to use; they offered products that delighted customers. Products that delight customers do the unexpected. They solve a problem customers didn't know they had, or they evoke a positive emotion. But how does a company create products that delight customers? The team discovered that design thinking offered critical new tools not in their familiar management tool set. Cook had the benefit of sitting on the board of Procter & Gamble and saw up close how P&G incorporated techniques like design thinking into product development. Drawing on design thinking principles, Cook, Hanson, and her team created a training program called Design for Delight (D4D), a program intended to transform Intuit into a design-driven innovation machine. Intuit's D4D initiative was based on searching for a big unmet customer need and then applying three principles. Gain deep customer empathy. Understand customers better than they understand themselves. Go broad to go narrow. Generate lots of solutions before winnowing the list. Experiment rapidly with customers. Seek feedback early and often. Hanson realized that to infuse D4D principles into the DNA of all eight thousand employees, she needed to get top management on board. To jump-start the process, Hanson and Cook helped plan a two-day offsite for Intuit's top three hundred managers. At first the group paid polite attention, but as the audience plowed through a five-hour PowerPoint presentation, Cook saw that the design thinking approach was falling flat. But then Alex Kazaks, a young associate professor at Stanford, led the team in a unique participatory exercise: Kazaks asked each person to design, and prototype, a wallet for the person next to him. As the managers worked through the design challenge, creating prototypes, getting feedback, and redesigning, the hands-on experience helped them see the value of design thinking as a tool to discover and deeply understand customer needs to create new value. Hanson then organized a series of design forums, typically attended by roughly three thousand employees, to teach people the key principles and let them practice D4D. However, after several forums and a huge effort, Hanson discovered a disappointing fact: the company wasn't changing enough to produce different results. "We did this for about a year," says Hanson, "and what I was hearing in the hallways—that made me feel absolutely nauseous—was that 'design for delight' is this flavor of the month. This was very disheartening, because we actually had senior leaders involved and engaged. As it turns out, senior leaders are not enough.

Problem: Discover the Job-to-Be-Done Managers tend to start by building solutions, but we emphasize the need to first deeply understand the problem. Keep in mind that "problem" may mean either a customer's pain or a customer's desire, such as a desire for connection, expression, fulfillment, and the like. At the core you are trying to discover the functional, social, and emotional elements of the job-to-be-done—the need for which customers might purchase your product. For example, although a BMW may do a similar functional job as another car (transport), a BMW can also accomplish important social jobs (prestige, status) or emotional jobs (feels "cool") that may be overlooked at first blush. At Intuit, teams follow up on an insight into an unmet customer need by using a technique called pain-storming. According to Rachel Evans, one of the innovation catalysts who developed it, "The purpose of a pain-storm is to get crisp on what we think the problem is so we can test our hypotheses." Pain-storming involves creating a customer's "journey line" to understand how customers now complete a task and identify their main pain points (and emotions) along the way. The team then conducts a root-cause analysis to understand the causes of the biggest pain points. Of course, it doesn't work if team members just sit in their offices and imagine what customers might want. Instead, Intuit's team members directly observe and talk to customers in their offices or homes. As CEO Smith told us, "To walk a mile in your customer's shoes, you have to take your own shoes off first." 17 In short, you must "be the customer." As Bachu and her team spent weeks living with, observing, and talking to farmers and middlemen in seven agricultural markets, she learned firsthand about the pain farmers felt when faced with a decision to sell perishable crops, whose prices might fluctuate as much as 50 percent in a single day. The team validated their initial observation that the farmers had no information on supply or demand to guide them, resulting in spoilage or suboptimal prices. They also validated the fact that farmers were often exploited by the middlemen, who had an incentive to minimize market price transparency. As the team members gained confidence that they had identified an important problem worth solving, they translated the problem into a vision statement for the customer: "10 percent higher prices for farmers." Drawing on the insights into the causes of the farmers' problem—and using the vision statement as a guide—the team then was ready to focus its energies on developing a solution. Solution: Prototype the Minimum Awesome Product After identifying a customer problem worth solving, most managers unleash the product development team to build a full-featured, error-free product to attract as many customers as possible. Although this approach makes sense in familiar markets, it is the wrong thing to do when you face uncertainty. Instead, managers should search broadly for a variety of solutions and then use a series of four prototypes to converge on the solution that best solves the job-to-be-done (theoretical prototype, virtual prototype, minimum viable prototype, and minimum awesome product). Although rapid prototypes may seem like old news, there is a subtle process to leveraging prototypes in the right way to rapidly validate your hypotheses. In the early days, although Intuit adopted the idea of rapid prototyping to test solutions, they found it led to premature development, as high-potential solutions were quickly thrown into Intuit's traditional software development process. This process often yielded long development cycles and disappointing results. Intuit's leaders soon realized that the better way to gain momentum was to fake the product in order to get something into users' hands more quickly. This virtual prototype, as we would call it, allowed the Intuit team to quickly test many, many solutions with customers to determine if they had any potential. For example, the Mobile Bazaar team (Intuit's name for the team searching for a solution to the farmers' pricing problem) experimented with several simple prototypes to test potential solutions. One prototype was an eBay-like auction where the farmers could auction their products directly to buyers. However, initial tests of virtual prototypes, drawn in PowerPoint, suggested such a system would be complex for farmers to set up and use (most of them were not well educated, nor did they have experience with computers). The team observed, however, that all the farmers had cell phones and knew how to send and receive text messages. So the team tested virtual prototypes, and then a minimum viable prototype, of a solution that involved gathering information on prices that buyers and middlemen were prepared to pay; this information was then sent to farmers in real time through text messages. Farmers then would use that information to decide when, and to whom, they would sell. The team "faked the back-end" by having three team members manually send text messages to farmers to see how they responded. Farmer response to this solution was extremely positive. Within one year, Mobile Bazaar had 180,000 farmer subscribers, and tests showed that farmers' prices had increased an average of 16 percent. average of 16 percent. In addition to demonstrating the use of specific prototypes, the Mobile Bazaar example demonstrates a more general principle of the innovator's method: "go broad to go narrow." At Intuit, teams apply this principle by generating as many solutions as possible during what the company calls a "solution-jam" before reducing the concepts to a short list for prototyping. After selecting at least three solutions, the team initiates a "code jam," with the goal of creating a working software prototype of each solution that isn't perfect but is good enough to test with customers. In this way, Intuit progresses from pain-storming to a customertested prototype within four weeks, thereby enabling rapid experimentation with customers numerous times before the solution is put into software development. However, as we will argue, truly delighting customers comes from the unexpected: it comes from understanding a problem in a way that others haven't and then going beyond customers' expectations in providing a solution. Therefore, the ultimate goal of this stage of the process is to create a minimum awesome product— one that remains "uncomfortably narrow" in feature set but is awesome at what it does. 18 Business Model: Validate the Go-to-Market Strategy At Intuit, Kaaren Hanson argues, "Until you've figured out how to delight a customer, don't even think about the business model." 19 But once you've discovered a solution customers want, you're ready to figure out the best way to get your solution into the hands of customers at a price that generates the revenues called for in your strategy. However, although most managers assume they understand how to get products to market, many companies have killed their new products by forcing them into existing business models. For example, managers often use the same distribution channels, a similar marketing strategy, a similar pricing strategy, and so on, as they use for existing products. But even when innovations appear similar, they often require their own unique business models. Properly aligning the business model involves discovering and validating your go-to-market strategy directly with your customers. This process requires validating how to acquire and influence customers, how to set price, and which resources will be required to deliver your solution to the market. Intuit currently manages this process by dividing innovation into groups. Innovations related to its core financial software products (Quicken, QuickBooks, and TurboTax) are labeled "Horizon 1" (H1) products and generally borrow the existing business model. But products only partially related to the core are labeled "Horizon 2" (H2), and new or unrelated products are labeled "Horizon 3" (H3). The new H3 and H2 products, in particular, require rapid experimentation to test assumptions about the new business model. Furthermore, H3 products require a unique set of metrics to measure progress in nailing the new business model. Rather than measure financial performance, such as ROI or contribution to top-line revenue, Intuit starts by measuring what it calls the "love metrics" (see chapter 8). The point is that you can't assume that new solutions will work with your existing business model. Mobile Bazaar typifies an H3 business, and the team is still in the process of experimenting with the business model. Unlike Quicken or TurboTax, the Mobile Bazaar distribution channel to customers will operate via cell phones (as will all digital marketing), and pricing must also be different (likely through subscription or a "free" advertising supported or freemium model). Intuit has not attempted to scale Mobile Bazaar at this point, because it has not yet validated a profitable business model. A New Style of Leadership Corporations are designed for execution, not innovation. But as uncertainty increases in the world around us, the way we manage has to change to meet these circumstances. To apply the innovator's method requires a new style of leadership. In the age of uncertainty, leaders are no longer chief decision makers. Instead, they're chief experimenters who formulate hypotheses with their team, conduct experiments, and let the data speak for themselves. "We want our leaders to be coaches and facilitators, not decision makers," says Cook. "The experiments that the team runs should provide the data to help the team make decisions so the leader doesn't have to." 20 Thus the manager's role shifts to coach and facilitator of "fast and frugal" experiments. If the manager, or anyone else on the team, says, "I think we should do X" or "I believe X," that statement is translated into a leap-of-faith assumption, and the next question should always be, "What's the fastest way to run an experiment to help us know whether we should do X?" 21 "With our new focus on experimentation, our leaders should stop trying to be Jobs or Bezos and predict the future," says CEO Smith.

"Our leaders should nurture innovation wherever it comes from. With lean experimentation, employees can come to leaders and have the boldness to say, 'I've got an idea, and here's the proof.'" 22 So within each of the first few steps (problem, solution, and business model), Intuit teams follow this process: (1) writing down the most important leap-offaith assumption, (2) designing an experiment to test it, (3) conducting the experiment to provide the answer, and then (4) looping back to figure out the next leap-of-faith assumption that the team needs to answer. Leaders have to walk the talk. Key decisions they want to make should be tested as leap-of-faith assumptions. Remember, in high uncertainty, anything you believe to be true is only your best guess. What is your leap-of-faith assumption? Intuit's Results How has Intuit's application of the ideas we describe here affected innovation at the company? First, Intuit has become an experimentation machine. In 2006 the TurboTax unit ran only one customer experiment; in 2012 it ran more than six hundred, and by 2013 it had run almost 2,500 customer experiments in a single year. Not surprisingly, this increase in market experiments has produced a plethora of successful new products. Mobile apps have increased from zero in 2008 to fifty in 2013, including the very successful SnapTax app, which generated 350,000 downloads in its first three weeks. But the proof is in the financial pudding. In 2010 Intuit generated $10 million in revenues from products launched in the prior three years. That number jumped tenfold—to $100 million—by 2012, and the company expects to earn much more as these nascent businesses mature. 23 Perhaps more important, Intuit's product launches and product improvements are being well received by the market, and profits are up considerably. Operating income has more than doubled, from 7 percent annual growth from 2004 to 2008 to 15 percent annual growth from 2008 to 2012. And investors have rewarded Intuit. Its market cap jumped from $10 billion in 2008 to $17 billion in 2013—a 70 percent increase (for comparison Intuit's market cap increased only from $9 to $10 billion from 2003 to 2008). Moreover, Intuit's innovation premium has jumped from 20 percent in 2008 to 30 percent in 2012—a 33 percent increase. Intuit is once again acting, and performing, like an innovative company and, some might say, like a start-up (see "Is Your Company an Eight-Thousand-Person Start-Up?"). Is Your Company an Eight-Thousand-Person Start-Up? If you're working in a larger organization, you may wonder, What does this start-up stuff have to do with me? Although we describe both startups and established companies, the issue isn't the size of the company. The issue is the type of problem you face and how you are solving it: uncertainty requires a different management approach that is critical for either entrepreneurial or corporate start-ups. However, because start-ups often spend their time solving high-uncertainty problems, you may incorrectly associate the innovator's method with start-ups rather than with the type of problem. with the type of problem. We define a start-up as does Eric Ries in The Lean Startup: as "a temporary organization designed to search for a business model under conditions of extreme uncertainty." 24 The definition includes three important dimensions. First, anyone (or team) who is creating a new product, service, process, or business—no matter the size of the company —is the founder of a start-up. The definition includes corporate and entrepreneurial start-ups. Second, a start-up has a special purpose and structure; it's a temporary organization focused on searching for a problem, a solution, and a business model. Third, the founders are trying to launch something new under conditions of uncertainty. It isn't clear whether there will be demand for the new product (demand uncertainty) or whether the technological solutions will work as desired (technological uncertainty). If you're a start-up founder (manager or entrepreneur), you should apply this method to avoid the number 1 pitfall that kills start-ups: scaling the business before you've nailed it. Similarly, we define "customer" as anyone with a problem or need, whether inside or outside the organization. You can apply the innovator's method to solve problems with some uncertainty inside your organization, whether in IT, HR, or finance. Wendy Castleman, an Intuit innovation catalyst, recalled such a process for an internal customer. An employee in IT observed that billing agents took fifteen minutes to answer customer questions. This spark of an insight and further observation identified the core problem: billing agents had to look across multiple systems to identify the various components of a customer bill. So she designed a series of experiments, testing different prototyped approaches to solutions for agents, ultimately finding a new tool that decreased call times from fifteen minutes to three! Using a similar approach, Intuit's Full-Service Payroll team wanted to see whether they could improve the customer experience of calling in for support. One idea was to answer the phone in a more personal way. Instead of saying, "What is your EIN number?" they hypothesized that they would get higher customer satisfaction by beginning with, "How can I help you today?" They tried it with one agent, and the results were stunning. The agent's NPS scores jumped more than 20 points, well beyond the rest of the team (or her prior scores).

CHAPTER ELEVEN

# Allocate Time for Innovation

We've often asked people who work for large companies, "What prevents you from moving more new ideas to market?" The most common answer? "I just don't have time. I have too much on my plate." That's what it's like to work in large organizations designed to execute routine tasks and processes. Good managers work to remove all slack in the system so that human resources (indeed, all resources) are fully utilized. But innovation takes time. We've seen companies specify 10 percent unstructured time for every employee (Intuit), 20 percent project time for engineers (Google), and, at the extreme end, as much as 100 percent self-defined time (Valve Software). According to Valve's employee handbook, "We've heard that other companies have people allocate a percentage of their time to selfdirected projects. At Valve, that percentage is 100. Since Valve is flat, people don't join projects because they're told to. Instead, you'll decide what to work on after asking yourself the right questions. Employees vote on projects with their feet. Strong projects are ones in which people can see demonstrated value; they staff up easily." 23 Although many companies have innovation boot camps or other innovation events, few provide ongoing time devoted to generating and testing ideas—even though it can make a significant difference. How much time companies allocate depends on the level of uncertainty they face and the importance of innovation (for example, Valve competes in a high-uncertainty market and believes it creates all its value through customer-focused innovation). Time has the power to let people explore new ideas that may not make sense at first; but the greater the variation in new ideas you test, the higher the probability that some will prove valuable. In fact, Google's "20 percent" projects have produced hits such as Gmail, Google AdSense, and Google Docs. One senior executive estimated that roughly half of Google's new products are generated in this way. 24 Such projects account for more than

25 percent of revenues. 25 Sadly, like other maturing companies, Google recently put constraints on the program, a move that many observers predict will shrink its innovation pipeline. However, Google appears to be pouring significant resources into its Google X lab with projects like Google Glass, Google Express, Google Loon, and Google Self-Driving. Just as Google is doing with Google X, some companies, such as Amazon, identify opportunities and form teams to generate solutions to the challenges of uncertainty. Innovation time is explicitly built in. No matter how it's done, leaders must make sure that employees are given the time—and the expectation—to conceive and test new ideas. It helps if leaders set an example. Facebook's Mark Zuckerberg tries to spend five hours a day on product development, and Scott Cook at Intuit tries to spend one day a week participating on innovation project teams. Ryan Smith, CEO of a billion-dollar survey company called Qualtrics, told us, "Every leader is a player and a coach. You have to get into the trenches if you want to innovate." 26 Provide Customers, Specialists, and Tools Another obstacle for start-up teams is a lack of tools. For example, teams need to run experiments with potential customers if they hope to discover the job-to-bedone and then nail the solution. Providing quick and easy access to various types of customers can facilitate rapid experimentation. Amazon provides employees a list of customers (and merchants) with which they can quickly test new ideas. Intuit invites customers to its headquarters one day a week for experiments. It also provides a list of nearby customers who have agreed to accept visits. These actions have doubled teams' face-to-face interactions with customers. 27 Numerous people told us that until Intuit started regularly bringing customers into headquarters, they didn't realize how easily they could test solutions with them. To help start-up teams generate a broad list of solutions, Intuit developed a technology palette. The company identified and hired experts in technologies related to mobile devices, social media, user interaction, collaboration, data, and the like. These experts are valuable for broadening solution searches, and they help teams identify what is technologically feasible. Google's leaders also provide tools for rapid prototyping, such as digital tools for making prototypes and mock-ups as well as flexible code structures for rapidly prototyping software. Google X's "design kitchen" was created to build simple prototypes for big ideas. Located in a building next to Google X's main offices, the design kitchen is a large-scale fabrication shop filled with 3D printers, high-end lathes, and other sophisticated prototyping

machinery. These tools can have a profound impact on the productivity of start-up teams. Remove Organizational Barriers For employees at companies that have ossified around execution, experimenting feels risky, unnatural, even against the (unwritten) rules. And because of the division of labor and accountability, employees need leaders' permission to test ideas that go beyond the scope of their business units. At Valve Software, leaders provide permission in a radical way: there are virtually no managers or formal titles among the software designers. 28 "Everyone is a designer," according to the employee handbook. "Everyone can question each other's work. Anyone can recruit someone onto his or her project." 29 Not surprisingly, Valve's approach to minimizing obstacles frees employees to pursue any start-up idea that interests them. Large companies also try to protect brand image and limit the liabilities of market experiments. In such companies, how do leaders give employees permission to take risks and freely run experiments? At Intuit, the legal team has assembled a list of guidelines; if you follow them, you're free to experiment without asking permission. For example, you don't need permission when these conditions are met. Testers (customers) understand they're participating in research. The experiment does not involve more than thirty thousand testers over two months. The experiment is labeled "Intuit Labs" to signal to testers that it is an experiment. The prototype does not actually complete transactions or collect user data. Intuit's data stewardship principles apply. Participants learn about the pilot via communication to the general public (and not targeted to government employees or agencies). Testers may be given a small token, if applicable, for their time. Intuit does a complete patent brainstorm before results of the experiment are shared publicly. 30 These guidelines serve as a signal to employees: "We expect you to run experiments! Don't ask for permission, just do it!" The I-School Leadership Curriculum If you attend business school, you take classes in finance, accounting, operations, organizational behavior, and similar topics, all of them drawing heavily on the logic introduced by Frederick Taylor. Rarely do you have a class on product development or the innovator's method as a core course (although many forward-looking professors teach some of these principles, mostly in elective courses). In most business schools, leadership is seen as the set of skills needed to manage mature organizations focused on executing under conditions of low uncertainty. But when you face uncertainty, you need a different set of management principles. Some of these principles are taught in design schools, led by Stanford's d.school.

But we think that beyond d.schools we need an innovation school—curriculum connected to B-schools that teaches innovation leadership across all of an organization's main functions. An I-school, in contrast with the B-school, would deal with the emerging science of managing uncertainty. Entrepreneurial leadership falls under the umbrella of the I-school, as do each of the other functional areas, which you also must manage differently when you face uncertainty.

For example, in B-school, when you study marketing, you typically learn the importance of building and protecting your brand, or doing quantitative analysis to identify customer segments and get customer feedback. But in an I-school we argue that you should initially ignore your brand and obtain all customer feedback through direct interaction, observation, or interviews. What's more, rather than emphasize building brands by satisfying a broad range of customers through perfected products, I-school emphasizes the need to test low-fidelity prototypes with small groups of customers, embracing errors as opportunities to learn. In B-school, when you learn finance you're taught about marginal cost logic: the importance of leveraging prior fixed-cost investments with new initiatives. But this approach biases you toward incremental innovation efforts. In I-school you learn about the dangers of marginal cost logic and other financial tools. 31 In a world of uncertainty, leveraging investments can often be a bad practice, because it may lead to building a workaround solution instead of one that nails the job-to-be-done. We aren't saying that one approach is good and the other is bad. Both are good. The key to management success is to recognize when to apply a more familiar B-school approach and when to apply I-school thinking—a decision that rests primarily on the degree of uncertainty. When uncertainty is high, apply an I-school approach. When the uncertainty has been resolved, use a B-school approach. After all, there's no reason to waste time running an experiment when there is a low probability that your choice of action is wrong. That being said, in our discussions with executives we see a rapidly increasing need for an I-school management approach. As Intuit's Cook observes, "We need to use these new leadership practices in our core business, because we face so much uncertainty and need to continue to reinvent ourselves." 32 For those of you reading this with a business degree, we have two questions: How many A/B experiments did you run in your classes before getting a business degree? How many prototypes did you build? For most of you the answer is: zero. That's got to change. The "I-school" label describes a group of emerging practices for managing uncertainty, especially in start-ups. But in the future, as uncertainty continues to grow, we will see changes in how we organize and manage all businesses. As the science of managing uncertainty develops, the I-school approach will need to be taught side-by-side with traditional management disciplines in B-schools.

If you want to innovate, savor the surprises. Too often we overlook the surprises. —Kim Clark, Former Dean of Harvard Business School FOR TEN YEARS (2000–2010) Hindustan Unilever (HUL), subsidiary of one of the world's leading consumer goods companies, experienced declining revenue growth, a flat stock price, and a falling market share. Efforts to improve execution and efficiency led to increased margins but little growth and even less innovation. Few new ideas bubbled up, and even the few that did seemed to struggle and disappear. As CEO Nitin Paranjpe and the management team wrestled to find ways to turn the company around, they hypothesized that the only way to save the company was to generate new ideas and insights. But how could it generate new ideas after ten years of the status quo? Fortunately, Paranjpe recognized that when you're in the routine of doing your current job well, you're not likely to have epiphanies. So to change course, the management team decided that the company needed to better understand their customers' needs and challenges. In 2010 Paranjpe launched a three-phase initiative called Project Bushfire, with the goal of getting every employee—more than fifteen thousand people in India alone—to visit customers in their workplaces and homes. In the first phase, HUL launched an internal campaign to create awareness, sending e-mails and hanging posters asking, "When was the last time you really listened to the customer?" Paranjpe also e-mailed employees to explain the program and to ask for ideas, adding that he would respond personally to every idea. But even with this appeal, skepticism remained high. In the halls, people whispered that the project was a "flavor of the season." 1 In phase two, the team selected hundreds of sites across India for managers to visit and then required them to reserve a date and time through an online system. Although the top management team made a show of logging in on the first day, resistance began to mount, with hundreds of requests to be excused. One factory manager argued, "My job is to maximize the production in the factory every day. I am convinced that my absence from the factory for an entire day will result in a greater loss for the organization than any observation or insight I might have from meeting customers, who meet with our sales and brand managers quite regularly." 2

Despite the protests, Paranjpe held firm, requiring 100 percent participation (he had assistants call and assign recalcitrant managers to observation sites). For the observations, managers were sent to shadow a frontline salesperson, meet consumers in their homes, or visit shops and ask questions. Each manager was given a sheet with questions such as, "What did I see that confirmed what I already know?" and "What did I see that was totally unexpected or surprising?" The goal was to capture the information in a central database. Then, as managers visited the field in phase three, their early observations proved transformational: some had never met customers before and were surprised to see the issues they struggled with. Others had such limited interaction with the real problems of their customers that they had overlooked interaction with the real problems of their customers that they had overlooked many opportunities. As the stories poured in (the Bushfire team made it a point to quickly share success stories), the recalcitrant attitude among many managers began to change. Just as important, ideas—small and large—began to flow in. Some of the insights prompted smaller initiatives. For example, when Paranjpe himself stood on the sales floor discussing the new Soya drink with customers, a woman asked why a "health" drink contained sugar. At that moment the CEO realized the team had overlooked a critical factor in the way most customers evaluate health products. Other insights had greater impact. For example, one manager was surprised to find that Shakti Ammas, women who sold HUL products in rural areas, couldn't sell other, noncompeting products. This led to an expansion in what the Ammas sell, including telecomm and banking services from other providers, as well as new HUL products, such as a low-cost water purification system called Pureit. Yet other insights led to the company's expansion into five thousand additional retail outlets and the adoption of a zero-inventory model. Other changes had a deeper impact on HUL's culture. For example, the project refocused HUL on generating insights from customers at all levels of the organization. Every member of the management team spends at least two hours every two weeks interacting with customers, and managers are expected to visit at least five customers per month. In addition, HUL captures insights differently than in the past: when an idea is proposed, a member of the management committee acknowledges it, and when ideas go into pilot testing, the person who generated the idea is acknowledged and invited to participate. The rewards for these efforts have shown up in HUL's financial performance. After a decade of a flat stock price, in 2012 shares climbed 34 percent (double the Sensex index), and sales spiked 40 percent. 3 Moreover, HUL's innovation premium climbed to 44 percent, making it the top-ranked consumer goods company (and number twelve overall) on the 2012 Forbes list of the world's most innovative companies. Generating insights represents the first step in our end-to-end innovation process. In this chapter, we show that insights are not the result of magic or of simply hiring "creative" people. Rather, they result from behaviors or processes you can apply. You'll learn how successful companies generate insights and how to effectively capture and select them. Four Key Actions That Generate Insights Innovations are only valuable if they solve problems. So the first step is to generate an insight about a problem worth solving. The insight could be finding a problem that others have missed or perhaps uncovering a potential new solution to a well-understood problem. We've found that the catalyst for an insight is a "surprise." A surprise is the clue that you've learned something new that might be a valuable insight—because if you are surprised then others may be as well. For example, when Intuit's Mobile Bazaar team was watching farmers conduct their business, they were surprised to find that crop prices could fluctuate by as much as 50 percent in a single day. This was a symptom of a problem that farmers were facing in their attempt to get fair prices for their crops. Similarly, when Michael Dell had purchased all of the components to build a PC in his dorm room, he was surprised to discover that they cost only $600 or $700 when an IBM PC was selling for $2,500. Dell told us this surprise raised a question: "Why does it cost five times more to buy a PC in the store than the parts cost?" 4 Intuit's Scott Cook teaches employees at Intuit to "savor surprises" and says that "at Intuit we teach our people to ask these two questions: What is surprising? What is different from what you expected? That is where true learning and innovation starts." 5 Our earlier book, The Innovator's DNA, explains how great innovators uncover surprises and generate new insights. 6 It describes four behaviors that provoke associational thinking: the ability to connect seemingly unrelated information or ideas and put them together in new ways—for example, crossing a kayak with a surfboard to come up with the idea for a paddleboard. Associational thinking happens as the brain tries to synthesize and make sense of information gleaned from questioning, observing, networking, and experimenting. As figure 3-1 shows, the four key actions of questioning, observing, networking, and experimenting are the key to triggering new insights through associational thinking.

First, people generate insights through questioning, constantly challenging the status quo with "why" and "why not" questions to turn things upside-down. They often ask "what if" questions to envision a different future. Questioning gives you the fuel to power new associations and insights. Hindustan Unilever's Bushfire project is an excellent example. The HUL team members started with a list of questions as they went out into the field, including "What surprises you?" and "What should HUL be doing that they are not doing?" These questions often acted as a catalyst. The manager of an HUL factory in Mangalore asked why he couldn't buy HUL products at the local store. The observation was a symptom of problems in the distribution network that, after study, led the company to expand into new retail outlets. Questions help you see things in a new light and open new avenues and possibilities. Second, managers garner new ideas by observing the environment as if they were anthropologists. They get out of their cubicles to closely watch the world around them—especially customers, products, services, and processes—to spark around them—especially customers, products, services, and processes—to spark unique ways of doing things. For example, an HUL manager observed that a shopkeeper didn't have inventory even though the distributor had a large stockpile. The observation helped the manager improve inventory by adopting a retail-driven model: shopkeeper orders are sent directly to HUL, and HUL ships the required product to distributors, eliminating stagnant inventory and improving fulfillment for the retailer. And don't underestimate the value of small, unexpected ideas. For example, one manager, an expert in product packaging, recalled his surprise at seeing a customer reengineering Tetra Paks to hang them from the ceiling, increasing their visibility to passing customers. Third, the successful innovators we studied excel at networking, talking with people to find—or spark a new way to solve—perplexing problems. They regularly talk with people who don't look, act, or (most importantly) think as they do. Instead of networking simply to gain resources, they interact with diverse people to get new ideas. Although the HUL initiative started with field visits, as managers met with people outside their discipline, they established new relationships that led to new ideas; for example, the managers in marketing and sales realized that a supply chain manager could solve a sales problem. As one manager put it, "You would be making a huge mistake by assuming that a Ph.D. in Organic Chemistry has no value to add to the selling process wired into a tablet PC." 7 Another noted, "A couple of years ago, a brand manager wouldn't be caught dead asking his finance counterpart for an opinion on a piece of advertising. Today, it is common." 8 Fourth, you generate insights by constantly experimenting. Innovators try out new experiences wherever they go. They take apart products or processes to see how things work—and how to improve them. Moreover, as you'll see in chapter 5, they rapidly pilot or prototype various solutions to find one that works. For example, when an HUL factory manager visited a shopkeeper, he was amazed to hear about a myriad of problems that could have been resolved by calling the factory's published help line number. So the manager tried an experiment: he printed the help line number on the outside of every box. Immediately, the number of calls increased dramatically, and the number of long-term issues plummeted. We studied a sample of founders and leaders of companies that enjoy a high innovation premium (those ranked in our Forbes list). We found that they spend 31 percent of their time engaged in the four discovery behaviors in pursuit of new insights. In contrast, leaders of companies having a low IP spent only 15 percent of their time thus engaged.

What kinds of things can leaders do to facilitate the process? And how can they make sure that insights are captured and the best ones are selected to be put through the innovator's method?

As you engage in the four behaviors, it's crucial to search broadly: look for ideas across countries, industries, companies, technologies, functions, and so on. Einstein called this "combinatorial play." A broad search leads to variation in the knowledge you gain—and that leads to more combinatorial thought trials, increasing the odds of discovering an insight. And we've found that people who searched broadly are much more likely to have an epiphany—an insight that seems to come from nowhere. Amazon's Jeff Bezos is an excellent example. Before deciding to sell books over the internet, Bezos researched the top twenty mail order products. He hypothesized that people would buy standard products (those that vary little) via the web. To his surprise, books—certainly standard—weren't in the top twenty products. Then he discovered why: there were so many books in print that no one catalog could cover them all. It would be huge and expensive to mail. As Bezos saw it, the internet was the ideal vehicle for offering such a catalog. Although rooted in books and positioned as a leading book retailer, Amazon has a track record of searching broadly for new business ideas. It has expanded into a wide variety of products and services, from electronic readers and tablets (with the Kindle) to cloud computing services (Amazon EC2) to video streaming services (through Amazon Prime) to daily grocery delivery (AmazonFresh). Amazon has recently moved into merchant lending (Amazon Lending) and reportedly is considering entering categories such as smart phones and TV settop boxes. Bezos encourages employees to search broadly despite criticism that Amazon is not focused enough. "Every new business we've ever engaged in has initially been seen as a distraction by people externally, and sometimes even internally," says Bezos. "They'll say, 'Why are you expanding into media products? Why are you going international? Why are you entering the marketplace business with third-party sellers?' We're getting it now with our new infrastructure web services. 'Why take on these new developer customers?' " 9 Bezos adds that most companies' big errors have been acts of omission and not acts of commission: "It's the opposite of sticking to your knitting. It's when you shouldn't have stuck to your knitting and you did," he says. "It's very fun to have a culture where people are willing to take these leaps. It's the opposite of the 'institutional no.' It's the institutional yes. People at Amazon say, 'We're going to figure out how to do this.'" 10 Most people naturally search narrowly, because they're told to leverage their expertise. Although this strategy makes sense for expanding into known territory, it limits you to only incremental insights. Searching broadly might include exploring new industries for your product, taking apart products from different industries, or asking yourself challenging questions that force you to look elsewhere ("How would we make money next year if we were legally prohibited from selling any of our current products to our existing customers?"). Searching broadly for new knowledge or new possibilities greatly increases the probability of uncovering a breakthrough insight.

In the past few decades, many companies have initiated processes to capture new ideas, such as idea repositories and knowledge databases, but many of them are glorified suggestion boxes that simply do not work. Successfully capturing ideas is a critical part of innovation, and managers need to use the right tools and the right process. A popular process we studied is the American Idol model. You challenge employees to submit ideas to be screened and selected by a panel of judges. For example, Google holds an Innovator's Challenge four times a year. Employees submit ideas for top management review; winning ideas receive the resources to be pushed forward (we discuss selecting ideas in the next section). Marissa Mayer (former director of consumer products at Google and now CEO of Yahoo!) championed regular brainstorming sessions during which engineers had ten minutes to pitch their ideas to Mayer and a group of as many as one hundred others. The goal of these sessions was not only to capture the insight but also to build on the initial idea with at least one new complementary idea. A second approach is to use a digital collaboration platform, sometimes called an idea management system. Google refers to its platform as an idea board, at Intuit it's called Brainstorm, and at AT&T it's called TIP. Many companies, such as Cisco Services, source from an outside company like Brightidea (Spigot and AHHHA are other popular tools). These tools allow employees (or outsiders) to post, view, sort, and filter ideas; vote and provide feedback; and use other social networking features like notifications and tagging. These tools use crowd-sourcing (outsourcing tasks to individuals or organizations) to encourage, refine, and advance ideas in ways that a static, centrally controlled suggestion box cannot. That being said, you must overcome challenges to encourage employees to participate. At Intuit, use of the Brainstorm platform is robust because it's embedded in the culture, but it's still necessary for innovation catalysts to pull out promising ideas to nurture and champion. Other companies, such as Cisco and Qualcomm, create engagement by using a batch-type process to focus everyone's attention on the idea platforms at particular times. Yet other companies, such as HUL, assign teams to respond to and develop each idea. The lesson is to marry crowd engagement with encouragement and cultivation from a trained team. AT&T's TIP is the largest idea board we've seen, with more than half of AT&T's two hundred thousand employees participating. It helps turn the company's typical innovation weakness—a vast employee base—into a strength. It's egalitarian; frontline employees participate in early stages with a voice equal to those of senior managers. The online platform allows employees worldwide to vote, comment, and collaborate on ideas. At the end of a designated time period, called a "season" (à la American Idol), the top ideas are evaluated by "angels," a group of high-level executives, who then select ideas to be presented in a live pitch session. Chosen ideas receive seed funding. Selected projects are managed by innovation champions: employees who act as "CEOs" of each project. They shepherd the idea through the proof-of-concept phase and receive additional funding if a business unit will match the investment for a second round. To illustrate, a call-center employee who lost a close friend in an accident caused by a distracted driver conceived of an app to help prevent texting while driving. Within one week of posting her idea on TIP, peers were providing helpful guidance on improving and implementing it. Ultimately, she was asked to present her idea to AT&T leadership, including CEO Randall Stephenson. Executives provided funding and moved the idea to an AT&T foundry, TIP's incubation process, where a prototype was developed and eventually released to the market. Dubbed DriveMode, the app has been downloaded hundreds of thousands of times and was a cornerstone of AT&T's "It Can Wait" public service campaign. Some companies also set up a database to capture ideas. For example, HUL entered all the Bushfire field observations into a database. To keep the ideas alive, it did two things: it promised to respond to every idea, and it assigned managers to probe the database, find strong ideas, and then push them forward with participation of the originator. Some companies set up processes to capture insights from outside the company. For example, Procter & Gamble has deployed seventy "technology entrepreneurs," who spend all their time searching for new ideas that will make a difference for P&G. These senior people help identify key customer needs and write the technology briefs that define the problems the company is trying to solve. They create external connections by, for example, meeting with university and industry researchers, and they combine aggressive mining of the scientific literature, patent databases, and other data sources with physical prospecting for ideas—say, surveying store shelves in Rome or attending product and technology fairs. It was a technology entrepreneur, exploring a local market in Japan, who discovered what ultimately became the Mr. Clean Magic Eraser. P&G's technology entrepreneurs work out of six Connect and Develop hubs in China, India, Japan, Western Europe, Latin America, and the United States. To date, they have identified more than ten thousand products, product ideas, and promising technologies. 11 Select the Insight Recently the editors at Budget Traveler magazine had a great idea to generate new material: Why not crowd-source an entire issue from readers? They sent out a call for submissions and received more than 2,800, including more than five hundred for a single piece on "50 Reasons You Love New York." Although the project generated new material, the editors now faced a monumental task: How to sort through almost three thousand submissions and then, for those chosen, rework and edit them to fit into an article. In the end, editor Erik Torkells reflected on the bittersweet experience, saying, "Let's be perfectly clear, making this issue was neither cheap nor easy." 12 Leaders at large companies can create similar problems when they succeed at inspiring—and capturing—insights but have broken mechanisms for winnowing them to those that are most promising. To solve the problem, most companies fall back on familiar techniques, usually a competition resembling a business plan contest, judged by senior executives. Unfortunately, this approach may not work well. Recall our earlier discussion of the problems of leaders making decisions under high uncertainty. We've found that leaders are more successful at selecting insights for their organizations to further explore by using either a "vote test" or a "proof test." Vote Test How could Budget Traveler have solved its editorial problem? What if the editors had used their readers to both source and evaluate the material? People both inside and outside your organization can be valuable for selecting insights through a form of crowd-sourcing we call "crowd-voting." One example is Threadless, an online community of artists and an e-commerce website. Threadless enlists its customers in a member community to submit ideas for Tshirt slogans and designs, tapping in to new artists and generating ideas without the need to hire professional designers. Just as important, Threadless uses crowd-voting (by customers and designers) to select which designs to take to market. By using the crowd, Threadless can better predict which t-shirts will sell. It has developed an enviable track record of never having produced a flop; every t-shirt ever produced has sold out. Crowd-voting works well when you use a crowd to evaluate an offering or predict uncertain events. However, use it with caution if you're trying to predict complex, technical, or radical problems or solutions. In these cases, expertise matters, and hands-on use can be a more viable predictor than opinions. As an alternative, you can create a system for choosing insights based on whether the advocate can get others to volunteer time to pursue it. This is what founders of start-ups must do. Similarly, Google and Valve Software, among others, challenge employees to recruit other colleagues to use their self-directed time on the employee's project. Compelling ideas are selected for further development because they draw volunteer resources.

## *How to Make Innovation Time Work*

Researchers asked students at Yale to do something for their own benefit: get tetanus shots. To one group, the researchers gave the time and location for the shots and then tried to scare them into attending. To the other group, they gave the same information but added a map to the building. All the students were familiar with campus, but when they received a map their attendance jumped from 3 percent to 28 percent. Even for students who knew what to do, providing a helpful tool increased participation. 13 Similarly, giving your team members time to innovate will be more effective if you provide a "map" to use it. For example, when Jeff Zias was put in charge of unstructured time at Intuit, he noticed that few people used it. To create a map, he started by encouraging people to mark their calendars with the days they would use unstructured time. This act increased employee engagement 20 percent. Then Zias recruited volunteers to share best practices and champion innovation time. Even so, Zias found that people didn't know how to use the time. So he created a series of "hack-a-thons": for twenty-four to forty-eight hours, people blocked out everything else and focused on innovation. At first, employees got together in "idea jams" and brainstormed problems and products. More than a dozen products, including TurboTax on the iPad, came out of the early idea jams. Then Zias created a pipeline of increasingly specific jams: "pain jams" to find problems worth solving, "solution jams" to brainstorm solutions, and "code jams" to develop prototypes or try variations to existing products. Zias argues that much of Intuit's success in new products can be traced to an overall increase in the use of unstructured time. But the greater benefit may be its role as a myth buster. Six years ago, Intuit was perceived as "an old, slow company," and people said it was too hard to be innovative and agile. The idea jams and code jams busted those myths by telling employees, "Go ahead—just hack that." 14 Even more radically, Valve Software has created an internal market for ideas —a true network of start-ups—by requiring that the generators of insights recruit others. From Valve's employee handbook: Since Valve is flat, people don't join projects because they're told to. Instead, you'll decide what to work on. Employees vote on projects with their feet (or desk wheels). Strong projects are ones in which people can see demonstrated value; they staff up easily. This means there are any number of internal recruiting efforts constantly under way. People are going to want you to work with them on their projects, and they'll try hard to get you to do so. But the decision is going to be up to you. . . There's no rule book for choosing a project or task at Valve. But it's useful to answer questions like these: Of all the projects currently under way, what's the most valuable thing I can be working on? Which project will have the highest direct impact on our customers? 15 This approach is unusual. As Valve employee Paul Kirschbaum (a former Amazon employee) observes, "It's different at Valve. You have to figure out where to allocate your time—which projects you think will create the most value. And if you want to pursue an idea, you've got to convince others that it's worth pursuing. No manager is telling you what to do. Ideas draw resources if others think they have merit." 16 The freedom to choose is critical for innovation success, because research shows that creative ideas come from folks who are intrinsically motivated to generate and pursue those ideas. 17 This approach also has the benefit of creating an environment where folks are happy and motivated because they work on things they care about. "We want innovators, and that means maintaining an environment where they'll flourish," say Valve's leaders in the employee handbook. "That's why Valve is flat. It's our shorthand way of saying that we don't have any management, and nobody 'reports to' anybody else. We do have a founder/president, but even he isn't your manager. This company is yours to steer . . . You have the power to green-light projects." 18 That's a powerful vote test for an organization to use to select ideas to work on. Proof Test It is possible that individuals (or teams) who are passionate about an idea but lack the "votes" may be on to something. How do you sort them out from the passionate individuals who lack votes because their idea is bad? Give them the tools we describe, and ask them to run a quick experiment. If the insight has merit, they'll return with data—the proof—that the idea is worth further exploration. For example, when Paul Buchheit, an engineer at Google, came up with the idea for a system that would read keywords distilled from your Gmail message and automatically find a related ad to display next to it, Marissa Mayer told him to drop the idea. "I was like, 'Paul, Paul, Paul—ads are never going to work,'" Mayer said in a Stanford University podcast. "We'll never make any money, or we're going to target the ads at their e-mail, which is just going to be creepy and weird. People are going to think there are people here reading their emails and picking out the ads and it's going to be terrible." 19 Luckily for Buchheit, empirical results trump opinions in Google's culture. So even after Mayer made him promise not to build a prototype, he stayed up all night and built one anyway, gambling that it would prove Mayer wrong. He released the prototype of his system, called AdSense, at 7 a.m. right before Mayer came to work. When Mayer first saw the prototype, she was annoyed. But when she checked her Gmail she saw there was an e-mail from a friend who invited her to go hiking—and next to it, an ad for hiking boots. Another e-mail was about Al Gore visiting Stanford University for a speech—and next to it was an ad for books about Al Gore. Mayer grudgingly admitted that AdSense was more useful, entertaining, and relevant than she imagined. 20 More importantly, the data from the prototype won out. (Buchheit's prototype led to additional prototypes, and AdSense was adapted to identify advertising opportunities through keyword searches, website content, and browsing that led to $10 billion in annual revenues.) In fact, Google CEO Eric Schmidt would often advise Googlers to get "100 happy users inside of Google" as proof of concept before launching a product to the market. In similar fashion, Regeneron, an emerging biotech star, has achieved a lofty 63 percent innovation premium (number 4 on our most recent Forbes list of most innovative companies) by placing many small bets in lots of places—and letting the experiments reveal which ideas are best. According to a Forbes analysis of 220 drugs approved over the past decade for publicly traded companies, the companies that invented three or more medicines spent an average of $4.3 billion in R&D per drug. Regeneron's cost per drug? Only $736 million. Setting criteria for success and then letting fast and frugal experiments show which bets to make is a far better way than having senior managers pick the insights to test and develop. According to Regeneron CEO Leonard Schleifer, having leaders pick the ideas to focus on is a bad idea. " 'Focus' is a dirty word for us, OK? It's a big mistake to think that you can pick the very best thing that you should focus on and then ignore all the other things." 21 The point: picking winners under conditions of high uncertainty is extraordinarily difficult: let experiments validate the best insights to pursue. Watch Out: Innovators Innovate, Customers Validate Most of your insights into problems to be solved will come from watching and interacting with customers and others. But don't fall into the trap of asking your customers to innovate for you. In later chapters we emphasize the importance of asking for feedback, but don't expect them to tell you what the innovation should be. Customers have a hard time imagining the future or resolving contradictory demands. For example, when customers told Kimberly-Clark they didn't want their toilet-trained children to wear diapers but they also didn't want them to wet the bed, those same customers couldn't imagine the solution: disposable underwear with the absorbent features of a diaper (called PullUps, they became a multimillion-dollar category). To avoid this trap, as we will teach in the next chapter, focus on the customer's job-to-be-done, come up with a variety of prototyped solutions, and then, using tools of the innovator's method, rely on customers to validate the solution. The Insight Business You cannot expect to see a flood of insights by doing the same things you've done in the past. But you can generate many new insights by changing what you do. Questioning, observing, networking, and experimenting will increase the probability that you will learn something new that will surprise you. Savor those surprises. They might be the catalyst to something big. Let us add that you cannot ignite more insights by just throwing money at people. Counterintuitively, some of the most successful innovators we studied offered almost no monetary rewards for innovation. Why did people participate? It's because many people, once they get a taste of it, find innovation the most fulfilling activity in their lives. People typically want to be acknowledged and want to be a part of taking their insights forward and turning them into real businesses, including taking time off to push the idea forward (many companies we observed offer three to twelve months of sabbatical for originators of the most promising ideas). You shouldn't forget to reward people, and it's a good idea to provide financial participation to retain your best innovators. But ultimately, giving people the time and opportunity to pursue their ideas may be the most important thing you can offer. And changing your behavior in simple and easy ways can make all the difference in helping trigger insights that can make a difference.

CHAPTER TWELVE

# Discover The Problem The JOB TO BE DONE

WHEN MIKE MAPLES JR., an experienced executive who had worked in telecommunications, decided to start a new venture with some colleagues, the problem was that they didn't know what type of venture to start. So Maples and his team made an unusual agreement: they would not start building anything until they found a problem that was worth solving. Maples and his friends began meeting several times a week to discuss problems they had seen. Then, then during the week they met individually with people in the industry to test their ideas. Although the group generated many interesting insights, Maples and his team kept pushing, recalling that they were looking for a problem so big that "you needed a tourniquet, or you were going to die." 1 Eventually, the team focused on the problem of the rapidly expanding help desk, a $70 billion problem bleeding the IT industry dry. Research revealed that as software solutions had become more complex, the help desk required increasingly knowledgeable staff to resolve customers' technical challenges. Help desk functions then consumed 80 percent of Microsoft's head count, and growing. Not surprisingly, several companies had developed solutions, usually knowledge databases of answers to frequently asked questions. Maples's team members felt that they, too, should develop a knowledge database—but it would need to be a better solution than competitive products. But because they had committed to deeply understanding the problem first, they agreed to devote serious effort to observing the challenges of the help desk. So the team went into the call centers and observed technicians, timing calls with stopwatches and recording the content. They also sat down with technicians, managers, and executives to discuss and understand the problem. They discovered something shocking: only 25 percent of the time on a call was spent actually resolving the problem. Up to 75 percent was spent gathering customer information, confirming whether customers had a support plan, and diagnosing simple items such as the operating system; knowledge databases were tackling only 25 percent of the problem. If the group could automate the simpler tasks, it could solve a problem consuming more than half the productivity of a $70 billion industry. Using this deep insight into the problem, Maples and his colleagues launched Motive Communications, a company that reached a multibillion-dollar market capitalization by providing a better solution to the real problem. 2 Maples's experience reinforces the importance of deeply understanding the problem before trying to solve it. Although such an observation may seem obvious, in fact, most managers actually start with the solution first, before ensuring that they've discovered a problem worth solving. As a result, although they develop highly innovative solutions, the product or service fails because they developed a solution that no one wants to buy. Therefore, the most important thing you can do next in the innovation process is to start by deeply understanding the problem you are solving—the job-to-be-done. Deeply Understand the Job-to-Be-Done Clayton Christensen argues that customers—people and companies—have "jobs" that arise regularly and need to get done. When customers become aware of a job, they look around for a product or service they can hire to help them get the job done. As well-known marketing professor Theodore Levitt once observed, "People don't want to buy a quarter-inch drill. They want a quarterinch hole!" 3 For example, customers may purchase an iron and ironing board to help them remove wrinkles from clothes. But they don't really want an iron and ironing board. They really want wrinkle-free clothing. By understanding what the job is, you can generate various insights about the problem or solution. Instead of thinking about ways to improve the iron or ironing board, you might consider creating a wrinkle-release spray for clothes, or perhaps a product to be used in the dryer, much as a fabric softener sheet is used. Or perhaps you could develop a product to be attached to a washer—or put in a shower—to steam out wrinkles. We've found that stepping back to deeply understand the job-to-be-done is a useful technique, not only for spawning ideas but also for laying the foundation to nail the problem and solution. Furthermore, it is important to recognize that every job has a functional, a social, and an emotional dimension—and the importance of these elements varies from job to job. For example, "I need to feel like I belong to an elite, exclusive group" is a job for which luxury brand products such as Gucci and Versace are hired. In this case, the functional dimension of the job isn't nearly as important as its social and emotional dimensions. In contrast, if you want to hire a delivery truck you're probably focusing on functional elements, such as the size of the truck or ease of loading. But even when a job looks purely functional, pay attention to hidden emotional or social dimensions. For example, even though a Harley-Davidson is highly functional, many people choose it for social reasons; they want to join the Harley Owners Group and be part of a club that rides motorcycles together. Understanding the functional, social, and emotional dimensions of a job is the most critical element of really nailing the problem you are trying to solve and setting yourself up for a successful innovation. It will lead you to solutions that you may never have considered but that will be much more successful. Another way of thinking about the job-to-be-done is to ask yourself, What outcomes do my customers want? Anthony Ulwick describes the efforts of outcomes do my customers want? Anthony Ulwick describes the efforts of Cordis, a struggling medical device manufacturer, to gain a foothold in the market for products related to angioplasty (a heart procedure in which doctors thread a device through an artery to reach the heart, where they inflate a balloon to place a stent, reducing blockage in a compromised heart artery). In the effort to improve their fortunes, Ulwick helped the Cordis team shift their focus from features to outcomes. Interviewers approached a sample of customers (surgeons and nurses) and asked them to talk through an angioplasty from beginning to end. As the customers talked, the Cordis team asked them what they would like, ideally, without focusing on existing solutions. Then they translated those desires into outcomes. For example, when surgeons said they wanted a smooth balloon, interviewers asked why; the surgeons wanted to avoid accidentally cutting a blood vessel. So the team translated this description into the outcome (the job-to-be-done). They then compared all the jobs to be done in the procedure and developed a hypothesis of the biggest unmet need (the most important outcomes having the least satisfaction): minimizing recurrence of artery blockage, which was rated 9.5 out of 10 on importance, but 3.2 on satisfaction. They then redesigned the stent to accomplish that job. Within one year, Cordis increased its market share from less than 1 percent to more than 10 percent. 4 In your search for jobs to be done, it is worth remembering that not all jobs are created equal. The world is full of opportunities; the only real question is which ones are worth solving. So how do you know if it's worth solving? Search for what we call a monetizable job: a significant need or problem for a large group of customers who: (1) have money and (2) will readily pay you to solve it. Too many innovators have chased very intriguing jobs but for very few customers or for customers who don't have money or aren't willing to pay! For example, while many elementary schools have a multitude of jobs to solve, they are often so budget constrained that they cannot pay to solve those jobs, unless you can find a way to also solve their budget constraint at the same time. As you think about different monetizable jobs, also consider that occasionally there can be multiple customers for a single job. For any particular job there may be up to three customers: the economic customer (the person who pays for it), the technical customer (the person who installs the solution), and the end customer (the person who uses the solution). Naturally you want to understand the jobs to be done for each customer type to avoid solving one customer's job while creating a problem for another customer. For example, if you solve a health care problem for a consumer (end customer) but insurers or administrators (economic customer) refuse to pay, you can't actually tackle the job. So (economic customer) refuse to pay, you can't actually tackle the job. So remember that you may need to find creative ways to solve the job-to-be-done for multiple customers. Lastly we recommend that you search for a monetizable job to customers' problems that can be described in terms of shark bites—and not mosquito bites. Many of us are bothered by mosquito bites, but we rarely buy the anti-itch cream. We just live with it. But if a shark bites you, then you will pay any amount of money to solve that pain—immediately. Your goal should be to look for shark bites that you can solve—the kinds of problems or needs that keep your customers awake at night, consume their time, engage them deeply, or cause them stress. When we are talk about shark bites, we're referring more to the degree of customer emotion and engagement than the size of the market. Of course, you want to solve a problem with big markets, but often the markets for new ideas are very small at the beginning. One of the biggest traps managers fall into is shooting down new projects because they're too small to satisfy the growth needs of large corporations. But seeds are small before they become trees—and they take time to mature. For that reason, even though you may be encouraged to start by sizing the market, we encourage you to pay more attention to the emotion of your customers. Strong emotion often leads to attractive markets. For that reason, don't be fooled. Some things that may appear to be a mosquito bite may be a serious customer need worth solving.

Is Instagram a Mosquito Bite or a Shark Bite? To find a monetizable job, you can focus on what causes your customers stress, what keeps them awake at night, where they spend their time, or what they hate to do: things we might label problems. But what about simple pleasures? Although we use the language of "problems" in the chapter, many important jobs are actually needs or pleasures sought by customers. When you explore customer needs, just think carefully about the difference between nice to have and need to have. Many of the things we see as simple pleasures actually solve a deep human need. Psychologist Abraham Maslow identified a hierarchy of human needs, arguing that beyond our basic needs for food and shelter, we have intense desires for belonging, love, friendship, and feeling important. Once those needs are met, we have a need for self-fulfillment, important. Once those needs are met, we have a need for self-fulfillment, including the need to create and experience new things. If you can solve one of these needs, something that looks like a simple pleasure may actually be solving a big unmet need. Consider Instagram, the photo-sharing application for smart phones. What problem is Instagram solving? Think of this question in terms of nice to have and need to have. Instagram solves a deep human need for self-expression, social connection, and prominence. But that's not all: the kicker is that it solves this need better than prior solutions. For example, internet blogs took off because they, too, solved a deep social need for self-expression and prominence. The problem with blogs is that writing them takes a great deal of time. Twitter solved this problem by reducing posts to 140 characters, allowing people to share their thoughts and achieve social prominence more quickly and with less work. Now consider the saying, "A picture is worth a thousand words." In some ways, Instagram allows users to share a thousand words with only a few clicks and, on top of that, receive social feedback. As you look for jobs, sometimes providing a simple pleasure may be solving an important customer problem, defined broadly. To find needs, you can also explore what customers love, want, and feel compelled to do. Only customers can reveal what's important. What looks small initially can sometimes be big. Even mosquito bites can be serious problems, especially if they carry malaria. Three Tools to Find the Monetizable Job To really discover the job-to-be-done, don't count on traditional marketing studies, analyst reports, news articles, surveys, or even focus groups. That may sound heretical, but in our opening example, if Maples had relied on an analyst report or a news article, he would never have discovered the job-to-be-done. Even if he had run a survey, he wouldn't have asked the right questions. Clearly these familiar tools have value under conditions of certainty, but they fail when you face uncertainty. So much so that Gianfranco Zaccai, the designer behind P&G's billion-dollar Swiffer product, said, "In my 40 years working in design and innovation, alongside some of the most brilliant minds in the business, I have never seen innovation come out of a focus group. Let me put it more strongly: focus groups kill innovation." 5 These tools fail because you can't get deep enough to observe real customer problems. For this reason we introduce a different set of tools to discover the job-to-be-done. Pain-Storming In chapter 1 we describe how Intuit started using "pain-storming" to ensure that the team had nailed a customer's biggest pain points before jumping to building solutions. The purpose of pain-storming is to gain clarity on what you think the problem is so that you can test your hypotheses. We've found that effective painstorming involves five steps. Step 1: Generate a problem hypothesis identifying the customer and the jobto-be-done. Step 2: Create a journey-line for the customer and identify pain points and emotions. Step 3: Select the biggest pain points, and conduct a root-cause analysis. Step 4: Pick a root cause that you think is most important to customers. Step 5: Identify assumptions behind the root cause, and then test them with customers. Let's look at each step. First, you create a problem hypothesis of the customer and the job-to-be-done. This involves identifying what you think is an important problem for a specific type of customer. For example, Motive Communications' problem hypothesis was that it could reduce the time (and costs) of help desks to solve customers' technical problems at large software companies like Microsoft. To identify a customer segment for your project, write down at least three identifying characteristics (for example, large software companies, with large numbers of unsophisticated customers, that have large customer support budgets, who want a reputation for good service). These are descriptors of the types of customers with the same job-to-be-done (see "Develop a Customer Profile to Segment Customers"). It may be helpful to fill in the following template from the perspective of the customer. I am _______________ (customer, with at least three characteristics) I am trying to _______________ (outcome/job trying to solve) But _______________ (problem I am facing) Because _______________ (the deeper root cause for why the problem is happening) Develop a Customer Profile to Segment Customers To effectively nail the problem, it helps to build a profile for each customer with a different job-to-be-done. Grouping customers based on shared needs or problems is a familiar marketing tool called customer segmentation. But in contrast to more familiar customer segmentation, the purpose of customer profiles is to build a deeply empathetic, intimate portrait of customers and the jobs they struggle to accomplish. To build customer profiles, you might start by first segmenting customers by the job-to-be-done, rather than more familiar metrics like age or income. The job is the critical unit of analysis, and your customer profile should aim to describe your initial hypothesis about the emotions around the job and how customers currently solve it. Then test your hypothesis by observing customers to understand their motivations (likes, dislikes, aspirations), behaviors (how they spend their time; how they purchase new products or services), demographics (income, industry, age, education, and available budget), and, most important, how they currently think about and solve the job-to-be-done. After these observations, you will see the world in a new way and will need to recreate a new set of customer profiles based on your observations. Each customer profile should be divided by the job-to-bedone, and describe all the elements above (emotions, current solutions, etc.) for that particular job. This profile will provide you the map of what problem to solve and how to solve it. But it will also provide your team focus and motivation, helping you avoid the trap of trying to solve every job, and in doing so, solving nobody's. To illustrate this danger, in one humorous example, the television show The Simpsons featured the main character, Homer Simpson, asking customers what they most wanted in a car. Homer then builds a car that includes every feature for every customer desire, such as "power like a gorilla, yet soft and yielding like a Nerf ball." Not surprisingly the car fails in the market, because, in trying to solve every customer's problem, the car actually solves no one's problems. The humor helps us see the absurdity of trying to serve every customer need, but it is inspired by real events. The failed Ford Edsel and Pontiac Stinger were designed to serve too many customer needs.

Step 2 is to create a customer journey-line: an in-depth visual portrait in which you identify pain points to understand how your customers do the job today and how they feel while doing it. Visually map out the steps customers take to achieve an outcome. It helps to assign a customer emotion to each step to identify how the customer is feeling. For example, Motive Communications first had to understand the journey taken by desk workers, including the tedious process of identifying a customer's software version. You may choose to develop a more simplified "storyboard" after completing your journey-line to share at a later time with customers for their feedback.

The third step is to select the biggest pain point and do a root-cause analysis (see figure 4-2). It's helpful to apply a "five whys" questioning process (developed by Taiichi Ohno, father of the Toyota production system). In most cases, we've found that asking "Why does this happen?" three times (going down three levels) is sufficient. As the Motive Communications team observed people working at the help desk, they measured the time taken by each step. They then broke out each step as a contributor to the overall time, and cost, required to serve a customer, asking, Why does this happen? They thus found out why the technicians had to gather the customer information, why they had to verify a support plan, why they had to search certain knowledge databases, and so on. You can brainstorm this information as hypotheses to be tested later, but ultimately you will need to gather it through observation (as we describe in the next section).

The fourth step is to pick a root cause to explore in greater depth because you think it's a critical reason for the customer's problem. As you develop a rootcause tree (the map of root causes uncovered by asking "Why" multiple times) for various problems, you may see that a particular root cause shows up in multiple places. This indicates an important root cause to explore. If you include customers in your pain-storming session, they can also help you identify which root causes are most important—and why. Step 5 is to create a list of questions about (or assumptions behind) the root cause—questions you need to answer through customer experiments. You can use the question-storming technique to develop the key questions, along with the customer activities or experiments that will answer the questions and validate your assumptions. 6 Motive Communications used help desk observations and stopwatches to answer their key questions.

Ethnography to Explore Assumptions Sitting in an air-conditioned conference room overlooking the sprawling city of Bogotá, the executives at Banco Davivienda became convinced they'd discovered a big problem worth solving. Although Banco Davivienda dominated the Colombian banking market, almost half the population had no bank account. Executives realized that if there was a way to tap in to this market of nonusers, they could dramatically grow their market share and help the Colombian people at the bottom of the income pyramid. They formed a cross-disciplinary team to develop an offering that would appeal to nonusers—a streamlined, easy-to-use version of existing bank accounts. After several months of hard work the bank launched the new product, and the optimistic team celebrated. Despite aggressive promotion, however, few customers adopted the new accounts. Even after several months, the team saw little growth, and by year-end they concluded that the project had failed. As team members analyzed the initial failure, they came to realize that although they had commissioned a market study and talked to a few customers, they hadn't understood the jobs to be done for the "unbanked." Rather, they had let their knowledge of existing customers and solutions distort their understanding of the problem. So the team decided to try a different approach: to go themselves into poor neighborhoods to interact with, and create profiles of, the target customers. They spent weeks living in various neighborhoods as they observed people's daily activities. Said one team member, "We decided to go out and try to understand what people wanted, not by asking directly 'what do you want,' but by trying to understand how people behave in real life without any kind of prejudice." 7 The team developed customer profiles (as described in the sidebar) of different target customers and the job-to-be-done, along with their motivations, behaviors, and other characteristics. For example, the team developed the following profile for "Martha." Martha is one of the 3 million low-income subsidy beneficiaries in Colombia. She wakes up at 2 a.m. to get ready to make the line at the bank at 3 a.m. in order to cash out her subsidy. She waits in line from five to six hours to finally get her turn, and cash the money. Then, she uses the cash to send a domestic remittance, paying a 10 percent fee for the service. In order to pay her utility bills, she will then move to a "district collections center" where she will wait in line for another two hours to get the payment done. The remaining cash will stay "under the mattress" because she hasn't had the opportunity to open a savings account due to the distance she lives from the bank and the high costs it will represent to her. 8 By building these customer profiles, the team at Banco Davivienda quickly identified the root cause of the failure of the mini bank account: it didn't directly solve any of Martha's biggest problems. In fact, Martha's main job-to-be-done was simply receiving money and making payments. Now that the team deeply understood Martha's problems, they were able to imagine a radically different solution: a mobile wallet that would allow Martha to make and receive payments from merchants directly using an account served by a mobile phone. This account, unburdened with unneeded features like an ATM card, would allow Martha to do everything by phone (including create the account) without ever having to visit a branch. Eventually the "Martha" solution that the team developed was adopted by hundreds of thousands of users. The product was then launched in several other countries targeted to customers like Martha. The Banco Davivienda team leveraged the number 1 tool for testing and validating the root causes of customers' problems: ethnography. This technique, which we might more descriptively call "fly on the wall" because that's how you do it, requires that you get deep into the lives of your customers by watching them in their natural habitat. You aren't trying to sell your solution or push your agenda. Instead, you're trying to deeply understand their activities, likes, dislikes, aspirations, challenges, and so on (see "What to Look For as a Fly-onthe-Wall"). Then, using this data, you build synthesized profiles of a prototypical customer—including his or her job-to-be-done and ways she or he currently solves it. You develop profiles for each customer segment and then use them to crystallize the biggest problem you can solve for each profile. You can take fly-on-the-wall further by actually doing the job your customers are trying to do, rather than just watching, through what we call role play research. This requires, as Intuit CEO Brad Smith suggests, that you "be the customer." Instead of watching, try to do the jobs with the current solutions whether that be riding in delivery trucks or balancing finances using software. We strongly recommend this powerful form of customer research, because you often get the most accurate and surprising insights from living the lives of your customers. What to Look For as a Fly on the Wall What to Look For as a Fly on the Wall What are you looking for when you are trying to find monetizable jobs? Start by looking for obstacles that get in the way of the jobs your customers are trying to do. Look for areas where customers are spending lots of time (time sinks) even if they don't realize it, workarounds they may have developed to solve a problem, or things that ignite their emotions. Cussing, crying, wasted hours, abandoned activities, or figurative "duct tape" where customers just make it work are great signs that customers are struggling to do the job. You might also look beyond the obstacles to the enablers that facilitate something customers want. Look for how people spend their time expressing themselves, connecting to others, or creating shortcuts. People invest time to solve needs and you may find a better way to meet that need. Lastly, don't forget to closely examine nonusers as well as extreme users. Although it can seem counter-intuitive these users can help you understand the problem more clearly than mainstream users. Most of all, look for surprises. It's easy to overlook them, because our minds try to conform what we see to fit our preexisting beliefs. But surprises provide the clues and bread crumbs to the real job-to-be-done. "Advice" Interviews A fast technique for developing your initial problem hypothesis is to interview customers using what we call the "advice" interview. Start by identifying a potential sample of customers that you think have a similar job to do. When you ask for interviews (via e-mail or cold call), always ask for advice about a specific customer problem. Advice is the magic word. In fact, you may want to mention that you aren't selling anything, just to put potential customers at ease. Then let them know you want to get their feedback on a problem you're trying to solve. Your goal is to listen and learn. Once you have interviews arranged, we suggest you ask three questions and then listen, listen, listen. These questions are as follows. 1. Quickly and clearly describe the problem you see. Describing the problem will make customers confident that you know something and will serve as an anchoring point to the conversation. Don't go to potential customers with a blank sheet and expect something to happen. 2. Ask, "Do you face this same challenge, too, or a different challenge? Tell me about it." This gives you a chance to find out whether customers really have the problem you hypothesized. If they don't, you can explore what challenges they really face. 3. Ask, "Would something like this solve that problem?" and then describe your theoretical prototype (see chapter 5). At this stage you shouldn't become too solution-focused, but discussing a potential solution will help you get better feedback on the problem. Customers react to the concrete, not the abstract. So you might think about bringing a drawing, storyboard, or PowerPoint slide to help them visualize a solution. This will help them talk about why the solution might, or might not, work to solve their problem. After five to ten interviews, patterns and trends will begin to emerge, which will allow you to test your hypothesis and change accordingly. Have You Nailed the Problem? Two Tests When ZipDx demonstrated its new teleconferencing solution, observers were surprised by the crystal-clear audio coming from the conference-call speaker. The new solution, which ZipDx described as "broadband audio," worked seamlessly with available Polycom phones and required little setup to achieve similar call quality. Despite the positive reactions, however, ZipDx couldn't seem to close any deals. Potential customers seemed interested but not enough to place an order. Like most innovators, the ZipDx team felt confident that it had found a pain point: the poor audio of conference calls. But had it really nailed the customer problem? When our team was called in to help close sales, we asked the ZipDx team members what customer problems they felt they were solving. Most answers involved vague responses about the poor audio quality of conference calls projected in a typical conference room. But when pushed, the team admitted that problem identification had come more from the ZipDx team than from customers. This led us to believe that they had built a solution before creating a customer profile and identifying the job-to-be-done. Because ZipDx had already developed a solution, it faced more constraints than if it had investigated customer problems first. So our team worked with ZipDx to use its existing customer knowledge to pain-storm a few hypotheses about the types of customers who might have a problem related to the ZipDx solution. They came up with three customer profile groups: (1) Polycom phone resellers (the original hypothesized customer), (2) voice over internet protocol (VOIP) service providers, and (3) companies attempting to capture bridging revenues. The team then identified nineteen customers by name (roughly six in each profile group) and cold-called them, leaving a voice mail about the problem ZipDx believed it was solving. Sometimes they left a second message. Then they waited to see who called back. Only five customers called back. But they had returned the cold call of a no-name company with an unknown product. Who were these people, and why did they call back? As it turned out, four of the five VOIP service providers they contacted returned the call. When the ZipDx team members described the problem and the solution (using the advice-seeking interview) and then listened, the results stunned them. VOIP service providers actually didn't care very much about audio quality—what ZipDx thought was the key feature. Instead, they struggled to differentiate themselves with reliable, easy-to-use conference-call software features. As it turns out, the ZipDx software that accompanied the "broadband features. As it turns out, the ZipDx software that accompanied the "broadband audio" had other attractive features that allowed users to schedule, join, and manage conference calls far better than most solutions on the market. These features solved the VOIP providers' most important job-to-be-done. Using this deeper understanding of the specific problems of a specific target customer, the team quickly refined its solution and the messaging to that target customer. The CEO then targeted key large customers with that profile. Within three days he closed the largest deal in company history. ZipDx was on its way to nailing a customer problem. 9 How do you know when you have nailed a problem worth solving? We recommend two tests: the cold-call test and the smoke test. In both tests, the measure of whether you have found a job-to-be-done is if customers give you their time. The Cold-Call Test One of the best tests of whether you've discovered a monetizable job is whether potential customers receiving a cold call (or e-mail) will give you their time. You start by identifying your hypothesized customer segments and their job-tobe-done. Then you reach out to each customer group via phone or e-mail (it's OK at this stage to use your contacts), briefly describe the problem, and ask for their advice on your theoretical prototype. Then observe who calls back, why they call back, and what they say. Initial call-back rates tend to be low (less than 10 percent), but we've seen some companies achieve call-back rates as high as 50 percent when they've hit on a monetizable job. Your final goal is to achieve a significant leap in the call-back rate. When people do not return your call or e-mail, it may be that you haven't clearly described the problem or haven't described a problem they care about. It's also possible you contacted the wrong customer profile or target group, or you contacted them at an inopportune time. As you work your way toward a 50 percent call-back rate, you need to ask yourself, Who returned the call (versus those who did not), and why? (If you're doing business-to-consumer e-mails, you'll achieve lower rates, so compare to the benchmark response rates for that channel.) For ZipDx most of the hypothesized customer groups did not call back. For these groups, the company needs to work through friends to get contacts with these customers and see where they went wrong. However, for one customer group, the VOIP sellers, nearly 75 percent called back—an extraordinarily high rate. The information from these customers helped the company understand the real problem it was solving. Naturally you may have to adjust the threshold depending on your context. For example, B2C e-mail return rates tend to be much lower (we all get a lot of e-mail). But ask yourself whether you're clearly and concisely describing the problem. What are the characteristics of the people who are responding? Remember, the real test that you are discovering a problem worth solving is whether people are giving you their time. The percentage of people giving you time should increase when you have discovered a monetizable job. The Smoke Test Smoke tests were first used in the 1800s by plumbers, who pushed smoke through a system to discover leaks. The idea of a smoke test proved so useful that the idea spread to engineering, instruments, and information technology, among others, as a way to test for critical flaws. We've borrowed the concept as a way to test for whether you've discovered a problem worth solving. Rather than use smoke bombs, we use a bit more smoke and mirrors to test whether customers care. To perform a smoke test, create a website, advertisement, phone number, or other channel that describes the problem, theoretical solution, and provides an option to "learn more," "buy now," "reserve now," or some other call to action. Find a way to get your smoke test in front of customers, perhaps by using Google AdWords, a print advertisement, a poster at a trade show, or another venue where you suspect customers will see the call to action. When customers activate (click, call, etc.) the call to action, they don't actually get to buy a product, but they effectively identify themselves as having an interest in the problem you are investigating. You can then follow-up to learn more about them and why they took the action. The test itself looks at the response rate (the conversion rate on the call to action), with anything higher than 5 percent suggesting that you've identified a real problem worth solving (although your early efforts won't achieve nearly this rate). But people's willingness to spend time with you and their general excitement about a potential solution will be the key indicators. You can easily use the smoke test for software or online products, but you can also use it for other services and products. For example, one of our students wanted to start a food truck, the latest rage in mobile cuisine. After learning about the regulations, including needing an inspected commissary, he wondered whether there might be a business opportunity to help would-be entrepreneurs jump this legal hurdle. Rather than write a business plan or rent a commissary, we encouraged him to conduct a smoke test. So he placed an ad in the local newspaper: "Want to start a food truck? We can help. E-mail or call . . ." That was it. Within one day our student received three calls, and by the end of the week had received more than a dozen e-mails. Perhaps more surprising, in conversations with these customers, he learned that people wanting to start food trucks didn't need his help finding a commissary or jumping through the legal hurdles. Instead, he found that the critical obstacle was affordable, lease-based access to the truck itself. His smoke test was key to discovering the problem and access to the truck itself. His smoke test was key to discovering the problem and the opportunity. Develop a Vision of the Customer Problem You Will Solve

Lastly, writing a clear statement of your vision of the customer problem can serve as a guide and an anchor as you begin to search for the right solution. It can also help unify your team and your organization around the big problem you're solving. A vision template helps you develop the articulation of your vision.

First, identify who the customer is—and who the customer is not. Use your customer profiles to define a narrow customer segment for which you will solve customer profiles to define a narrow customer segment for which you will solve a big problem. Second, describe this big problem—the most critical job-to-bedone—that you hope to address, with supporting data and insights about that problem. Third, create a short, focused vision statement for the job you will do, with supporting data. Consider the development of Amazon Lending. As described in chapter 2, Jeff Bezos has set himself up as Amazon's chief experimenter and has vocalized the grand challenge. As a result, everyone in the company recognizes the importance of searching for and generating insights. For example, every spring, the company sets aside time when any employee can propose new ideas for customer problems to solve. One new business, described in the Wall Street Journal, is Amazon Lending. 10 The original idea came from the front line: customer service representatives assisting small merchants noticed a common theme: small merchants complained about their capital constraints leading to early stockouts. The discussion of this potential problem made it all the way to Bezos, who asked a small team to explore the problem. The team started by examining the customer feedback and then talking with customers. While as a general rule, "we always put ourselves in the shoes of customers," another observer noted that "The team's goal was to understand the biggest customer need that was not being met. Once they confirmed their belief regarding what customers wanted, then they thought about how they could implement a solution to solve their challenge that will work for Amazon." To explore the need, the team conducted advice interviews and also employed ethnography: "They would call up small merchants and ask, 'Hey, would you be willing to spend an hour with us so we could get your advice?' Since some of them are here in Seattle, they would go visit them and see what they were doing and talk to them." 11 Using the data from interviews and observations, the team then developed customer profiles and made a list of problems faced by them. Team members noticed that many small merchants faced stockouts because they lacked capital. Brick-and-mortar merchants often can borrow capital for inventory using their store buildings as collateral, but online merchants don't have these kinds of assets and so cannot easily access traditional bank lines of credit. Other credit options are typically complex, and the paperwork can be overwhelming. Some of these merchants, which the Amazon team labeled "curators," carried unique items that broadened the Amazon.com product catalog. By contrast, other merchants, labeled "resellers" by the team, focused on identifying a low-cost source of common items and then providing these lower-cost options for Amazon.com buyers. These different merchant groups had some needs that were similar, and others that were different. Recognizing that Amazon could not solve every customer problem, the team wanted to focus on a specific customer group. Based on the size of the problem, the team decided the target customer was not low-volume merchants (including curators) and low-volume resellers. Rather, it was high-volume resellers that repeatedly stocked out. Their biggest problem was limited (or hard to access) capital for short-term inventory financing, as the team learned from customer interviews and observations and by examining data on how often these customers lost sales because of stockouts. Having created a clear problem statement, the team then moved to creating a vision of the job-to-be-done: quick, easy-to-access inventory financing.

With the clarity and energy of this vision statement, the team moved to the next stage: prototyping the solution. It started by brainstorming a wide variety of potential solutions, including lines of credit, loans, private label cards, and so on. Then, after exploring the challenges, and legal limitations, of each solution, the team went back to customers with a series of prototypes. The team started with theoretical prototypes to quickly get initial customer reactions, then virtual prototypes mocked up in Amazon's web lab, and finally minimum viable prototypes tested with actual customers .

With each test, the team discovered many surprises about the features customers wanted most (for example, customers wanted financing only for four to six months and not a few years; furthermore, most customers struggled initially to understand the program and the true cost of lending). Ultimately the team iterated, tested, and validated an invitation-based loan program in which Amazon uses existing data to preapprove loans and eliminate the tedious paperwork of a typical loan. After receiving the invitation, a merchant can quickly accept the loan and have funds transferred to its account with only a few clicks. Although we cannot reveal specific performance figures, the new business has provided a significant lift in sales to resellers (and transaction fees to Amazon), and the team has discovered a solution and business model.

Having nailed the problem and solution for the original customer group, the team is now working to nail the biggest problem for a different customer segment, beginning with the vision statement. "Right now the team is exploring another group of customers," said another observer. "But I can tell you they haven't touched the solution yet, not until they get more feedback from customers to make sure they are going down the right road first." 12 This Amazon Lending team understands the importance of deeply understanding the biggest problem for a specific customer segment before spending time developing a solution.

Watch Out: Incremental, Urgent Problems Create Limited Growth Large companies fall into traps when it comes to finding jobs to be done. Their existing customers often come to them with incremental problems related to their core activities. They want fewer defects, a new feature,faster service, lower price, and so on. There's always something more that customers want—and it's always urgent. So large companies—in an attempt to be responsive—try to listen to customers and end up solving their incremental problems. This creates a dilemma: Should you focus on solving the urgent problems of your existing customers? Or should you try to solve a problem for noncustomers that could create growth in the future? We all tend to choose the urgent over the important. This is a big watch out. It's not that the urgent problems of existing customers aren't important, but solving these concerns usually gives you less bang for the buck than bringing a new solution to new customers (or even a new solution to existing customers). It's a matter of diminishing returns: after you've solved the most important problem that affects the greatest number of existing customers, you then work on solving a problem for a smaller set of customers. So you must carefully consider the criteria you use in selecting problems. Disruptive innovation projects must be in the innovation project portfolio—and that means trying to solve the problems of noncustomers. Unfortunately, it's hard for prospective customers to tell you that their problem is urgent, too. First Things First Although it may feel "slower" to start with the customer problem rather than the solution, you save time by deeply understanding the customer's job-to-be-done. You avoid wasting resources in pursuit of a solution that doesn't solve a monetizable job. Your first task as a manager is to deeply understand customers and the problems you're trying to solve for them. You cannot ask customers what innovations they want, or rely on their feature requests. Instead you have to observe their jobs to be done, propose a solution, and then watch their reaction. As we like to say, innovators innovate, customers validate, and not the other way around.

CHAPTER THIRTEEN

# Solution:Awesome product

If you can increase the number of experiments you try from 100 to 1,000, you dramatically increase the innovations you produce. —Jeff Bezos, CEO, Amazon.com

WE describe how Banco Davivienda (BD) tried—and failed— to reach the large "unbanked" population in Colombia by creating simple bank accounts with lower fees. After its initial, solution-first approach failed, the bank sent teams into poor neighborhoods to understand the problem through ethnography. This fly-on-the-wall approach gave managers a deep understanding of the job-to-be-done and a vision of what the solution would have to do for customers. But how did they actually develop a solution? To get outside the box, the BD team tried some unusual things. First, the team members listed the key elements of a bank account, such as branches, accounts, debit cards, forms, signatures, paper, fees, and so on. Then they subtracted one item at a time and asked, "Can we build a business around this one item?" 1 Initially most team members scoffed. How could you build a solution using only one element? But when they suspended their disbelief, they realized that, for the unbanked, a simple solution to a specific problem might be the best approach. During their field research, teams noted that virtually everyone, including the unbanked, had cell phones. So the team studied wireless service providers and found that some companies had developed products that the unbanked would pay for, such as virally adopted games or a joke of the day. The team also began looking at other industries, such as internet retailers, to see how they provided solutions through mobile phones to a lower-income customer segment. Lastly, the team observed financial institutions in Asia, Africa, and other areas of Latin America to see how others were solving similar problems. As mentioned earlier, eventually the BD team tested a mobile phone wallet that customers could use to do one thing: receive and make payments. The new solution stripped away traditional elements such as application forms, debit cards, and so on. Customers didn't have to come into a branch to sign documents or present personal ID; everything could be done on the mobile platform. To overcome compliance and regulation issues, Banco Davivienda borrowed emerging big-data techniques to analyze typical behaviors for similar customer groups and monitor or reject atypical usage. When the team hit a substantial roadblock—how to let customers withdraw cash without adding an expensive and cumbersome ATM card program—the bank tried something highly unusual in banking but common among internet retailers: a one-time password, which, in this case, let customers withdraw cash from any ATM. Banco Davivienda's solution produced significant growth, with BD quickly enrolling more than a million users in various countries. 2 Solution-Storming to Generate Solution Options To develop its novel solution, the team at Banco Davivienda used a tool we call solution-storming (brainstorming multiple solution options) to help it search broadly for solutions before using customer tests to help it narrow the options to a single solution. Going broad in the search for a solution is a foundational principle for solution-storming—and for innovation generally. It leads to more options and combinations, and that in turn leads to novel solutions. For example, most people credit Henry Ford with developing the modern production line—an invention that allowed him to make the automobile affordable. Ford radically transformed the auto industry and American life. How did he do it? We see the production line as a "solution," but Ford actually developed it by searching broadly, borrowing ideas such as interchangeable parts (used in sewing machines, firearms, and watches), continuous-flow manufacturing (used in processing flour, canning food, and making cigarettes); and assembly-line techniques (used in meat-packing plants and breweries). 3 In similar fashion, the BD team generated solution options by first searching broadly, in part by observing practices in other industries and other countries. Starting Solution-Storming Start your solution-storm with a problem and customer vision statement like the one . As with all kinds of brainstorming, a key principle of successful solution-storming is that you don't shut down any proposed solution or solution process too early. Recall that Banco Davivienda was skeptical that subtracting the elements of a familiar solution would work. We can top that: we once had a participant in a solution-storm for Leatherman, a manufacturer of multitools and pocket knives, propose shipping a live monkey with each tool to assemble the product. It took all we could muster to not shut down that idea immediately. But then the idea turned out to be pivotal in helping the team discover a super-simple assembly— one even a monkey could do easily. To help you brainstorm solutions, we suggest you choose from a menu of techniques (see figure 5-1). You won't use all these techniques at once; instead, think of them as choices or options. Analogs: Close and Far Away Think about the possible solutions around you on a spectrum from those that are close to your industry to those that are far from your industry. Closest to you, check to see whether one of your customers has already developed a workaround. Usually, these make-do solutions are held together by figurative duct tape, but they provide insights into ways you could solve the problem. For example, one entrepreneur we interviewed initially felt discouraged when he discovered a potential customer had already developed a workaround to solve the problem. But then he licensed the solution for a small royalty and used it to build a solution and company that eventually reached a market value of well over a billion dollars. Look for analogs and complements to your existing solutions that can suggest alternative solutions (be aware that there may be novel solutions in adjacent industries). For example, one fuel cell company we studied borrowed newspaper printing techniques to print fuel cell membranes. These examples of borrowing demonstrate the power of analogs of what to do or what not to do. For example, Rent the Runway borrowed analogs from Netflix and from airline reservation systems, and Banco Davivienda borrowed analogs from internet retailers and financial institutions in other emerging markets. FIGURE 5-1 Tools for solution-storming Elements: Parts and Wholes Consider solutions in terms of parts and wholes. At one end of the spectrum, as with Banco Davivienda, subtract one element of an existing solution and try to build on it as the essential component. Or consider how you could swap in or swap out parts of a solution, as the iPod did by swapping in the movement of a combination lock to search rapidly for songs. Also think about how you could multiply, divide, or unify features. In the classic example, Gillette multiplied the blades in a razor to create a new solution. Or you can consider stealing the entire solution from another company by asking yourself questions like, "How would Amazon (or Apple, or Disney, or . . .) solve this?" Observables: Visible and Invisible Think about solutions that might be nearby but difficult to see. For example, others may have tried and failed to create the solution you seek. What can you learn from searching the graveyard of prior failures? Next, consider unrelated markets or disciplines to borrow an idea that could transform your industry. For example, ideas from biology (such as fitness landscapes or the process of variation, selection, and retention) have changed how we think about strategy and change. And look for ways to break the conventional wisdom of your industry. For example, IKEA broke the convention that furniture had to come assembled and thereby revolutionized its industry. Lastly, daydream about the future by ignoring the current technological limitations you see and imagine what the perfect solution might look like. For example, what would the perfect portable music device look like? The iPod is a great solution, but perhaps a better solution would be to allow customers to speak the song they want to listen to, say "play," and then hear it in stereo sound. How might you make something like that happen? Examining "awesome" new products is an activity that might inspire you to imagine novel solutions. Selecting Solutions to Prototype After you've generated a range of solution options, you're ready to select the most promising ideas to test with customers. Recall Intuit's experience from chapter 1: when the team voted on the "best" ideas, they tended to pick those that were easiest to understand and implement. Wendy Castleman, the innovation catalyst community leader at Intuit, comments: Project teams had truly mastered "going broad"; they were good at generating lots and lots of ideas . . . But teams did a bad job of picking the best ideas to work on because our selection criteria were generally faulty. The problem stemmed from the team voting on ideas, a classic design thinking approach . . . The ideas with the most votes get explored further. But it turns out that people often vote for what is easy to implement and familiar, and that rarely yields ideas that will surprise and delight customers. 4 Based on our observations at Intuit and other companies, we recommend you post the solution options on the wall and use the following process. First, think of the different themes or characteristics represented among the solutions, such as "ease of use" or "high performance." Then select an option from each theme to explore so that you can observe how customers respond. Second, define the proposed solutions along a dimension or spectrum. For example, one spectrum might involve ranking solutions from low to high on dimensions such as "game changing," "bold/risky," "most easily attainable," "technical difficulty to deliver." Then select solutions to test at different ends of the spectrum. This approach will help you to go broad in the solutions you test. Third, once you've selected solutions to test, write down your leap-of-faith assumptions or list them as questions to be answered. Then prioritize the assumptions based on those that you think are most important to validate in order for a solution to succeed. For example, when the Banco Davivienda team was brainstorming solutions for the unbanked, they wanted to test whether customers would sign up for bank accounts through their smart phones without visiting a branch or speaking to a person. It was critical to test this assumption for target customers, who didn't have the time or means to get to a branch. Once the critical assumptions have been made explicit, the team can design experiments (use prototypes) to test them. Four Kinds of Prototypes In a semisecret location, the Google X lab has been exploring crazy new technologies such as flying wind turbines and wifi balloons. These are the kinds of technologies, given the level of technical and demand risk, that most companies don't even consider. The first product, Google Glass, began to roll out in early 2012, with customers lining up to pay $1,500 to try a beta version. Although the success of Google Glass is anything but assured, the product development process offers lessons on prototypes. The Google Glass team originated with a project by University of Washington professor Babak Parviz. 5 Although initially an interesting technology, it became an interesting solution when the team noticed a problem: How often in social interactions people "check out" to check their smart phones. The Google X team asked, "What if you could use this technology to stay engaged with the world around you while also using the internet?" At the same time, you can imagine the immensity of the technical challenges: How could you allow someone to connect to the internet using a lightweight, touchless device? Given the technical risk, ask yourself, How long should it take the team to create the first fully operational, wearable prototype that projects live images from the internet? Ready? It took one day. In a recent presentation, Tom Chi, head of experience at Google X, described how the team created and tested the first prototype.After creating a wearable device, Chi and the team needed a way to navigate it. If you've seen the movie Minority Report, you probably remember Tom Cruise moving his hands in the air to manipulate the computer. The Google X team also saw the movie and asked, "Why not try it?" Any guesses as to how long it took to prototype the motion detection system? Ready? About forty-five minutes. Chi and the team allowed users to manipulate the device by attaching borrowed headbands (worn around the wrist) to a clicking device (made from a pencil, a binder clip, a chopstick, and a mouse) via a taut fishing line (run over the back of a whiteboard) so that any movement by the user put tension on the line and clicked the device.

The Google Glass experience shows how quickly a company can move in developing prototypes, whether hardware, software, or services. And Google Glass is not an outlier. Gmail and AdSense (Google's content-targeted advertisement product that has made billions) were each prototyped in a day. 7 Indeed, we have found that at companies like Google, Intuit, and Valve, it is typical to build a prototype in twenty-four to forty-eight hours. Although many people have heard about prototypes, few people understand the various types or know how to use them properly. Managers often go wrong by forgetting that every prototype should answer a specific question or by putting more effort into the prototype than is justified, simply because building stuff feels like progress. Based on our research and practice, we recommend four types of prototypes. Here they are, in order from the simplest—with the fastest learning cycle

Theoretical prototype Virtual prototype Minimum viable prototype Minimum awesome product

Theoretical Prototypes The number 1 thing you can do to avoid the trap of building products customers don't want is to not build anything. We're not advocating inaction. But we are advocating a theoretical prototype as a tool to help you survive the early days of innovation ambiguity without falling into the Field of Dreams trap (the "build it and they will come" myth portrayed in the film). A theoretical prototype expresses your idea as a well-structured mental image in which you outline the general shape of the solution, but not the specifics. An example of a theoretical prototype might be to ask customers, "If you could check on your house visually from your smart phone, would you want to?" The beauty of a theoretical prototype is that it's fast and cheap. You can test dozens within a week. For example, AT&T recently held a series of workshops with the members of its leadership team to build their innovation skills and consider ways to improve customer service. The attendees took fifteen minutes to solution-storm pilots or experiments to test new ways of delivering the industry's highest-quality customer experience. These were simple theoretical prototypes, such as testing a way for customers to walk into an AT&T store and make purchases without needing to interact with a human. These sessions led to the testing of a number of virtual and minimum viable prototypes during the next twelve months. By contrast we've watched many teams dive into building products based on their intuition alone before they've even tested whether anyone cared about the solution. In fact, the biggest problem for most corporations is that when they do a prototype, they do it in a complicated, expensive way, using lots of 3-D modeling and other techniques that are inappropriate at such an early stage. A theoretical prototype gives you a cheap and easy way to "test" and adapt solution concepts with customers. Generally when you talk to customers about the jobs to be done, you will use a theoretical prototype (or sometimes a hyper rapid virtual prototype) as a straw man for the conversation. At the point when you're getting enthusiastic, positive responses to your theoretical prototype from potential customers, you're ready to create a virtual prototype. Virtual Prototypes Several decades ago, IBM wanted to test an unusual solution to a common customer problem: transforming spoken words into type. A team of computer scientists and executives envisioned highly sophisticated voice recognition software that would transform dictation into text. In addition to the core software, the solution would require high-quality microphones and an adaptive algorithm to parse differences in dialect and diction. Although the technical risk seemed high, the team believed that if it could overcome the technical challenges, it would solve a huge customer problem. But before it made a big investment, how could IBM test whether customers cared about the solution? At a minimum, it seems that some primitive beta software would be needed to test whether the solution would be worth building. Instead, the IBM team hung a sheet across a room, and, when the customer spoke, a hidden typist on the other side of the sheet captured what was said and projected it on a computer screen for the customer to see. Essentially IBM "pretended" to have the solution to answer the question, "Do customers care?" 8 Like IBM and the Google Glass team, most successful managers use virtual prototypes (VPs)—"pretend-otypes"—to answer key questions while avoiding the costs of developing expensive, unwanted solutions. To develop a VP, ask yourself a simple question: If I had to sell the solution today, how could I fake it in a way that feels realistic? The answer should be a good guide for what you could develop and how fast. Our favorite VPs use PowerPoint, sketches, off-the-shelf components, or other mock-up tools. For example, PowerPoint can mimic software by creating invisible click-through hot spots to quickly simulate what might take months in development. Similarly, Kaiser Permanente faked various service innovations through a combination of storyboards and rehearsed service simulations. One observer said, "There's something magical about low-fidelity ways of trying something out. It automatically allows people to feel like they can put their fingerprint on it. The more polished, the more people feel like it's already done." 9 Whatever tool you use—including advanced tools like 3-D printers, video, or flash demos—remember that all prototypes should be designed to answer specific questions. Your VP will likely be an imperfect representation of the product, but the goal is to start answering your key questions, or hypotheses, about what customers want. By doing only the minimum to get feedback on the most relevant uncertainty you face, you speed up your learning and preserve your flexibility. The ability to learn quickly through prototypes (especially VPs) may be your most important advantage over slower rivals. In the words of one innovator, "A chess novice can defeat a master if moving twice each round." 10 Minimum Viable Prototypes When someone at social gaming giant Zynga has an idea for a new game, no one starts the process by building the game. Instead, the team members boil the idea down to five words and perform a smoke test, to see whether there is any customer interest. For example, suppose someone has an idea for a game about running a hospital. She would put up a low-cost ad on a high-traffic web page that simply says, "Ever fantasize about running a hospital?" The users who click on the link receive a brief description of the theoretical prototype and are told they will receive an e-mail when development is complete. If the ad produces enough response, Zynga designers then spend a week or less building a minimal, stripped-down version and launch it to the e-mail list. Then they see what they can learn about the solution: How many users sign up, how long they play, what features they like, what they hate, and so on. 11 This one-week test, or what has been called a minimum viable prototype (MVP), helps them learn crucial lessons about what customers actually want and guides them in deciding whether to perform another iteration or go explore different ideas. A minimum viable product has been defined as a product having the minimum feature set required to work as a stand-alone product while still solving a "core" problem (we use the word prototype rather than product as used by Eric Ries in The Lean Startup, to emphasize that your objective is to test your assumptions rather than build a product). 12 You build an MVP to rapidly test which features are most likely to drive customer purchases. It's like an exercise in archery: your goal is to hit the bull's-eye features that drive purchases and put other features on the back burner. Why? It's easy to be swamped with feature ideas that could add value. Adding features feels as if it will increase the chances customers will like the product, but actually it can decrease customers' ability to recognize how your solution solves their problem (see "Don't Forget to Go Narrow"). Worse, you waste time building features that don't motivate customers to purchase. You may not fully identify the bull's-eye in the beginning, so use the VPs and MVPs to identify those features that matter most to customers. At first, the process may feel haphazard and random. But remember that you can use many MVPs to test minimal feature sets, as quickly as you can, to get multiple points of useful feedback from target customers. Don't Forget to Go Narrow When the cofounders of an educational software company first met with the chief technology officer at the University of Southern California, his feedback on their beta product seemed fairly positive. Earlier conversations with other faculty and university officers had established a significant problem with existing learning management software. But to get a sense of how well they were solving the problem, members of the team showed the CTO their minimum viable prototype: essentially an inexpensive flash-based version of the software that highlighted the top twenty features they believed would be most valuable for educators. Then they asked a critical question: "How much would you be willing to pay for a solution like this?" Despite the CTO's early enthusiasm, his response—$2,500 per year—dimmed their hopes of building a sustainable business. But before leaving the room, they tried a tool we recommend called the $100 R&D game. 13 You ask customers to allocate $100 of an R&D budget to the features they most want. When the developers asked this question, they were surprised that the CTO allocated $80 to a simple drag-and-drop feature and then split the remaining $20 between two other features, a pattern repeated in visits to other universities. Using this data, the team crafted a new flash prototype and returned to the first CTO, this time with a minimum viable prototype that contained only three features, the most prominent being the drag-and-drop feature. What does your intuition tell you about how the CTO responded to the stripped-down prototype? In fact the CTO liked the product more and offered to license the product for $12,500 per year. By focusing on the minimum feature set, the team sold an early product with only one-tenth the features for five times the original expected price. 14 Throughout the book we emphasize the importance of diverging and going broad first, but as you develop MVPs, don't forget to converge and go narrow to really nail the solution. In addition, rather than add many features to a single prototype, it's a good idea to develop several prototypes that emphasize different key features, and see how customers react (see "Won't an MVP Hurt My Brand?"). Even testing a solution missing the key feature has power. Remember, the goal is to learn, and it's easier to learn when you're testing fewer dimensions in a single MVP. One team we worked with tested a medical device lacking the key feature they felt added value (which was also slowing FDA approval) and discovered an entirely new market that didn't actually want that "critical" feature. Won't an MVP Hurt My Brand? Some folks are concerned that offering a low-fidelity MVP to the market might damage the company's brand. For products in mature categories where customers have a developed understanding of the product and clear expectations (conditions of lower uncertainty), it's true that MVPs can be dangerous because customers will demand what Geoffrey Moore calls "the whole product solution." 15 But when companies launch new products that are not well understood, they're often adopted first by innovators who have lower expectations and are more forgiving of an MVP. Therefore, when you test your MVP with a sample of customers, you can get away with a minimal prototype. Of course, you will be embarrassed about it. In fact, as Eric Ries argues, if you're not embarrassed, you've done too much work. You didn't develop an MVP. To help allay this concern, we recommend several tactics. First, create a separate brand or sub-brand that clearly communicates the preliminary status of the product. For example, Intuit launches all MVPs with the "Intuit Labs" brand, and Google uses "Google Labs." Second, flip the liability of testing an MVP on its head by providing higher levels of service and satisfaction for the MVP test. For example, when Samsung launched an experimental refrigerator in Southern California, it offered customers a hotline with white-glove service (the company would replace the fridge and all its contents within twenty-four hours if something went wrong). An acquaintance actually participated in this experiment, and his fridge had a problem. He told us, "They responded so well to my problem that I'm only going to buy Samsung products from here on out." 16 And remember, you are testing the MVP with a sample of customers and not the entire population. You may think of a sample in terms of limited geography (e.g., a particular town), type of customer (e.g., early adopters), or a limited number of customers.

Minimum Awesome Products Once you have a minimum viable prototype and have validated your core assumptions, your next step is to develop something that customers cannot resist, something that customers love, something awesome. We first heard the term minimum awesome product (MAP) while spending an afternoon observing Intuit's globally broadcast training session for all the product designers, developers, and user-interface architects in the company. The training was focused on a single issue: What is "awesome"? Intuit had presented lean start-up training, and everyone was familiar with the concept of a minimum viable product. However, founder Scott Cook was uncomfortable with some aspects of the concept. "When you say 'minimum viable product,' engineers naturally focus on the word product. So they want to jump to building a product," says Cook. "At the early stages of a new product idea, we want our engineers to just be experimenting, answering their leap-offaith hypotheses." 17 We agree with Cook, and that's why we prefer to substitute the word prototype for product in our use of the term minimum viable prototype. But once the MVP has revealed which features are most likely to drive a customer purchase, it's time to go beyond viable and reach for awesome. The goal of a minimum awesome product is to deliver a solution that is so extraordinary on the most important dimension that it inspires positive emotion in your customers. As Scott Cook explains, "You don't want to be viable in the dimension that matters—you want to be awesome in the dimension that matters, all while maintaining an uncomfortably narrow focus." In other words, you want to identify the minimum feature set possible and then relentlessly focus on making your solution awesome on those dimensions. But what is awesome? And how do you get there? Customers describe products as awesome when they inspire positive emotions, such as creating deep satisfaction, calming anxiety, or giving confidence. Often "awesome" solutions do unexpected things that inspire positive emotion. When a product or service surprises you by doing something you didn't expect—something you may not have even thought was possible—it can evoke positive emotion and prompt you to say, "That is awesome!" Apple has often achieved awesomeness in this way. When the first iPod launched, customers said, "Wow! I can really carry my whole library of songs with me everywhere I go. That is awesome." When the first iPhone launched, many customers said, "Wow! I can do this (listen to music, take a photo, find an many customers said, "Wow! I can do this (listen to music, take a photo, find an address, etc.) on my phone. That's cool." Steve Jobs was known to say that Apple's job was not to give customers what they wanted. It was to give them what they didn't know they wanted (or needed). That's when you evoke positive emotion. Of course, that's a high hurdle. What if the product just nails the job-to-bedone perfectly but doesn't do it in an unexpected way? For example, Dyson vacuums are touted as having "twice the suction of any other vacuum." Can better suction really create positive emotion? The answer: absolutely. But the solution must be noticeably better than alternative solutions (and of course, the customer must care about suction). The solution evokes positive emotions because the customer is surprised by how much better the offering is than competitive offerings. To illustrate, Intuit identified what it thought was a problem for a large group of Americans: simple tax filers struggling to fill out their complicated tax forms. One thing Intuit learned from early experiments—using theoretical and virtual prototypes—was that simple filers often had trouble figuring out which information from their W-2 statement to plug in to their tax form. (For tips on getting the most from your experiments, see "How to Run a Good Experiment.") So the Intuit designers tested an MVP that let filers take a photo of their W-2 form with their cell phone or camera and upload it to their computer; then the software pulled the data from the W-2 into the right location on the tax form. Tests showed that filers loved the idea of taking the photo and having the data magically appear at the right location. But they didn't like the ensuing steps of uploading it to their computer, because it was both time-consuming and complex. "Why can't I just take the picture of the W-2 and finish my taxes on my phone?" many asked. Intuit listened, creating a prototype that took the W-2 photo, plugged the data into a tax app, and quickly completed the taxes (after asking the user a few basic questions) on the smart phone. This dramatically cut the time and complexity of tax preparation for the simple filer. Initial tests revealed that the app, dubbed SnapTax, let simple filers take the photo and finish and file their taxes in less than ten minutes (something Intuit touted in ads). That was unexpected. And it evoked strong positive emotional responses from users. One early user of SnapTax gave it a five-star rating, gushing that it was so easy to use he literally completed his taxes during a Valentine's Day date. The couple were so happy to be finished with their taxes they had one of their best dates ever. Can you imagine a tax preparation product inspiring that kind of a response from a user? To develop a minimum awesome product, Intuit focused on simple filers (some 59 million people), identified the key pain points, and then persisted in searching for a solution to that pain in an unexpectedly easy way. Of course, minimum awesome products start out as satisfactory MVPs. In fact, with the first smart phone version of SnapTax, more than 90 percent of users abandoned the app after three touches on the phone. Why? It was because "the first screens required people to create an account with name, password, et cetera," says SnapTax product development head Amir Eftekhari. "But users just wanted to check out the app to see how it worked. They didn't want to create an account." 18 So Intuit redesigned the app so that within three touches, users could see the three steps to complete their taxes and capture a photo of their W-2 to start the process. Account setup, and payment, wasn't necessary until the user was ready to file—but that was typically within ten minutes. The point is that you use the MVPs to quickly improve those dimensions of your solution that can inspire emotion—and turn your MVP into an MAP—a Minimum Awesome Product. As you refine your prototype, remember that your customers are hiring your solution to do a job for them—and that every job has functional, social, and emotional dimensions. Your solution may inspire awesome by doing the unexpected on any of these three dimensions of the job. But beware: it can be difficult to be awesome to everyone. Stay "uncomfortably narrow" as you build your minimum awesome product. How to Run a Good Experiment Most people believe they understand experimenting, but when we teach executives and students, 90 percent of the time they get it wrong at first. What are the mistakes they make? No hypothesis or metrics. Don't conduct an experiment without a clear hypothesis or without defining how you will measure what you learn. Wrong tools. Don't rely on focus groups. They tend to get stuck in groupthink. And avoid starting with surveys. You don't yet know what questions to ask. Bad samples. Make sure you talk to a relevant sample of customers. Often experimenters pick the wrong people (for convenience), or they talk to everyone (the population). Also, don't reformulate your solution between every conversation; wait for a pattern to emerge, and then reformulate. In contrast, good experiments test the most important assumptions quickly, reliably, and affordably on a relevant customer sample. And they measure the results. Consider the following simple experiment at Intuit. The finance operations team wanted to retain small-business subscription customers whose credit cards were about to expire. It had been sending e-mails to these customers, but a large percentage didn't respond and when credit cards lapsed, the income stream from a customer was typically lost. So the team, looking for a better way, wanted to verify that customers were receiving the e-mails and whether the e-mails were effective at triggering a response. "The idea was to call customers to see if they had received our communication and get them to take action immediately, instead of putting it off—small-business people are busy folks who forget about things that aren't urgent," said Wendy Castleman, an Intuit innovation catalyst. So the team ran an experiment to test the hypothesis that many customers weren't getting Intuit's e-mail. When team members called a dozen customers selected because they represented different customer segments, they discovered that about a quarter had an outdated e-mail address and weren't getting the e-mails. Others didn't feel the urgency with an email communication. The team then tried another experiment: they hired a small team of temp workers to call businesses as their credit cards came due for renewal. The new communication process resulted in more than $8 million in recovered revenues in FY2013. This experiment quickly tested a clear hypothesis, using customer behavior as the data, with clear metrics of success. Although this experiment worked out, Intuit has conducted hundreds of experiments in which the team quickly learned what doesn't work and why, and pivoted to explore other ideas. Have You Nailed the Solution? Three Tests Using virtual prototypes and MVPs can be an illuminating but ambiguous process. How do you know if you have it "right," the kind of solution where people say, "Wow, they really nailed it"? There are a few tests we recommend that you can use to "nail it, then scale it" rather than the other way around.

The Wow Test If you're in the early days of theoretical or virtual prototypes, we recommend the wow test to measure how excited customers are about your solution. The wow test has two parts. First, qualitatively, when you show customers your prototype, can you see their enthusiasm, or are they only being polite? If you can't see the enthusiasm in their faces or hear it in their voices, then you probably need to make a change. Second, quantitatively, ask customers, on a scale of 1 to 10, how excited would you feel to own the solution (10 being "extremely excited" and they're ready to buy the solution, and 1 being not at all excited)? You should be aiming to improve the wow score over time, shooting for an average greater than 7. Anything significantly lower than 7 may suggest customers are only being polite and you need rethink your solution. 19 The NPS Test Once you have an MVP or MAP that customers can start using, you can apply the promoter test. There are a few variants on this test, our favorite being the net promoter score (NPS). Recall that NPS is based on a single question: how likely are you, on a scale of 1 (not at all likely) to 10 (extremely likely), to recommend this product or service to a colleague or friend? "Promoters" answer 9 or 10, "passives" answer 7 or 8, and "detractors" answer from 1 to 6. A company's (or product's) NPS is the percentage of promoters minus the percentage of detractors.

Your ultimate goal is to score 9 or higher with your core customer group. But you won't start there, so don't get discouraged. Instead, use the prototypes we've discussed to iterate there. When 80 percent or more of your core customers rate a solution 9 or 10 and your average NPS is higher than 60 percent, then you've not only nailed the solution but also created evangelists for your product. Notice, too, that we said "core" customer group, and not all your customers: one of your too, that we said "core" customer group, and not all your customers: one of your greatest challenges is to stay narrowly focused on a customer group. Ten customers may ask you for dozens of features that can pull you in multiple directions. As mentioned earlier, if you try to please everyone, you will never nail the solution or turn your customers into evangelists. As you get feedback on your prototypes, look for the themes that segment customers into groups based on the functional, social, and emotional dimensions of the job-to-be-done, and then remove some customers from your focus (tell yourself you'll serve them later). For example, when Google engineer Paul Buchheit was building a prototype of Gmail he was told to find one hundred "happy" users. "I was like, 'Oh, that's easy, Google has like thousands of employees,'" said Buchheit. But it turns out that happiness is a really high bar, and to get people to say they're happy is actually sort of challenging. We literally did it one user at a time. We would go to people and ask, "Okay, what's it going to take to make you happy?" And in some cases they would ask for something really hard, and we'd be like, "Okay, well, you're not going to be happy with Gmail, quite possibly ever." But with other people it turned out there would be something really small we could do and then they'd be happy. So we'd do the really easy things until we got 100 people who were happy. And 100 doesn't sound like a lot but it turns out people are pretty similar to each other so if you can make 100 happy, you can usually make more [happy]. 20 So start by shooting for a 9 or 10 NPS score with ten people, and then you can think about progressing to the hundredth.

The Payment Test The ultimate test of whether you've nailed the solution is that people will pay you for it. Understandably, some managers may be afraid to ask the hard questions about whether customers (or end users) will pay. But delaying the question delays discovery of whether you have a viable solution. We've seen many instances when potential customers responded enthusiastically to prototypes, but when it came time to open their wallets, they lost their enthusiasm. In other cases, we've seen customers prepay for a product that doesn't yet exist. In one of our favorite examples, Coin (a single card device that stores multiple credit cards) presold millions of cards that weren't delivered until a year later. In truth, its story is nothing special: crowd-funding—which resulted in more than $5 billion in transactions in 2013—employs a form of the payment test in which funders prepay for an item. 22 At the core, the payment test involves asking customers to pay for your solution, whether or not you actually collect the money. In most cases you conduct the payment test during the MVP stage or later. During the test, you need to get a credible commitment from customers. Just asking customers whether they will pay yields weak results. Actual behavior counts. For example, Intuit gives testers of its prototypes the opportunity to preorder or purchase using a credit card. After testers enter the first four numbers, a message pops up saying their contact information has been registered and they'll be contacted to purchase the product after it has passed final testing. At this point, we should clarify a critical point: we are not asking you to go out and sell. Although that may sound contradictory, selling often reinforces a one-way communication pattern that shuts down your openness to feedback. Rather, when you conduct the payment test, keep in mind you're actually seeking customers' feedback. If your customer prepays, wonderful! But if customers hesitate or stall, then view that as a good outcome, too: it gives you the opportunity to directly ask customers what is still missing from the solution. Don't wait too long to apply the payment test, because it's the ultimate test of whether your solution does the job. We've heard too many stories from managers who delayed the payment test, only to realize much later that their solution was neither viable nor awesome.

A Solution Process Template To map the process you'll use to nail the solution, consider applying the solution process template The template reflects the approach we've suggested, starting with a solution-storm that generates a wide range of solutions. Then select several solution options to rapidly test with customers using theoretical prototypes. Then use the wow test to identify which solutions attract the most attention. Next, develop at least three virtual prototypes that embody different aspects of the solution, and test them with customers. Eventually you will converge to one virtual prototype using the tests described here, and you can develop it into a minimum viable prototype. Once you reach the MVP stage, you should use the NPS or payment test to determine which key features to highlight and perfect as you iterate your way to a minimum awesome product.

Large companies develop core competencies that are key to their success. And executives are often encouraged to stick to their knitting—to apply the competencies that got the company to where it is now. But large companies that stick to their knitting face a big watch out. Although there are a handful of companies that have strayed from their core competencies and failed, there are mountains of cases in which companies, in times of uncertainty, stuck to their knitting and missed a huge opportunity or were killed by innovation. Going beyond your current competencies is important for another reason: people typically develop new solutions by combining technologies and ideas from different fields. This means that a broad search typically outperforms a narrow search in generating solutions. While it feels more efficient to search narrowly within the company.

Searching a broad range of technologies and firms (possibly through alliances) is critical for large companies if they hope to solve new problems and enter new markets. Amazon is one of the few large companies we know that has developed a broad range of technologies internally—and with other firms in partnership—that it draws on to generate solutions to help it enter new businesses.

Getting to Awesome Some 90 percent of initial proposals don't nail the solution to a significant problem. This explains why it's folly to start by building a product or service before you've discovered how it falls short. It also explains why it's important to know how to test many options by using prototypes. Adopting solution-storming and prototyping will minimize your investment, accelerate your learning, and allow you to test the assumptions that can kill your idea. We encourage you to use the cycle of searching broadly and then creating theoretical, virtual, and minimum viable prototypes, along with a minimum awesome product, to test your hypotheses and answer crucial questions. Remember to design your prototypes to answer specific questions and to use clear metrics to assess them. Embrace the freedom of using prototypes to validate your solution as the key to success under conditions of uncertainty.

CHAPTER FOURTEEN

# Go To Market Strategy

GODREJ & BOYCE MANUFACTURING is a 115-year-old company that sells consumer goods in India, most notably household appliances. For years it succeeded by bringing technologies developed abroad, such as refrigeration, to the wealthiest segment of the population. But as low-cost competitors from elsewhere in Asia entered India, Godrej's market share began to erode rapidly. As company leaders looked for ways to respond, they discovered a surprise that had the kernel of a problem worth solving: 80 percent of Indian households lack refrigeration. As a company run for more than a century according to the best Bschool thinking, it immediately leapt to developing solutions. As Navroze Godrej, director of special projects, recalls, "We imagined we would be making a shrunken-down version of a refrigerator. Make it smaller, make it cheaper. And we had preconceived notions of how to build a brand that resonated with these users through big promotions and fancy ad campaigns.

The Godrej team, with the help of Innosight (an innovation consulting firm cofounded by Clayton Christensen), quickly learned the error of a solution-first approach and instead decided to first try to understand the problem. To start, team members traveled all over India and were shocked by how wrong their initial guess had been. As Navroze Godrej recalled, it was a "long and fascinating journey. We were surprised by many things, we were shocked by many things." 2 As they talked to customers they realized that women managing households in rural India faced many challenges. One was that they could not store food, so they had to buy and prepare it every day, something that was timeconsuming and expensive. Moreover, most potential customers had intermittent power, and that would rule out a standard refrigerator like they initially imagined. Furthermore, if the refrigerator broke down, the cost of repair would likely be prohibitive, because there were few local repair shops or servicers, especially in rural areas. As Navroze Godrej recalled, "[W]ith all this information we realized our original hypothesis was quite wrong. We knew we couldn't just repackage and reconfigure an existing refrigerator and just pass that off." 3 Based on their understanding of the customers' jobs to be done, the team decided to tackle the problems faced by lower-income women. As they explored solutions, they tested a number of virtual prototypes and minimum viable prototypes and discovered the crucial features for any solution. For example, the customer group they were targeting needed much less space than that found in a traditional refrigerator. The target customer simply couldn't afford to buy, and store, large amounts of food. They also learned that the refrigerator needed a battery to operate during power outages, and given the 90 degree or higher heat in some regions of India, it would be critical to minimize cooling loss when the door was opened. So the team iterated to a solution more akin to a cooler: the chotuKool opened at the top, preventing cold air loss, and cooled by using solid-state thermoelectric technology rather than the familiar refrigerator coolant. Furthermore, they placed all components, including the battery, in the lid so that they could easily be removed for servicing.

Because the team appeared to have nailed the problem and solution, most companies would assume it had succeeded and would assimilate the product into its existing business model—its approach to communicating with and capturing value from customers. Unfortunately, such an assumption often kills innovations. For example, Godrej originally assumed that it could simply "launch the product the way we used to with a big advertising campaign." 4 But as team members talked to customers, they realized that for their women customers, their local community and support groups played a much more powerful role in their purchasing decisions. If the chotuKool team was to succeed in convincing women to buy the product, it needed to find out how to communicate with these women. The team conducted a number of business model experiments. In one test of the business model, it "launched" the new chotuKool (which means "little cool" in Hindi) at a village fair attended by more than six hundred women and the local support groups. It was in the discussions at the fair that the team discovered how best to communicate with this customer segment (which message, which channels). They also discovered that, given the low household incomes among their target customers, the price of chotuKool would probably need to be less than $50 USD—and even then a large percentage would need financing. This pricing constraint meant that the traditional appliance supply chain (which had been operating for fifty years) did not work well for distributing a low-cost, low-margin product to customers in rural areas having few appliance stores. The team experimented with several approaches, talking to as many people and experts as possible to find ways to solve the problem. Finally, the people and experts as possible to find ways to solve the problem. Finally, the team had a breakthrough when G. Sunderraman, Godrej vice president and leader of the chotuKool project, sat next to a university vice chancellor on an airplane. As Sunderraman talked to the vice chancellor about obtaining application forms for his youngest son, the university official pointed out that Sunderraman could get the forms at any post office. The next day, when Sunderraman went to the post office and asked for the forms (which the post office offered for a fee), what surprised him was the helpful clerk, who then promoted several other universities and their accompanying application forms. It dawned on Sunderraman that the post office—which had offices in every area of rural India—might be an ideal distribution channel for chotuKool. In further discussions in the field, the Godrej team also learned about the central importance of the post officer in rural villages, where the postal representative is treated like a trusted friend and may even be invited into the house for tea. At this moment the team realized that it could effectively turn postal officers into the sales channel and leverage the post office to create an entirely new distribution chain, which, in combination with a novel microfinancing scheme, would allow Godrej to distribute, sell, and make money from chotuKool, all while improving the lives of local villagers. 5 The chotuKool story shows that even after nailing the problem and the solution, the team's job was not finished. They had to develop the business model that would allow them to successfully take the solution to market. In this chapter we will focus on how to validate the unique go-to-market strategy for your innovation projects. Validate Each Component of the Business Model The term business model refers to a firm's overall strategy for delivering value to—and capturing value from—customers. The most important dimension of a business model is the solution—the value proposition—that a firm offers to a target segment of customers. Once you've nailed the solution to an important problem for a particular group of customers, you're ready to test and validate the other critical components of a business model to build an effective, data-driven go-to-market strategy. Several tools are available to help you think through the dimensions of a business model. One of our favorites is the Business

Model Canvas template, developed by Alex Osterwalder and Yves Pigneur. The template shows nine business models components, starting with the value proposition. We highly recommend these authors' excellent book Business Model Generation for a deeper exploration. 6 From our experience and research we've identified six business model components—a subset of the template—that you need to validate when you're taking your value proposition to market.

We refer to this as a business model snapshot -

The six components of the business model snapshot are as follows. 1. Value proposition (solution). What is the solution that you're offering to provide value to your target customer segment? (The value proposition emerges from your earlier efforts to nail the problem and solution.) 2. Pricing strategy. How should you price your solution to optimize revenue streams and generate profits? How much are customers willing to pay? How do they prefer to pay? 3. Customer acquisition: relationships. How can you communicate with and convince your target customers that they need your solution? 4. Customer acquisition: channels. How do you make it easy for customers to access your solution? Through which channels do your target customers most want to be reached? 5. Cost structure: activities. What key activities do you, or your partners, need to perform well in order to deliver your solution? 6. Cost structure: resources. What resources or assets are most critical for delivering your solution? Fortunately, once you've developed an awesome solution, you know the value proposition you want to offer. Now you're ready to explore and validate the proposition you want to offer. Now you're ready to explore and validate the other five components. We recommend starting with pricing strategy so that you can figure out your customers' willingness to pay and the kinds of revenue streams you will likely generate to cover your costs. The next step is to figure out your customer acquisition and education strategy and the channels you will use. Succeeding here requires a deep understanding of the customer consumption chain (described later). Then you turn to figuring out which activities are most critical. These activities may be conducted internally or with partners. You also need to determine which resources (assets such as brands, patents, installed base, physical locations, plant and equipment, etc.) are most important and how you can effectively access or build them. The emergent chotuKool business model snapshot would look something like figure 6-4. The chotuKool product required a different business model because it targeted a new customer—low-income women—with a value proposition that solved a significant problem. This new business model demanded a low price, paid either at purchase or under a microfinanced payment plan. It also required new customer acquisition, using women as a communication channel and the post office as a distribution and communication channel. Finally, it required new activities (low-cost manufacturing) and resources (solid-state thermoelectric cooling and batteries). The completed business model snapshot describes how chotuKool creates and captures value To underscore the importance of validating each of your assumptions with customers in a world of uncertainty, in launching the chotuKool, the team actually discovered a new customer segment: vendors of items like cold soda or chocolate in hot climates. Many sales have shifted to this new customer segment. Serving these customers uses some of the same resources but requires a new approach to customer acquisition. The business model snapshot is a template to capture your hypotheses: what you believe to be true about the business model. Writing down your hypotheses at the beginning, as at any other stage of the innovator's method, will help you focus on asking the right questions, running the right tests, and recognizing whether you've validated the assumption. Your goal should be a validated business model snapshot like the chotuKool example.

Nail Your Pricing Strategy We recently advised a team that was developing wireless pulse oximetry socks, which allow parents to monitor their infant's breathing during the night in hopes of preventing tragedies like sudden infant death syndrome. The team members followed our process to identify the problem, first interviewing and observing nurses and mothers to understand the problem and then using a smoke test to gauge customer interest. In the smoke test, the team posted a video on its website describing how the product—which didn't yet exist—worked to see whether customers cared about the idea. By accident, the smoke test generated national media coverage, along with e-mails from more than five hundred parents asking to buy the product immediately. Convinced it had found a problem worth solving, the team started prototyping solutions, first using theoretical prototypes to discuss with experts and customers, then using virtual prototypes—simple drawings of the product—to show parents as they came out of stores like Babies 'R Us, and then finally minimum viable prototypes that they tested with infants and parents. As the team members gained confidence that they were converging on a solution, they asked, "What price can we consistently charge?" As a first step, they sent a survey asking potential customers how much they would be willing to pay. Surveys are not the ideal way to figure out how to price a product, because buyers typically don't tell the truth about their willingness to pay. Because you're facing uncertainty, the sooner you can observe customer behaviors, the better. That being said, what people say they will pay gives you a starting point for your pricing hypothesis, and you can later observe their behavior. For the pulse oximetry socks, most survey respondents stated they would expect to pay around $100. Unfortunately, given the estimated costs of production and the margin required by wholesalers and retailers, that price would leave little room to produce the device at a profit. Rather than give up, we suggested the team look at customers' actions, rather than their words, comparing what they actually pay for a product that solves a similar problem. So the team members drove to the nearest Babies 'R Us and checked the prices on baby monitors, finding that most were priced higher than $200. Furthermore, when they asked the store clerks which products sold in highest volume, the clerks reported that most parents bought the more expensive monitors. Intrigued, the team then called thirty-one other stores around the nation and found the same thing: most parents bought the more expensive baby monitors. more expensive baby monitors. Using the information from the survey and the price comparison of close substitutes, the team then conducted a payment test experiment. On its website it listed the baby monitor at different prices (starting with higher prices and then moving to lower prices) and displayed a "Buy Now" button. When customers selected the button, they were told they would be put on a preorder list and notified when the product became available. Using data from this payment test, the team estimated the price elasticity of demand (how the number of purchases changes as the price changes) by observing customers' actions—their actual purchase behavior. The team learned that a price around $200 would maximize revenue streams while leaving plenty of margin for profit. The Price Sensitivity Meter Tool The team roughly followed a process that we recommend for testing your pricing hypothesis. The first step is to look at the price of current solutions that are the closest substitutes for yours. Potential customers will use those solutions as price reference points, and you can use these prices as a reference point for your initial pricing hypothesis. Second, create a price sensitivity meter (PSM) using a customer survey to further refine your initial pricing hypothesis. Developed by Dutch economist Peter van Westendorp, a PSM lets you estimate optimal pricing by surveying target customers. We suggest a simplified version of the traditional PSM approach that involves two price-related questions: 1. At what price would you consider the product to be so expensive that you would not consider buying it? (Too expensive) 2. At what price would you consider the product to be priced so low that you would feel the quality couldn't be very good? (Too cheap) The standard method requires that the percentage of respondents indicating a specific price is "too expensive" or "too cheap" are plotted as cumulative frequencies. A PSM analysis for the innovator's DNA selfassessment, an assessment of an individual's innovation and execution skills that was developed by Jeff Dyer and Hal Gregersen. 7 You graph the "too expensive" line by plotting the percentage of respondents who said a particular price was too expensive. The "too cheap" frequency is plotted starting at 100 percent of those who find a particular price too cheap and then eventually going down to zero at higher prices. The intersection of the two lines reveals the optimal price point (OPP). This is the price (in this case, $44) at which the number of consumers who rated the product too expensive equals the number rating it too cheap. It is the equilibrium price between customers' not buying the product and doubting its quality.

The bottom line is that a PSM analysis can give you a reasonable range of prices to test with your payment test and a proxy for your ultimate goal: discovering the demand curve where you can garner the greatest revenue and profit. In the case of the innovator's DNA assessment, the estimated optimal pricing was $44. Although this example is for product-based pricing, it can be done for subscription pricing, licensing, upsells, and so on. 8 Once you have a reasonable range of prices, you conduct a payment test to validate your hypothesis. The pulse oximetry team conducted a payment test through its website, but it also tested simply by standing outside Babies 'R Us with pictures of the product, including prices, and asked customers whether they would preorder. If you do this with three sets of one hundred randomly selected target customers using three price points, you will have the data to estimate how demand will change at different price points, what economists call the price elasticity of demand. As you conduct the test, consider the advantages of starting with a price higher than the OPP and then gradually move to test a price lower than the OPP. As you apply the pricing tool, remember you're trying to discover the price at which you can create a repeatable business model, which requires a price at which you can make profit (and leave extra margin in that price for the inevitable errors).

Scott Cook generated the insight for Quicken, Intuit's first product, while sitting at his kitchen table while his wife complained about the hassle of manually keeping track of their finances. (The table is now at Intuit's headquarters, and Cook regularly sits there to meet with employees.) With an insight into a potential problem, Cook spent the next several months exploring the problem by discussing his hypothesis with potential users. When he became convinced that easing the tasks of bill payment and personal finance was a big problem to solve, he partnered with Tom LeFevre to develop a solution. The duo did an excellent job of testing multiple prototypes with customers to nail the solution. For example, Cook famously lugged a computer to a meeting of the Junior League of Palo Alto and challenged the participants, many of whom had never used a computer, to write a check in less than fifteen minutes using his prototype software. Some users were so unfamiliar with computers that they had to be told where to find the Enter key. But when even these users were able to print a check using Quicken, Cook felt he had nailed the solution and was ready to take it to market. At the time, consumer software was sold primarily in large retail outlets like CompUSA, and the typical customer acquisition strategy was to mount a big advertising campaign. With this typical model in mind, Cook went to venture capitalists in Silicon Valley to raise money. To his surprise, the venture capitalists turned him down. Even though initial tests showed that Quicken was far easier to use than other financial software solutions, the doubters pointed out that Quicken would be the forty-third financial software package in a crowded market. Not dissuaded, Cook approached retail outlets directly. He recalls the ominous feeling as he approached the door of one store and noticed a large bin of software titles marked "90% Off" just outside the door. When he asked the retailer to sell Quicken, the manager simply pointed to the discount bin and said, "These were the titles I decided to sell." 9 Increasingly desperate, Cook tried to stir up PR for the new PC-based software and succeeded in generating several articles, but few sales resulted. Finally, as company funds dwindled, in a bid to sell some software Cook approached a friend at Wells Fargo about selling Quicken in its branches. Although this did generate some sales, it was not enough to cover costs, and soon Intuit's CFO approached Cook with the bad news: they had less than $100 in the bank. It was over. Cook returned all the office furniture and, for desks, used pieces of plywood on top of stacked copies of Quicken. When the landlord began nosing around, asking why they didn't have furniture, Cook dodged the question, saying they were redecorating. Cook then tried, and failed, to place Quicken in more retail banks while LeFevre raced to code an Apple-based version of the software in hopes of selling a few more copies. The end of the company seemed imminent. Then a surprising thing happened: when the Apple software hit the Wells Fargo branches, Cook started to get phone calls from customers wanting to buy the software. Surprised, he asked how they found out about it, and callers replied they had read about it in a magazine featuring new Apple software titles. Call by call, Cook pieced together what he and LeFevre had missed: although they had put a good deal of effort into promoting the PC-based version, most PC customers used their computers in their businesses. In contrast, people who wanted personal finance software used Apple computers at home. Furthermore, these users found out about, and were influenced to purchase, new software based on reviews in a few key software magazines. With this deeper understanding of customers and their preferred way to learn about and purchase software, Cook scraped together $125,000 and ran a big advertising campaign in the Apple software magazines his target customers read. The phones soon rang off the hook, and Quicken quickly became the number 1 personal financial software in the United States. 10 The Consumption Chain Tool Intuit's experience is not unusual. Like Intuit, many companies develop an innovative solution to an important problem, but they have a hard time communicating and distributing the solution to customers. Because established companies already have a familiar business model, they often fail to realize that, for an innovative product, they often need a different business model—one that includes new ways to communicate with customers. It's critical to develop a relationship with, and a channel to, customers. Success usually requires testing a number of messages, at different points in the consumption chain, with different channel options. Channel options include a direct-to-customer website or a sales force, distributors (such as pharmaceutical distributor McKesson), focused retailers (Wells Fargo, Best Buy, Zappos), mass merchandise retailers (Walmart, Amazon), original equipment manufacturers (such as General Motors), or value added resellers (e.g., system integrators like IBM and Accenture). Fortunately for Intuit, Cook was persistent in experimenting with different channels and different customer acquisition strategies. His initial guesses about the best channel to the customer were wrong —and it almost killed the company. But as he continued to test channel options, he developed a deeper understanding of how customers find out about, decide to use, and purchase personal finance software. A tool that can be extremely helpful for understanding your target customer and developing a customer acquisition strategy is the consumption chain—a term popularized by Ian MacMillan and Rita McGrath. 11 The consumption chain is the series of steps through which customers pass from the time they first become aware of a need for your solution, to evaluating your solution (relative to others), to purchasing, using, and even staying connected to it.

Ten Questions to Ask about the Consumption Chain To help you understand the factors that influence customer acquisition, here are ten questions you should ask. Awareness 1. How do customers become aware of a need for your product or service? Is there a way to make it easier or more convenient for them to find your offering? Evaluation 2. What is your product really used for? What job is the customer hiring your product to do? 3. What does the customer ultimately consider the most important features when making a final product selection? (If they had 100 points to allocate across all the features they consider important, how would they allocate them?) 4. Which influencers (reference customers, critics, experts, press, media, peers, direct referrals) are most likely to influence the customer's evaluation of your product? Purchase 5. How do consumers order and purchase your product? Is there a way you can make it easier, less costly, or more convenient to buy? How is your product delivered? Can you do it faster, cheaper, or in a different way? Use 6. What frustrations do your customers have when trying to use your product? Do they use your product in ways you didn't expect? 7. What do customers need help with when they use the product? 8. Do customers do things that hurt the longevity or reliability of your product? 9. How is your product repaired, serviced, disposed of? Are there opportunities to make this easier or more convenient (or teach the customer how to use the product so that it requires less maintenance, or do self-maintenance)? Connection 10. How might customers connect to and promote your product? How could you leverage customers' connections to each other to influence parts of the consumption chain for your customers and noncustomers? Scott Cook's experience with customer acquisition at Intuit illustrates the importance of understanding how target customers become aware of and evaluate new products, which lies at the heart of your unique go-to-market strategy for your innovation. Just getting Quicken into various channels wasn't enough. The consumption chain reminds you that you first need to generate awareness and favorable evaluation before you will acquire a single customer (see "The Customer

Influence Pyramid" for more about how to create awareness, and positive evaluation, of your product through influencers). Even if you have the right channel, it can be challenging to create awareness, positive evaluation, and purchase. Consider Merck, which launched a new serotonin reuptake inhibitor (SSRI), an antidepressant. In the crowded market, the new drug, although performing essentially the same task as Prozac via the same chemical mechanism, fared poorly, and initial revenues were disappointing. Merck returned to the drawing board to explore the customer need from the perspective of physicians who prescribe the product as well as consumers who felt depressed, worried, or anxious. Through extensive interviews with physicians and customers, the company learned that before the decision to prescribe or purchase, physicians as well as consumers associated certain products with certain labels. For example, Prozac was closely associated with the "depression" label. As a result, when patients came into the office complaining of depression, physicians often intuitively leaped to prescribing Prozac (in part because patients requested it based on the recommendations of friends and family).

What's more, sometimes you can't use an existing distribution channel. You need to create a new one, as Godrej did for chotuKool. But note that Godrej didn't create the distribution channel from scratch. Instead, it piggybacked on the activities and resources of the Indian post office. In other cases, companies have built their own distribution channels. For example, Cemex did this in the late 1990s when it discovered that its distributors were not effectively meeting the needs of its poorest customers. After adopting a radical approach to understanding customers—literally living with the poorest customers for several months—the Cemex team realized that customers didn't really want the solution it had been selling: bags of cement. Instead they wanted houses built with cement, which Cemex distributors either could not or did not want to provide (many distributors actually engaged in corrupt practices that damaged product quality). The Cemex team developed its own distribution channels to deliver cement, advice, and financing to customers—products and services that allowed customers to do the job of building a house. In this way, Cemex achieved significant growth in what had appeared to be an unattractive market. The Customer Influence Pyramid Most managers who have a marketing background understand that we rarely directly influence customers; their purchase decisions are influenced by many other forces. The customer influence pyramid complements the consumption chain by mapping influence forces.

The forces closest to the company represent those you have most control over, and those closest to the customer represent forces that have the most influence over the customer purchase decision. At the level closest to you, partners include channel partners, resellers, and complementors that sit on your side of the table and attempt to sell to customers. Although you have greater influence over their message, the message typically has less impact on customer purchases compared with other influences. For example, Godrej could have worked with appliance stores as partners in selling chotuKool, and together they could have stores as partners in selling chotuKool, and together they could have marketed the benefits of the product to customers, but this likely would have been less effective than getting respected women to be advocates. Next, as a company you may construct marketing messages in the form of advertising, promotions, and social media blasts, but they typically have a modest influence on the customer purchase decision. We cannot cover the science of optimizing these campaigns, and it may be irrelevant; when you face uncertainty, the key idea is to understand what your customers pay attention to and the elements of the job-to-be-done (social, emotional, functional, etc.) that they want to accomplish. Using these two elements you can design a customer acquisition strategy that works because you target the customer's job-to-be-done in the channels they pay attention to. Influencers can profoundly shape customer decisions. Influencers fall into four categories: experts such as product reviewers, thought leaders, or product evaluators; peers such as bloggers, customer reviews, and forum discussions; media and press, whose attention shapes customer perception; and reference customers, who create legitimacy and comfort with your solution in customers' minds. For Godrej, the key influencers proved to be prominent women in the local community—socially central individuals. For other companies, these influencers may be online or in the real world. For example, Skull Candy made a successful business of branding headphones and then sponsoring extreme athletes to wear them, thereby influencing other customers to buy them. Understanding and managing your influencers can be keys to success. Everyone understands that word-of-mouth recommendations from someone you know and trust have the greatest influence on individual purchase decisions. Having a solution that delights customers is the best way to get word-of-mouth referrals. But you should explore different ways to create word of mouth using the principles we've discussed. For example,

Dropbox relied on an intuitive but ultimately costly approach to acquire early customers, paying almost $300 on AdWords to capture subscribers, who ultimately paid only $100 in annual fees. As Dropbox experimented, it discovered it could more effectively acquire customers by offering current users free storage space to invite new users, a promotion that cost pennies on the dollar while increasing the virality of the solution.

As you try to acquire customers, pay attention to your customer acquisition costs. As a rule, customer acquisition costs should be less than one-third of customers' lifetime value, leaving plenty of room for the inevitably inaccurate assumptions one makes under uncertainty. As your innovation matures, you can move from simple metrics such as customer acquisition costs or virality to an optimization approach, measuring the funnel of customer acquisition, activation, retention, referral, and revenue.

Once you've figured out your value proposition (solution), pricing strategy, and customer acquisition strategy, you're closing in on a scalable business model. The final challenge is to determine the right cost structure—the key activities and resources—for delivering your solution. Key activities are those processes the firm or its partners must engage in to operate successfully—from software design to manufacturing to product delivery or service. These are the activities that are most critical to delivering your value proposition. Key resources are those assets that are most important to your value proposition. They could be physical resources (land, plants, equipment), intellectual resources (brands, patents, databases), human resources (scientists, engineers, salespeople), or financial resources. Understanding your cost structure is critical, because if you can't figure out how to deliver your solution at a cost that is lower than the customer's willingness to pay, then you aren't ready to launch and scale your product. Webvan, an online grocery-delivery start-up, represents a spectacular cautionary tale, having racked up losses of almost a billion dollars before flaming out after the dot-com crash. The Webvan team assumed there was proven demand for grocery delivery, so the Webvan team's plan was to replace the expensive brick-and-mortar grocery retailers with centralized distribution centers that delivered groceries to the customer's door. The company spent a billion dollars developing the distribution centers and networks, only to discover that it had made critical untested assumptions. For example, it assumed that the average customer order would be $100 and that it would generate enough orders to operate its expensive distribution centers at full capacity within three months of opening. But demand turned out to be much lower, orders were much smaller ($81 on average), and the real killer—delivery—ended up costing about $27 per order. In the end, executing on the plan rather than testing the overlooked uncertainties killed Webvan. How could Webvan have tested the uncertainties about customer demand and the cost of delivery without investing the money? The answer: borrow, defer, or pretend rather than build the resources. Webvan could have partnered with local grocery stores to do the distribution as it figured out the actual sizes of customer orders (thereby validating demand). It could have experimented with various ways to most efficiently pick and deliver customer orders, thereby learning about the challenges of delivering ice cream on a 100-degree day during rush hour. At the very least, it would have learned the true cost of delivery. By leveraging the the very least, it would have learned the true cost of delivery. By leveraging the activities and resources of other firms to experiment with the cost structure— essentially making all of its costs variable instead of fixed—Webvan could have resolved key uncertainties about the cost structure before making huge fixed-cost investments. Webvan didn't figure out, until after it spent the money on expensive resources, that its cost structure was too high for customer demand and willingness to pay. It's interesting that Amazon.com has recently moved into grocery delivery with the AmazonFresh service in the Seattle area. At this point it appears to be a limited experiment. But Amazon, as the largest online retailer, has now had years of experience in the activities of fulfillment: managing the supply chain, using robotics, picking inventory, packing products, and shipping. Amazon understands the activities required to be successful at grocery delivery in a way that Webvan could not. Moreover, Amazon has critical resources that Webvan didn't have, including large fulfillment distribution facilities, equipment, a trusted brand, and employees who have deep knowledge of the technologies that are critical to effective fulfillment. It has even experimented with delivering products via drones. Even with all this going for it, Amazon is experimenting with the business model (in particular, the activities and resources required for efficient grocery delivery) before a full-scale launch. If anyone can make it a success, we expect AmazonFresh to have a serious chance. Stay Variable, Stay Flexible One of the first steps toward nailing your cost structure is to make a list of the key activities and resources and estimate the cost of each. Traditional management thinking would then encourage you to lower your per-unit costs by investing in fixed costs (investments such as buying custom injection molds, building a proprietary back end, or purchasing equipment). But fixed costs require more up-front capital and are naturally sensitive to volume, and that makes such investments more dangerous under conditions of uncertainty. We have seen many failed innovators make seemingly logical fixed-cost investments with their precious capital, only to discover demand was lower than expected. Hence, we strongly recommend flipping traditional financial logic on its head: take any fixed cost, and turn it into a variable cost as you experiment. For example, an acquaintance wanted to launch a snack business, but rather than buy kitchen equipment he leased a kitchen at a restaurant during the offhours. Only after building a significant revenue stream—when he had enough sales—did he build a multimillion-dollar factory, with cash, for nationwide expansion of the business. As you're testing your business model, if you have to lose some money on each unit sold to preserve your flexibility, it will be worth it in the short term. These are investments in learning. To judge when to accept higher variable costs, recall that the greater the uncertainty, the greater the value of the flexibility. As a general principle, borrow, defer, or pretend wherever you can. Today, most of the capital-intensive equipment or service resources that companies formerly owned and paid for have become easy to access through outsourcing. For example, companies that need computing and server capacity can buy processing power and storage in the cloud from companies like Amazon rather than set up servers themselves. Manufacturing that used to be capital intensive can now be outsourced on a small scale to local flexible manufacturers or on a large scale to Asia. IT and services can be outsourced to India, with an equally significant reduction in cost. The trick is to defer costs while you resolve the uncertainty about which activities and resources are most critical to delivering your solution to customers. Rather than invest in facilities, equipment, leases, rentals, salaries, or any other expense, defer it as long as possible. Use every free tool (e.g., Google Docs, Skype, Quora) that you can find. Also consider outsourcing, crowd-sourcing, open sourcing, licensing, or substituting some component of the solution rather than developing it yourself. than developing it yourself. Putting the Pieces Together: Business Model Snapshot Template Example For an example of how to capture your initial hypotheses about your business model and then record your validated hypotheses, see the before and after snapshots for the chotuKool business model. captures the starting hypotheses for the chotuKool, with the value proposition (and resulting resources and activities) being fairly clearly defined but with the pricing and customer acquisition elements being uncertain and in need of validation.

Large companies love it when they can sell a new value proposition to (a) the same customer, (b) using the same pricing strategy, (c) through the same distribution channel, (d) using the same marketing messages and process, (e) leveraging the activities, capabilities, and resources they already have. In other words, companies always want to do the efficient thing. They want to take any new solution and apply the same business model, preferably in their existing business units. The reason is that big companies are designed for execution, not searching for new opportunities. This is a big problem for innovation, and here's why. First, it means companies often refuse to consider developing a solution that doesn't fit the existing business model—and this means they miss many new growth opportunities. Second, most business models have interdependencies among elements, and so if you change one or two, you often must make changes to other elements. For example, when Netflix first shipped DVDs by mail to customers they iteratively discovered and then optimized their business model. In particular, Netflix acquired resources such as distribution warehouses and specialized sorting equipment and developed capabilities for efficiently acquiring and allocating DVD inventory. When video on demand (VOD) first emerged, Netflix experimented with VOD as an add-on, and soon discovered the technology had greater capability and demand than initially predicted. But the new solution also required different resources: distribution warehouses were worthless in a VOD world as were many of their prior capabilities. To Netflix's credit, the executives recognized this and tried to create space for a new business model when they tried to split off mail order DVDs in the Qwikster business. By trying to organizationally divide those two business models into separate businesses, they initially confused and upset many customers. Although they perhaps could have handled the division better (Netflix's stock price dropped from over $300 to $50), in the long run separating the businesses has produced some advantages of being able to focus and align the business models to fit different customer profiles. Today over 75 percent of Netflix's business is VOD and their stock price is over $300. By contrast, Blockbuster, who ignored DVDs by mail and VOD for a long time because it conflicted with their business model eventually went bankrupt. Large companies prefer to leverage rather than build, but that is a big watch out. As companies like Godrej, Intuit, Cemex, and others have watch out. As companies like

Godrej, Intuit, Cemex, and others have discovered, the right business model for an innovation can be much different from what you expected—and different from your existing business model. Trying to force disruptive innovations into the existing business model will almost certainly destroy them. Don't be afraid to make room for new business models by creating new business units or by spinning off or even creating a separate business unit that incubates new business models themselves. Making It Pay It's crucial to nail the six components of the business model snapshot before you're ready to fully scale. As with each phase of the innovator's method, nailing the business model depends on generating explicit hypotheses, in this case about the optimal pricing strategy, customer acquisition strategy (customer relationships and channels), and cost structure (activities and resources), and then testing them by conducting experiments with customers. There are many ways to take your solution to market, so use your business model exploration to test various combinations of approaches.

www.ingramcontent.com/pod-product-compliance
Ingram Content Group UK Ltd.
Pitfield, Milton Keynes, MK11 3LW, UK
UKHW021907190726
13853UKWH00002B/561